The C. S. Lewis Chronicles

Also by Colin Duriez

The C. S. Lewis Encyclopedia

The Inklings Handbook (with David Porter)

Tolkien and The Lord of the Rings

Tolkien and C. S. Lewis: The Gift of Friendship

A Field Guide to Narnia

The

C.S. LEWIS

CHRONICLES

The Indispensable Biography
of the Creator of Narnia
Full of Little-Known Facts,
Events and Miscellany

COLIN DURIEZ

DARTON · LONGMAN + TODD

Published in Great Britain in 2005 by
Darton, Longman and Todd Ltd
1 Spencer Court
140–142 Wandsworth High Street
London SW18 4JJ

Published in the USA in 2005 by
BlueBridge, an imprint of United Tribes Media Inc.

Cover design: Stefan Killen Design
Cover art: Per-Henrik Gurth
Interior design: Stefan Killen Design

ISBN 0-232-52646-X

A catalogue record for this book is available from the British Library

Printed in the United States of America

TO

Emilia Duriez

"The history of a given period is not exclusively, or even mainly, the history of its famous men and women. The real history of the past lies in the answer to the question, 'How did the ordinary, undistinguished man live?' . . . It is with a view to providing posterity with an addition to such all too scanty material, that the papers which follow have been embodied in a permanent form."

From the foreword to *Memoirs of the Lewis Family 1850–1930*, edited by Warren Hamilton Lewis

Contents

Foreword

There are various ways of writing a book. You can plan and plot in microscopic detail, as most mystery and thriller writers probably do, applying the tenacious logic of a crossword-puzzle setter or a chess grand master. Alternatively, you can just take a leap, dive right in and see where the current of your imagination takes you, going with the flow, enjoying the unexpectedness of every swirl and eddy.

The latter method is, for some of us, the more appealing, and, certainly, many great books have been written in that way. A nineteenth-century Oxford don famously sent a child named Alice plunging down a rabbithole without, as he later admitted, the remotest idea of what was to become of her. And a twentieth-century Oxford don pushed a child called Lucy through the back of a wardrobe without, initially, knowing how she came to find herself in a snowy wood illuminated by a London gas-lamp, let alone why she would suddenly encounter a faun carrying an umbrella and a pile of parcels!

In any story where the process of creation is truly extemporaneous, the characters embark on journeys—real or fantastical, physical or emotional—while the writer dashes off in hot pursuit, observing and chronicling with a sense of immediacy that, eventually, hooks readers and draws them into the same urgent chase.

One reason, therefore, why we respond so strongly to such tales is because they carry with them their own internal excitement and suspense, borne out of the author's state of unknowing. But also, arguably, it is because the process is intrinsically like Life.

Each day, each hour, is an unknown void as likely to be filled with the unexpected as with the expected. Our lives unfold, however much we might wish or dream to the contrary, through a succession of singular happenings, tiny and inconsequential or huge and significant. The past—the chapters that have already been written and read—are the only constants; the rest is the Voyage, the way from Here to There and Beyond, the storyteller's glorious "What if?"

Biographies, however, are not written in this way. They are written with hindsight. How could it be otherwise? If we didn't know that a man or a woman had grown to greatness, what would be the point of writing the story of his or her life? If he or she was not already famous or infamous, why would anyone want to *read* it?

The biographer writes with an eye applied to the telescope of fame: viewing the colossus, up close and dominant, rather than from a distance and in relation to landscape, and then sets out to demonstrate how every aspect of the journey between smallness and greatness delineates and explains some feature of the known final destination.

But what if it were possible to reconstruct a life, not with the benefit of hindsight but by following a person's growth and development—day by day; year in, year out—setting down the life-patterning events as they took place, from the cradle to the grave, and placing them within the context of the comings and goings and dramas being enacted on the wider stage of the world? Then might not a new and compelling portrait emerge from the process?

Certainly, that is what Colin Duriez has done in *The C. S. Lewis Chronicles*. He has taken for his subject a man whose life has already been extensively, exhaustively, explored and examined by biographers, novelists, and filmmakers. Undaunted, he has looked at Lewis through what conventional biographers would think of as the *wrong* end of the telescope and, in so doing, has shed new light, opened new perspectives, and brought fresh insight to the life of a man who—through his philosophy, writing, and experience of living—has deeply enriched, and continues to enrich, the lives of others.

This book incisively charts the journey of a lifetime— a journey eminently worthy of being followed.

Brian Sibley

Preface

C live Staples Lewis is known throughout the world as the creator of *The Chronicles of Narnia*. A number of biographies of him have been written, attempting to catch in their nets the elusive character of the brilliant Oxford don who was also a master storyteller. Even his appearance presented an enigma—he looked like a farmer, remarked some who knew him, but spoke like a philosopher. (He did indeed have Welsh farmers among his ancestry.) The onetime British poet laureate Sir John Betjeman, who was one of his earliest students, described Lewis as "breezy, tweedy, beer-drinking and jolly."

Though I am on the same quest, my approach is rather different from the conventional biography. I go through the years of his life, from birth to death, selecting varied but representative days throughout each year. These give vivid insights into the events of his life, his books, his attitudes, sense of fun, wit and wisdom, beliefs, and friends. I also include a miscellany of the kind of facts that make C. S. Lewis's life endlessly fascinating.

As the daily events unfold we meet his friends, such as J. R. R. Tolkien, Owen Barfield, and Charles Williams, as well as his mentors past and present. We discover his unforgettable quasi-adoptive family, and his late marriage with the much younger American poet and novelist Joy Davidman—a marriage of deep and unexpected happiness, leading to profound grief at her untimely death. And we become increasingly aware of the bond between Lewis and his brother, Warren.

Sometimes, I have found, it is not absolutely clear upon which day an event occurred or a letter was written. In such a case I have indicated this with a question mark after the conjectured date. In referring to C. S. Lewis, I have usually called him by his self-chosen name of Jack during his boyhood and youth. When I refer to him as an adult, I do so by his surname because I do not consider that I have the right to be overfamiliar.

In writing this book I must acknowledge my particular debt to the Wade Center at Wheaton College, Illinois, and to Walter Hooper, compiler and editor of the letters and diaries of C. S. Lewis. Without the Wade Center and its staff, and without the labors of Walter Hooper, this book would not have been possible. I must also express my thanks in particular to my publisher and friend, Jan-Erik Guerth, for his vision and encouragement, and to the members of the Leicester Writers Club, who have enriched my life.

Colin Duriez

CHAPTER ONE

Childhood in
the North of Ireland
(1898–1908)

Clive Staples Lewis was born on November 29, 1898, in prosperity, in suburban Belfast, Ireland. He had one older brother, Warren ("Warnie") Hamilton Lewis (1895–1973). Much of their childhood was spent in an untidily constructed house, "Little Lea," "almost a major character in my story," Lewis later wrote. He was the second son of a solicitor, Albert James Lewis (1863–1929), and a clergyman's daughter, Florence ("Flora") Augusta Lewis, née Hamilton (1862–1908). His grandfather Richard Lewis lived with the family for a while (he was a devout Welshman and engineer who had settled in Ireland and had been a partner in a shipping company in the nearby docks). Lewis's mother was from a cultured family and hailed from County Cork in the south. She died when Lewis was not yet ten. As a child Lewis soon became aware of his parents' contrasting temperaments—Albert, passionate and emotionally unpredictable; Flora, analytical (she achieved a First Class degree in logic), sunny, and stable. Flora was the young boy's dependable Atlantis (as Lewis was to put it later), a great island continent of tranquillity that soon was lost forever under the waves. Her personality is captured in letters she wrote to Albert while (rarely) he was away from home, or (often) while she was away on long summer vacation with their boys.

Belfast in 1898 and into the twentieth century was a buzzing industrial city. It was proud of having one of the world's busiest shipyards, which launched what was then the world's largest ship, the *Oceanic*, and later the short-lived *Titanic*. The Lewis home was bursting with books, lodged into every conceivable space, even the attic. From the moment he could read, Lewis ("Jacks," or "Jack," as he named himself) gave his allegiance, he tells us, to books of romance—stories and poems that carried glimpses of other worlds. This attraction was reinforced by the tales told him by his nurse, Lizzie Endicott, rooted in the folk-culture of County Down—upon which the later Land of Narnia was to be built. Lewis and his brother sat enraptured as she recounted stories of leprechauns and pots of buried gold, and immortal worlds, such as the Isle of Apples and the Land of Youth.

Into this imaginative world of Lizzie Endicott's story-telling came Jack's discovery of the early Beatrix Potter books. Stories like *The Tale of Benjamin Bunny* and *The Tale of Squirrel Nutkin* told of talking animals, accompanied by exquisite colored illustrations. The stories were set in the northern Lakeland of England. *Squirrel Nutkin* gave him a clear experience of beauty and what he later described as "the Idea of Autumn." This was one of several qualities, often evoked by northern lands, which enchanted the young Lewis and nourished his growing sense of "sweet desire," or inconsolable longing, so important in his writings as an adult.

Little Lea was chosen by Albert and Flora because of its view. The north side of the house looked down over fields to Belfast Lough, with the "long mountain line of the Antrim shore" beyond. The view to the south side revealed the Holywood Hills, "greener, lower, and nearer" than the Antrim slopes. The boys walked and cycled around those hills. From them one could see Strangford Lough, a green world of pastures and woods, and, in the distance, the blue Mountains of Mourne. In the imagination, one could be looking southward across Narnia to the mountains of Archenland in the dim distance, with the Eastern Sea to one's left.

During this happy period Jack, wielding pen and paintbrush like Beatrix Potter, began making a cycle of junior stories about "chivalrous mice and rabbits who rode out in complete mail to kill not giants but cats." These stories were his attempt to bring together his two great pleasures, which were knights in armor and "dressed animals." In collaboration with Warren, Jack developed the stories into an "Animal-land" with a considerable history. This land of talking animals is strikingly different from the later Narnian Chronicles. It is full of a child's view of adult preoccupations.

The weather was an important feature of Lewis's early life. Parental wisdom of the time, darkened by a real fear of tuberculosis, was to keep children indoors during the frequent squalls and showers. A cousin, Claire Clapperton, was three years older than Jack and a visitor to Little Lea. She remembered long after a large oak wardrobe, hand carved and built by their grandfather Richard Lewis. The wardrobe made a den for the children. In its gloom they would listen silently "while Jacks told us his tales of adventure." This became the inspiration for Professor Kirk's wardrobe, which provided a gateway into Narnia.

The Lewis family was Church of Ireland (Anglican) and worshiped at nearby St. Mark's Church, where Lewis had been baptized as an infant. Flora Lewis's father, Thomas Hamilton, was rector of the church. Through the services, the young Lewis became familiar with the litur-

gy of *The Book of Common Prayer* and *Hymns Ancient and Modern*.
When his mother became seriously ill with cancer, the
boy found it natural to pray for her recovery. Her death, on
August 23, 1908, removed all hopes for a miracle. Nearly
fifty years later Lewis wrote: "All settled happiness, all
that was tranquil and reliable, disappeared from my life."
In a matter of weeks after his mother's death Jack traveled
in a four-wheeled cab to Donegal quay, in Belfast's dock-
lands. In uncomfortable school clothes he caught the ferry
to England and to boarding school.

This time period saw the end of the reign of Victoria,
monarch of an empire where the sun never set, and the
beginning of a new world that was to see Cubism, Dada,
modernism in art and literature, and global wars. Lewis's
infancy coincided with a flowering of children's literature,
as fantasy writing found few outlets in grown-up reading.
It was the period of the Bastable family in Edith Nesbit's
The Treasure Seekers, and of Digory and Polly in Lewis's
Narnian Chronicle *The Magician's Nephew*. It was the era of
the new motorcar, cableless communication across the
Atlantic, and heavier-than-air flight. The issue of Home
Rule for Ireland was becoming increasingly urgent.

1862

MAY 18 (Sun)

Birth of Florence (Flora) Augusta Hamilton, mother of
C. S. Lewis, in Queenstown, County Cork, in the south
of Ireland.

1863

AUGUST 23 (Sun)

Birth of Albert James Lewis, father of C. S. Lewis, in
Cork, in the south of Ireland.

1872

MARCH 28 (Thu)

Janie Moore (née Askins) is born; she will later become like a second mother to Lewis.

1886

SEPTEMBER 20 (Mon)

Charles Williams is born in Holloway, north London; close friend of Lewis and member of the Inklings.

1892

JANUARY 3 (Sun)

John Ronald Reuel Tolkien is born of British parents in South Africa; close friend of Lewis and member of the Inklings.

1894

AUGUST 29 (Wed)

Albert Lewis and Flora Hamilton are married in St. Mark's Church, Dundela, Belfast, where Flora's father is rector.

1895

JUNE 16 (Sun)

Warren (Warnie) Hamilton Lewis, brother of C. S. Lewis, is born in the first Lewis family home, named "Dundela Villas," in Belfast.

AUGUST 27 (Tue)

Arthur Greeves, lifelong friend of Lewis, is born in Belfast.

1898

NOVEMBER 9 (Wed)

Owen Barfield is born; close friend of Lewis and an intermittent member of the Inklings.

NOVEMBER 29 (Tue)

Birth of Clive Staples Lewis at home, in Dundela Villas.

1899

JANUARY 29 (Sun)

C. S. Lewis is baptized in St. Mark's Church, Dundela.

NOVEMBER 29 (Wed)

C. S. Lewis's first birthday.

1900

The British Labour Party is founded. The Boxer Rebellion is happening in China. In the course of the Boer War in southern Africa, Ladysmith is relieved by Redvers Buller.

Basil Bunting, Geoffrey Household, Richard Hughes, Stephen Potter, V. S. Pritchett, and Antoine de Saint-Exupéry are born.

R. D. Blackmore, Ernest Dowson, James Martineau, Friedrich Max Muller, Henry Sidgwick, Oscar Wilde, Stephen Crane, and Friedrich Nietzsche die.

JANUARY 20 (Sat)

Death of art critic, social reformer, and writer John Ruskin, author of the influential series Modern Painters *and the children's story* The King of the Golden River, *and acquaintance of George MacDonald, J. M. W. Turner, and Sir John Millais.*

MAY 3 (Thu)

Flora Lewis, as "Doli," writes to Albert ("dearest old Bear"), who is away in London on legal business: "If you ask [Baby] where Daddy is, he says 'gone.'" [*Warren is nicknamed "the Badge" or "Badgie," and Lewis is "Baby," "Babsie," or "Babbins."*]

MAY 8 (Tue)

In a letter to Albert, Flora mentions looking after "Babsie" and "Badgie" the previous Sunday while suffering a headache. She tells him how she had then lain awake all night listening to the "wretched" dog barking. It had been a very stormy night, with hard rain. She tells Albert of her sister-in-law, Annie, coming around, bringing her second baby child, Ruth, with her. Flora notes that "Clive is about, and was anxious to look at it [the baby], but objected to be asked to kiss it."

AUGUST 6 (Mon)–27 (Mon)

Flora (with the assistance of a nurse) takes her two sons on a holiday to Ballycastle, on the coast of County Antrim, to the north of Belfast. Albert, as usual, stays behind at home to work. [*Jack is not quite two years old.*]

AUGUST 6 (Mon)

Writing to Albert from Ballycastle, Flora notes that today there is a "nice crisp feel in the air." Of her younger son she

Warren, Hamilton, and Ewart Family Genealogy

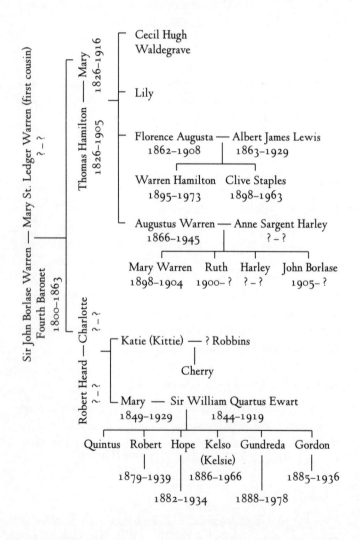

Lewis Family Genealogy

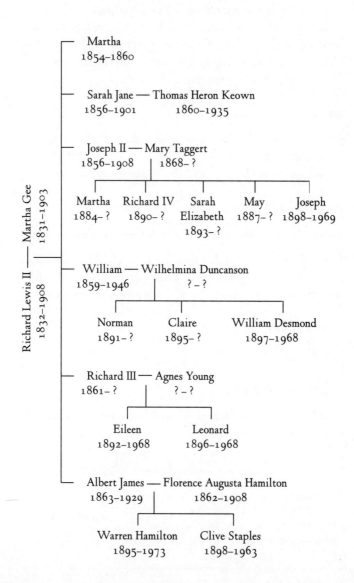

Richard Lewis II —— Martha Gee
1832–1908   1831–1903

— Martha
1854–1860

— Sarah Jane —— Thomas Heron Keown
1856–1901   1860–1935

— Joseph II —— Mary Taggert
1856–1908   1868– ?

Martha   Richard IV   Sarah   May   Joseph
1884– ?   1890– ?   Elizabeth   1887– ?   1898–1969
                            1893– ?

— William —— Wilhelmina Duncanson
1859–1946   ? – ?

Norman   Claire   William Desmond
1891– ?   1895– ?   1897–1968

— Richard III —— Agnes Young
1861– ?   ? – ?

Eileen   Leonard
1892–1968   1896–1968

— Albert James —— Florence Augusta Hamilton
1863–1929   1862–1908

Warren Hamilton   Clive Staples
1895–1973   1898–1963

observes, "Babsie is talking like anything. He astonished me this morning; Warren sniffled, and he turned around and said, 'Warnie wipe nose.'" Flora continues, "There are some nice girls in the house next to us who talk to him and Warren in the garden. Baby calls them the 'Joddies.'" She remarks that "Baby" enjoys the story of the three bears that Martha, the maid, is reading to Warren.

AUGUST 21 (Tue)

From their holiday letting in Ballycastle, Flora writes to Albert in Belfast, "There is a fair on today, and Babsie is delighted with the pigs and sheep passing up and down."

OCTOBER 14 (Sun)

Sigmund Freud publishes his seminal The Interpretation of Dreams.

[*As an undergraduate and then young scholar at Oxford, Lewis will be much exercised by Freud's views on fantasy, dreams, and wish-fulfillment, and throughout his life continues to reflect on Freud's ideas.*]

NOVEMBER 29 (Thu)

Jack's second birthday.

DECEMBER 24 (Mon)

Max Planck of Berlin University unveils his revolutionary quantum theory of energy.

─────── *Lewis's Childhood Pets* ───────

Tim—dog (Irish terrier); "He never actually obeyed you; he sometimes agreed with you." Though epileptic, he had a long life, not dying until 1922.

Tommy—black and white mouse.

Peter—canary.

1901

Australia becomes a dominion. U. S. President McKinley is assassinated and succeeded by Theodore Roosevelt. The British Academy is established.

Roy Campbell, James Hanley, Rosamond Lehmann, Gladys Mitchell, Marlene Dietrich, Walt Disney, André Malraux, and Laura Riding are born.

Sir Walter Besant, Robert Williams Buchanan, Mandell Creighton, Kate Greenaway, William Stubbs, Henri de Toulouse-Lautrec, Giuseppe Verdi, Brooke Foss Westcott, and Charlotte Mary Yonge die.

JANUARY 22 (Tue)

Queen Victoria dies. She is succeeded by her son Albert, as King Edward VII.

About this time Warren Lewis brings the lid of a biscuit tin into the nursery of his younger brother, who is enchanted by the miniature garden Warren has made in it. [*Lewis (he later remembers) experiences beauty for the first time, an "incurably romantic" epiphany. It allows him to see his Belfast garden in a new way—almost seeing its beauty for the first time. His brother's toy garden contributes to his imagination of Paradise ever after.*]

JUNE–JULY

Flora, Warren, Jack, and the boys' nurse Lizzie Endicott vacation at the small seaside resort of Castlerock, on the coast of County Derry, north of Belfast.

JUNE 1 (Sat)

Writing to Albert from Castlerock, Flora tells of Jack's delight in the train journey from Belfast the day before, "only he could not be induced to use the closet, and so wet his drawers." On the train they had had a lunch of hard-boiled egg and milk. [*The train had departed from Belfast at 12.25 p.m., arriving at Castlerock at 3.10 p.m. This was "no very distinguished performance," Warren will observe in his diary many years later, "as this represents an average speed at 24.7 m.p.h."*] Both boys, Flora continues in her letter, have spent the morning on the sandy beach, with Jack "much concerned" because he couldn't find a crab. She tells Albert that Lizzie Endicott is "delighted with the place." [*Lizzie is a much-trusted and -loved nurse-cum-housemaid who will have a significant impact on Lewis's development with her Irish folk tales.*]

JUNE 10 (Mon)

As this turns out to be a showery day, Flora keeps the boys near the railway station or the house in which they are staying so as not to get caught in the rain. The station is as big an attraction as the beach, with the steam engines puffing through the small town and into or out of the tunnel to the west, in the direction of Downhill. Flora writes to Albert in Belfast, explaining that she had forgotten to bring a small cardboard box with "the precious 'Miss Noah' in it," together with the paint brush—they were "the only things Baby wanted." She asks Albert to address the package to "Baby," if he can find the box, as "he is much concerned because the postman doesn't bring him a letter." [*Flora pays a local girl a penny a day to bring up a bucket of water to give the boys a warm salt bath at night.*]

JUNE 13 (Thu)

Today is very blustery—one of the storms from the Atlantic that from time to time gust onto the Antrim coast. The long beach at Castlerock, interrupted by the Bann estuary before resuming as Portstewart strand, affords a dramatic view of huge gray waves transforming into surf. Flora remarks in a letter to Albert, "Such wind I've never heard in my life before."

JUNE 14 (Fri)

Flora has to go out into the rain, and buys Jack and Warren two little boats with toy figures in them. She records for Albert, "We made paper fishes and Baby spent most of the day making his man catch them by the primitive method of jumping over the side and bringing the fish back with him." She tells Albert that Jack has made friends with the station master. She had taken Jack along to pick up a newspaper, "and as soon as he saw him in the distance he called out, 'Hello, station master.'" [*Within a few weeks the toddler will be insisting upon calling out "Good morning, Robert" every morning to the station master, and getting a smile in return. Jack continues to be "infatuated" with the steam trains stopping at Castlerock—if he sees a "siglan" down he has to be taken back to the station.*]

JUNE 17 (Mon)

In today's letter, Flora tells Albert another railway tale about Jack. "Here is a story to amuse the old people. I took him to buy a [toy] engine, and the woman asked him if she should tie a string to it for him. Baby just looked at her with great contempt and said, 'Baby doesn't see any string on the engines what baby sees on the station.' You never saw a woman so taken aback as she was."

JULY 10 (Wed)

Flora writes to Albert, "We had heavy fog yesterday, which turned to rain, and some three or four claps of thunder after dinner. The first clap came at once after a very bright flash, and was a bit startling. Poor Babbins, whose first experience it was, was very much frightened, he sat on Lizzie's knees with his face hidden, till long after it was all over, and had to be taken down to the kitchen before he could get over it. Then he told us he thought it was his nursery falling down."

JULY 14 (Sun)

A letter comes for Flora from Albert, in which he has included a poem for her. She expresses pleasure at the poem in her reply, considering that it has real feeling in it, rather than (as usual with Albert) being "written for the sake of the verses." Poignantly—in the light of her early death a little over seven years later—Flora writes about their love: "I don't see that there is anything else to look to in this life for comfort or happiness, at least for you and me. I don't think either of us could ever find pleasure in outside things in which the other had not a part; it is

Important People
in Lewis's Childhood

Florence (Flora) Lewis—mother, who taught Lewis French and Latin. When she was twelve she witnessed an apparent miracle in one of the churches in Rome, where the eyes of an effigy of Mary opened, which she later concluded was "all done by cords." At Queen's University, Belfast (then called the Royal University of Ireland), she gained very high grades in examinations in Geometry and Algebra, and later in Logic, obtaining a B.A. She was, recalled Lewis, a "voracious reader of novels." She also wrote short stories and other pieces, including "The Princess Rosetta," in _The Household Journal_ of 1889, and a parody of a sermon.

Albert Lewis—father, who, like his wife, aspired to write, and read and collected numerous books. He was a member of the local Belmont Literary Society, and involved in the grassroots politics of his day. He was a very successful solicitor, serving the Belfast City Council, Belfast and County Down Railway Company, and the National Society for the Prevention of Cruelty to Children. For many years he was church warden of St. Mark's Church, Dundela. Some of his sayings were collected by Jack and Warren in a notebook titled "Pudaita Pie." They called him between themselves the "Pudaitabird," after his pronunciation of the word "potato."

Warren (Warnie) Lewis—older brother of C. S. Lewis, inseparable com-

going to be so with us always, isn't it dear?" In the same letter she mentions carpets being put down in Dundela Villas before her return to Belfast at the end of the month, suggesting "Mrs. McCredy could be there while the men are at it." [*There will be a Mrs. Macready looking after Professor Kirke's large country house in the Narnian Chronicle* The Lion, the Witch and the Wardrobe.]

SEPTEMBER

Flora and Albert visit Dunbar, Scotland, where Albert's older brother Richard lives.

---

panion and collaborator on juvenile writings and illustrations. Warren was more practical and technically minded than his brother.

Lizzie Endicott—nurse, who told Jack and Warren Irish folk stories.

Sir William and Lady Mary Ewart—relations and friends. Sir William Quartus Ewart was a wealthy Belfast linen manufacturer and one of the city's most prominent industrialists. Mary was a first cousin and close friend of Flora's. They lived at Glenmachan House, less than a mile away from Little Lea.

Gundreda, Hope and "Kelsie" Ewart—daughters of the Ewarts. The youngest, Gundreda, was ten years older than Lewis, who confessed in later years, "She was the most beautiful woman I have ever seen, perfect in shape and colour and voice and every movement." Warren agreed with this judgment.

Annie Harper—Lewis's governess, and responsible for his early education. In a drawing she is quoted in a speech balloon as saying, "Don't say can't to me, Jacksie."

Maude Scott—housemaid.

Martha (Mat)—cook and housemaid.

SEPTEMBER 11 (Wed)

Warren writes a letter to his absent parents, referring to his younger brother as "Jacksie." [*C. S. Lewis reveals in his autobiography* Surprised by Joy *that he decided as an infant that he should not be called Clive, but "Jacksie," which is later shortened to "Jacks" and then a few years later to Jack, the name by which he is known to his family and friends throughout his life.*]

NOVEMBER 29 (Fri)

Jack's third birthday.

1902

The Boer War is ended by the Treaty of Vereeniging. The Triple Alliance between Germany, Austria, and Italy is renewed. The London Times Literary Supplement *begins publication.*

Lord David Cecil, Stella Gibbons, Georgette Heyer, Nikolaus Pevsner, John Steinbeck, and Stevie Smith are born.

Lord Acton, Philip James Bailey, Samuel Butler, S. R. Gardiner, Francis Bret Harte, "Mrs. Alexander" (Annie French Hector), G. A. Henty, Lionel Johnson, Cecil Rhodes, and Émile Zola die.

MAY 31 (Sat)

The Boer War is over.

JULY 12 (Sat)

Arthur James Balfour becomes Britain's prime minister.

[*Balfour is also a philosopher; his book* Theism and Humanism *will have a profound influence on Lewis in later years, especially in his argument against naturalism in* Miracles.]

NOVEMBER 29 (Sat)

Jack's fourth birthday.

DECEMBER

Beatrix Potter's The Tale of Peter Rabbit *is published.*

1903

King Edward VII is proclaimed Emperor of India. Physicist Marie Curie becomes the first woman to win a Nobel Prize.

Kenneth Clark, Cyril Connolly, George Orwell (Eric Blair), William Plomer, A. L. Rowse, Evelyn Waugh, and John Wyndham are born.

F. W. Farrar, George Gissing, W. E. Henley, William Henry Lecky, Herbert Spencer, Paul Gaugin, James Abbott McNeill Whistler, and Camille Pissarro die.

JANUARY

Charles Williams, later a core member of the Inklings, begins studying at University College, Gower Street, London. [*He is only able to complete two years of study before his scholarship money runs out and he is forced to find a job.*]

MAY

Flora, Warren, and Jack vacation at Spar Hotel in Ballynahinch, a few miles south of Belfast, in the heart of County Down.

JUNE 16 (Tue)

Henry Ford begins selling the "Model A" car for $850. Original Model A
not the big seller one

NOVEMBER 29 (Sun)

Jack's fifth birthday.

1904

An entente cordiale is formally established between Britain and France. War between Russia and Japan begins. The Abbey Theatre,

Dublin, is opened. Admiral Fisher becomes First Sea Lord in Britain.

Harold Acton, Margery Allingham, C. Day Lewis, Graham Greene, Patrick Hamilton, Christopher Sherwood, Patrick Kavanagh, and Nancy Mitford are born.

Sir Edwin Arnold, Lafcadio Hearn, Samuel Smiles, Sir Henry Morton Stanley, Sir Leslie Stephen, and Anton Chekhov die.

JUNE–AUGUST

Flora, Warren, and Jack vacation at Clifton Terrace, Castlerock (County Derry). The boys happily play on the sandy strand, digging and wading in the cold Atlantic.

AUGUST

Construction of the new Lewis family home, Little Lea, begins in the outer suburbs of Belfast, not far from Dundela Villas.

NOVEMBER 29 (Tue)

Jack's sixth birthday.

1905

In Ireland the Sinn Fein party is founded by Arthur Griffith and Bulmer Hobson. Sir Henry Campbell Bannerman becomes Britain's prime minister. The British Automobile Association is founded.

H. E. Bates, Norman Cameron, Henry Green (Henry Vincent Yorke), Geoffrey Grigson, Arthur Koestler, Anthony Powell, Greta Garbo, Jean-Paul Sartre, and C. P. Snow are born.

George MacDonald, William Sharp, Guy Boothby, Sir Henry Irving, and Jules Verne die.

JANUARY 22 (Sun)

Workers are fired on in St. Petersburg, Russia, on "Bloody Sunday," leading to a general strike in July.

APRIL 21 (Fri)

The Lewis family moves to Little Lea. The house is close by the village of Dundonald. [*In later years Warren comes across a novel by Agnes White called* Romily. *A description in the book reminds him of Dundonald:* "Halfway up the hill they looked back and saw Slieve Donard peer over the shoulder of the Castlereagh Hills inquiringly, and at the summit the long blue range of the Mourne

——— *Nicknames and Pseudonyms* ———

Jacksie, Jacks, Jack—C. S. Lewis

Warnie, Badge—Warren Lewis

SPB aka Smallpiggiebotham—C. S. Lewis

APB aka Archpiggiebotham—Warren Lewis

(SPB and APB derived from an occasion when the exasperated Lizzie Endicott had threatened to smack their "piggiebotties"—the Lewis brothers ever after referred to each other by these initials.)

Pudaitabird—nickname for Albert, based on the way the word "potato" came out in his brogue (strong characteristics of Albert were considered "Pudaitabirdisms")

Doli—Albert's affectionate name for Flora

Old Bear—Flora's affectionate name for Albert

Leeborough—Little Lea

Uncle Pumblechook—the brothers' nickname for G. Herbert Ewart, brother of Sir William Ewart of Glenmachan House

Clive Hamilton—first name and mother's maiden name used as a combined pseudonym in Spirits in Bondage and Dymer

N.W., Nat Whilk—used as a pseudonym in some published poems. "Nat whilk" is early English for "I know not whom."

N. W. Clerk—used as a pseudonym in the original edition of A Grief Observed ("clerk" is a medieval term for "scholar," combined with "N. W.")

Mountains huddled and linked together, came suddenly into view."
That view across County Down, familiar to Lewis and Warren in boyhood, was later to inspire the landscape of Narnia, with the mountains
of Archenland in the blue distance.]

MAY 10 (Wed)

Warren is sent to Wynyard School, in Watford, England.
[Late in his life Warren will describe going to Wynyard as "when I
descended into the pit in May 1905."]

JUNE 7 (Wed)

Jack receives a letter from Warnie, away at school, asking
him to send the "new paper" he is writing.

JULY 1 (Sat)

Albert Einstein proposes his theory of relativity, beginning a scientific
revolution.

Little Lea

Little Lea still stands today. In 1957 it was advertised by a real estate
agent as a "residence of distinction" with about two acres of land.
Structurally it was then still like the original 1905 house:

"This Well-Built Residence is situated in a secluded position on
the Circular Road, convenient to Campbell College and Stormont, and
is approached by two gravel drives.

"The Grounds are tastefully laid out for ease of management in
lawns, rose beds, rock gardens, etc.

"Lounge Hall with Fireplace; 3 Reception-rooms; 4 Principal
Bedrooms; 2 Secondary Bedrooms; Dressing-room; 2 Bathrooms;
Kitchen (Esse cooker); Double Garage; Greenhouses. The Rooms are
spacious and the excellent woodwork includes parquet flooring in the
Principal Bedrooms and oak and maple floors in the Hall and Reception-
rooms...."

SEPTEMBER

Flora, Warren, and Jack vacation at the seaside resort of Killough, County Down, not far from Newcastle and the Mourne Mountains.

SEPTEMBER 12 (Tue)

In Killough, the family is staying at the Bangor Arms Hotel, which Flora finds a noisy place. [*The previous Sunday night it was rowdy until 2 a.m., disturbing her sleep.*] Today she takes the boys to the lighthouse at St. John's Point, where the keeper lights it up for them and shows them around. The brothers bathe in the sea, as they do every day.

SEPTEMBER 18 (Mon)

The Scottish writer George MacDonald, who postmortem is going to have a great influence on Lewis, dies in Ashtead, Surrey. His ashes are taken to Italy and buried beside his wife's body in Bordighera.

[*Ashtead is very near to where, momentously, Lewis will find a copy of MacDonald's book* Phantastes *on a railway station bookstand ten years later.*]

SEPTEMBER 25 (Mon)

Jack receives a letter from Warren, back at school in Watford, in which he asks his brother about the "secret dark hole upstairs" in Little Lea. He wonders whether "Jacks" has been to it lately.

NOVEMBER 29 (Wed)

Jack's seventh birthday.

1906

There is a Liberal landslide in the British general election.

Samuel Beckett, John Betjeman, Catherine Cookson, William Empson, Richard Llewellyn, R. K. Narayan, Michael Innes (J. I. M. Stewart), A. J. P. Taylor, Vernon Watkins, and T. H. White are born.

Charles Hamilton Aïdé, John Oliver Hobbes (Pearl Mary Craigie), Richard Garnett, F. W. Maitland, Charlotte Elizabeth Riddell, Paul Cezanne, and Henrik Ibsen die.

FEBRUARY 10 (Sat)

The British navy launches the battleship Dreadnought.

JUNE 14 (Thu)

Parliament in London passes a bill banning women from dangerous sports following the death of a female parachutist.

AUGUST 19 (Sun)

Maureen Moore, daughter of Janie Moore and Courtney Edward Moore, is born in Delgany, County Wicklow, Ireland. [She will spend much of her life with C. S. Lewis.]

SEPTEMBER

Flora, Warren, and Jack holiday at Castlerock.

SEPTEMBER 4 (Tue)

From the lodgings of a Miss Gilkey, Flora informs Albert, "We had a great time in the afternoon watching a boat from America with a cargo of timber. She had gone ashore at the mouth of the Bann, and a tug had to come down from Derry to get her off; it was great sport for the boys."

SEPTEMBER 5 (Wed)

The afternoon turns wet and stormy in Castlerock.

SEPTEMBER 15 (Sat)

Flora writes to Albert of a trip with Jack and Warren to Dunluce Castle the day before: "We went to Portrush again yesterday; they wanted to go to Dunluce and to the white rocks where there is a cave to be seen. We had a very nice day and they enjoyed it. The bridge you have to cross at Dunluce is quite a dangerous place without any climbing; it was there that Mr. Lanyon was killed. I did not like going over it at all, and I would not have taken the boys if I had remembered what it was like; however they were not nervous about it, so it was not so bad." [*The childhood memory of Dunluce Castle may well have inspired Lewis's*

Narnia and the North of Ireland

The north of Ireland, as Lewis remembered it from childhood, inspired the geography of Narnia, with its Eastern Sea, the wild lands to the north, and the mountains of Archenland to the south. There are a number of resemblances to Narnia in actual landscapes, while other Narnia localities have none (for instance, there is of course no desert to the south in Ireland).

The Great River of Narnia—River Lagan

The Kingdom of Narnia—the pastures, woods, and gentle hills of County Down

The Mountains of Archenland—the Mourne Mountains

The Wild Lands of the North—the Glens of Antrim

Cair Paravel—Dunluce Castle, County Antrim

Mountains of the Western Wild—northwestern Ireland (including Donegal)

Eastern Sea—Irish Sea

The Lone Islands—Rathlin Island (visible from Ballycastle) and the nearby The Skerries (out at sea from Portrush)

creation of Cair Paravel in The Chronicles of Narnia. Nearly
ten years later he will record his memories in a letter to Arthur
Greeves, who had written while staying in or near Portrush: "I . . . certainly wish I could have been with you; I have some vague memories of
the cliffs round there and of Dunluce Castle, and some memories which
are not at all vague of the same coast a little further on at Castlerock
where we used to go in the old days. Don't you love a windy day at a
place like that? Waves make one kind of music on rocks and another on
sand and I don't know which of the two I would rather have."]

NOVEMBER 11 (Sun)

Warren, boarding at Wynyard School in Watford, writes
to his parents and includes an enquiry about "Jacks"—is he

——— *Important Childhood Places* ———

St. Mark's, Dundela—the local church, where Flora Lewis's father was
rector and where Lewis as an infant was baptized at a font.

Dundela Villas—first home until 1905 (now demolished). It was here
that Warren showed his younger brother the miniature garden in a biscuit tin lid that awakened longing for, and a sense of, beauty in nature.

Little Lea—the new house in Strandtown, Belfast, that the Lewis family
moved to in 1905, now numbered 76 Circular Road. Overlooking
Belfast Lough, it is near Stormont Castle. In 1905 it was on the edge of
suburbia, with open fields and hills the other way.

Bernagh—nearly opposite Little Lea, the home (now demolished) of
Lewis's boyhood friend and later soulmate, Arthur Greeves.

Glenmachan—nearly a mile from Little Lea, and home (now demolished)
of the Ewart family, relations and friends of the Lewis family.

Lisnadene House—about half a mile from Little Lea, and home of Jane
McNeill, lifelong friend of the Lewis brothers. *That Hideous Strength* is
dedicated to her, as is Warren Lewis's volume of French history, *The
Sunset of the Splendid Century*.

Ty-Issa—near St. Mark's Church, in Lower Sydenham, home of paternal

still thinking of making a tepee in the garden, Warren wants to know.

NOVEMBER 29 (Thu)

Jack's eighth birthday.

1907

The Second Hague Peace Conference takes place. Lenin leaves Russia. The Boy Scouts movement is founded by Sir Robert Baden-Powell.

W. H. Auden, Daphne du Maurier, Peter Fleming, Christopher Fry, Rumer Godden, John Lehmann, and Louis MacNeice are born.

Mary Coleridge, David Masson, Francis Thompson, Edvard Grieg, and J.-K. Huysmans die.

---

grandfather Richard Lewis.

Harland and Wolff docks—visible from Little Lea. The *Oceanic* and *Titanic* were constructed here. Grandfather Richard Lewis had been a partner in the company MacIlwaine and Lewis: Boiler Makers, Engineers, and Iron Ship Builders.

Donegal Quay—embarkation point in Belfast for the ferry to England.

Castlereagh Hills and Holywood Hills—hills near Little Lea frequented by the Lewis brothers. These hills had helped to awaken longing, the quest for joy that was a central theme in Lewis's life. They afforded a view over County Down, with the Mountains of Mourne in the distance.

Castlerock—an Atlantic seaside resort on the north coast of Ireland (County Derry) with a long, sandy strand at which Flora and her sons vacationed for several summers, and regarded by Lewis as one of the most beautiful places in the world.

Ballycastle—a popular resort on the Antrim coast north of Belfast, where the Atlantic meets the Irish Sea. Rathlin Island is visible in the near distance, and Scotland towards the horizon. Ireland's oldest fair, *Ould Lammas*, takes place here, dating from the fifteenth century.

MARCH

The landmark appearance of Picasso's painting Les demoiselles d'Avignon.

JUNE 26 (Wed)

Oxford University bestows upon Mark Twain an honorary Doctorate of Letters.

LATE AUGUST–SEPTEMBER

Flora, Warren, and Jack holiday at Berneval, in northern France. [*Nearly eleven years later, during World War I, C. S. Lewis, then seriously wounded, will be hospitalized a few miles up the coast from here.*]

AUGUST 20 (Tue)

In London, on their way to France, Flora (writing from Morris's Private Hotel, in the Strand, at 2 Craven Street) reports to Albert that Jack was delighted with Trafalgar Square. They took the bus to London Zoo, in Regent's Park, where both boys were overjoyed to see the animals.

SEPTEMBER 4 (Wed)

By now the three are settled into "Pension Petit" in Berneval, near Dieppe. In a dutiful letter to his father Warren mentions that "Jacks" has begun a "new book." [*It is an addition to what would later become known as* Boxen, *entitled, "Living races of Mouse-land."*]

SEPTEMBER 19 (Thu)

Writing from London, on the return journey from France, Flora informs Albert that they plan a trip to the Tower of London, followed by the British Museum, before "hair cut-

——————— *The Kingdom of Boxen* ———————

Boxen is an imaginary kingdom created through stories by Lewis as a young child, together with his brother, Warren. (The stories have been collected and edited by Walter Hooper and published as *Boxen* in 1985.) In his autobiography, *Surprised by Joy*, Lewis described the origin of *Boxen*. The first stories were written, and illustrated, "to combine my two chief literary pleasures—'dressed animals' and 'knights-in-armour.' As a result, I wrote about chivalrous mice and rabbits who rode out in complete mail to kill not giants but cats." In creating an environment for the tales, a medieval Animal-Land was born. In order to include Warren in its creation and shaping, features of the modern world like trains and steamships had to be included. Thus Lewis had to come up with a considerable history and geography. Unlike in *The Chronicles of Narnia*, the focus in *Boxen* is on Lewis's contemporary milieu.

———————————◆—◆———————————

ting," and then the short train journey to Watford to take Warren to Wynyard School for the new term. [*This will be Lewis's first sight of the school he will be sent to a year later, shortly before his tenth birthday.*]

NOVEMBER 29 (Fri)

Jack's ninth birthday.

DECEMBER

Jack is writing a journal, entitled "My Life. By Jacks Lewis," 1907. The following excerpts retain the original spelling: "Papy of course is the master of the house, and a man in whom you can see strong Lewis features, bad temper, very sensible, nice wen not in a temper. Mamy is like most middle-aged ladys, stout, brown hair, spectaciles, kniting her chief industry etc., etc." He adds that he is "like most boys of 9 and I am like Papy, bad temper, thick lips, thin and generaly wearing a jersy." Miss Harper, his governess, "has fair hair, blue eyes, and rather sharp features, she generally wears a grene blouse and a dress of the same hue." He also notes: "I told Maude [Scott, the house maid] and Mat [Martha, the cook] that I was a home-ruler."

DECEMBER 25 (Wed)

One of Jack's Christmas presents is a toy boat called the *Mayflower*, equipped with sails. He adds a pasteboard poop and forecastle, and is pleased with the result. [*This toy boat may have been a forerunner of the* Dawn Treader *in the Narnian Chronicles.*]

1908

Austria-Hungary annexes Bosnia-Herzegovina. Herbert Asquith becomes British prime minister. The English Review *is founded by Ford Madox Ford.*

Ian Fleming, Pamela Frankau, Osbert Lancaster, Norman Lewis, Simone de Beauvoir, and Kathleen Raine are born.

Edward Caird, John Churton Collins, Lanoe Falconer (Mary Elizabeth Hawker), Mrs. Cashel Hoey (Frances Sarah Hoey), "Ouida" (Marie Louise de la Ramée), Joel Chandler Harris, and Nicolai Rimsky-Korsakov die.

Kenneth Grahame's The Wind in the Willows *is published.*

[*Lewis would not come across* The Wind in the Willows *until a later year. It was to affect his thinking about fantasy and the presence of the spiritual in nature.*]

FEBRUARY 7 (Fri)

Flora's health is causing great concern. From the pocket diary of Albert Lewis: "[Drs] Campbell and Leslie, 1st Consultation at Little Lea."

FEBRUARY 11 (Tue)

Flora writes to Warren, away at school in Watford, that she is to have an operation on Friday.

FEBRUARY 15 (Sat)

Flora undergoes major cancer surgery at home under chloroform. From Albert's pocket diary: "Operation on Flora lasted from 10 till 12 o'c. Drs. Campbell, Leslie, and Fielden, a nurse. Horrible operation."

MARCH 24 (Tue)

From Albert's pocket diary: "My father had a stroke this night."

APRIL 2 (Thu)

From Albert's pocket diary: "My father died at 1 o'c today, Mary and the nurse alone being present." [*Mary was Albert's sister-in-law.*]

MAY 20 (Wed)

Flora and Jack are at Larne on the Antrim coast, north of Belfast, as she recovers from her operation; Warren is away at Wynyard School. From "Tigh-na-mara," Larne Harbour,

—————— *Lewis's Writings at This Time* ——————

My Life (a journal)	*Relief of Murry* (a history)
Building of the Promenade (a tale)	*Bunny* (a paper)
Man against Man (a novel)	*Home Rule* (an essay)
Town (an essay)	

Flora writes to Albert, "Jacks has a great time watching the boats, there is a pair of opera glasses here that he looks out at them with. . . . Jacks and nurse were over on Island Magee today, I think Jacks thought the ferry the best part of the trip."

EARLY JUNE

Warren, still away at school in Watford, frequently asks for news of his mother. In one letter he asks his father, "From your letters you don't seem to think she is likely to live. Do tell me plainly next time you write."

JUNE 9 (Tue)

Charles Williams begins working as a proofreader for Oxford University Press in London.

JUNE 24 (Wed)

From his office at 83 Royal Avenue, Belfast, Albert writes words chosen in great pain to Warren: "My dear son, it may be that God in His mercy has decided that you will have no person in the future to turn to but me."

JULY 8 (Wed)

Warren comes home from school early, before term ends, due to Flora's terminal illness.

AUGUST

A few days before her death Flora gives a Bible to each of her sons.

AUGUST 21/22 (Fri/Sat)

Albert records some of Flora's last words in one of his notebooks: "In the middle of the night of the 21st August

while at times she was wandering and at other times perfectly possessed, I spoke to her (not by any means for the
first time—nor was it the first time by any means that a
conversation on heavenly things had taken place between
us—sometimes begun by her, sometimes by me), of the
goodness of God. Like a flash she said, 'What have we
done for Him?' May I never forget that!"

AUGUST 23 (Sun)

Florence Augusta Hamilton Lewis dies today, on Albert's
forty-fifth birthday. On Albert's Shakespearean calendar
for that day the inscription runs: "Men must endure their
going hence." [*Fifty-five years later Warren will have those words
engraved on his beloved brother's grave.*]

SEPTEMBER 3 (Thu)

From Albert's pocket diary: "Poor dear Joe died at 7 o'c
this evg." Joseph was Albert's brother, uncle of Warren
and Jack, and born in 1856.

SEPTEMBER 18/19 (Fri/Sat)

Jack and Warren travel from Belfast to Watford. It is Jack's
inauguration at Wynyard School. [*Jack, like his brother, would
come to hate the school.*]

SEPTEMBER 29 (Tue)

Warren incurs the fickle wrath of the brutal headmaster at
Wynyard, Robert Capron (who would later be certified
as insane). That evening he writes home, "You have never
refused me anything Papy and I know you won't refuse me
this—that I may leave Wynyard. Jacks wants to too."
Albert has no idea of the cruel circumstances at Wynyard
and ignores the plea.

OCTOBER 22 (Thu)

Capron writes to Albert about his sons, "Not only is Clive an exceptionally bright, intelligent, and most loveable little boy, but he is very keen and eager to learn. Would that I could write to you in the same strain of Warren! Ever averse to effort, physical and mental, he grows worse, and I am almost driven to regard his indolence in the light of a disease."

NOVEMBER 29 (Sun)

Jack's tenth birthday.

_____ Some of Lewis's Reading _____
(up to age twelve)

Beatrix Potter, *The Tale of Squirrel Nutkin*, etc.

Punch, *Strand*, and *Pearson's* magazines

Edith Nesbit, *Five Children and It*, *The Phoenix and the Carpet*, and *The Story of the Amulet*

Sir Arthur Conan Doyle, *Sir Nigel* (These stories of Doyle and Nesbit were serialized in *Strand* magazine between 1902 and 1906.)

Mark Twain, *A Connecticut Yankee in King Arthur's Court*

Jonathan Swift, *Gulliver's Travels*

Henry Wadsworth Longfellow, *Saga of King Olaf*

Esaias Tegner, *Drapa* (Longfellow's translation)

John Milton, *Paradise Lost*

F. Anstey, *Vice Versa*

A. E. W. Mason, *At the Villa Rose*

Hall Caine, *The White Prophet*

Henryk Sienkiewicz, *Quo Vadis*

Dean Farrar, *Darkness and Dawn: or, Scenes in the Days of Nero*

George Whyte-Melville, *The Gladiators: A Tale of Rome and Judaea*

Lew Wallace, *Ben Hur: A Tale of the Christ*

H. Rider Haggard, *The Ghost Kings* and *Pearl Maiden, a Tale of the Fall of Jerusalem*

H. G. Wells, miscellaneous science-fiction stories

DECEMBER 17/18 (Thu/Fri)

Jack and Warren's train journey home for the holidays from Wynyard School to Belfast is as follows: They travel to Euston Station from Watford on the 3.28 p.m., arriving at 4.05 p.m. The brothers sit "for an interminable time" before catching the 5.30 p.m. for Fleetwood, Lancashire. The Fleetwood Boat Train stops at Stafford, Crewe, Warrington, Wigan, and Preston. It arrives at Fleetwood at 10.25 p.m. They then embark on the steamer for Belfast, which deposits them on Donegal Quay at 5.45 a.m. the next morning.

DECEMBER 25 (Fri)

Lewis, we may surmise, is given for Christmas *Blackie's Children's Annual* for 1909. [*In it appears for the first time Edith Nesbit's short story* The Aunt and Amabel, *in which Amabel finds her way into a magical world through a "Bigwardrobeinaspareroom."*]

CHAPTER TWO

School Days and Tutorage: Watford, Malvern, and Great Bookham

(1909–1916)

────────•═══•────────

Within weeks of his mother's death in August 1908, Jack was enrolled at Wynyard School, Watford, near London. Warren had entered there in May 1905 and so was worldly-wise to its brutal ways. Jack found the regime at Wynyard little short of unbearable. Educationally, it was barren. "The only stimulating element in the teaching," he recorded years later, "consisted of a few well-used canes which hung on the green iron chimney-piece of the single school-room." The headmaster, Rev. Robert Capron, ran the school rather like Crichton House described by F. Anstey in his *Vice Versa*, observed by the bitter Lewis to be "the only truthful school story in existence." Warren added his own condemnation: "In spite of Capron's policy of terror the school was slack and inefficient, and the time-table, if such it could be called, ridiculous. When not saying lessons, the boys spent the whole of school working out sums on slates; of this endless arithmetic there was little or no supervision. Of the remaining subjects, English and Latin consisted, the first solely and the second mainly, of grammar. History was a ceaseless circuit of the late Middle Ages; Geography was a meaningless list of rivers, towns, imports and exports."

The school closed ingloriously in the summer term of 1910, and by September 1910 Jack was enrolled as a boarder back home at Campbell College, Belfast, just one mile from Little Lea. He only lasted there until November, when he was withdrawn with worrying chest problems. These difficulties were not eased by the fact that Jack by now, like his brother, was a confirmed and secret smoker. Once again in Warren's larger footsteps, Lewis was sent to Malvern, in the English West Midlands. The spa town was famous as a health resort, especially for those with lung problems. He was enrolled as a student at Cherbourg Preparatory School (which he referred to in *Surprised by Joy* as "Chartres," to hide its identity), a small school close by Malvern College where Warren was enrolled as a student. Jack remained there until June 1913. It was during this time that he abandoned his childhood Christian faith in favor of materialism (which he later, in his book *Miracles*, called "naturalism") and sought solace in his imaginative life.

In *Surprised by Joy* we learn how he lost his faith during his terms at Cherbourg School, which had much to do with esoteric religious interests of the matron, Miss Cowie. Other reasons conspired to make him drop his faith with no sense of loss but with the greatest relief. An unnatural preoccupation with prayer had made it a painful penance. A native pessimism had evolved from his clumsiness with his hands, his mother's death, the shadow of Wynyard School, and his father's unconcealed fears, usually unwarranted, such as of bankruptcy. A sweet sexuality, too, was awakened at this time by the beauty of his dance teacher. She was the first woman he ever "looked upon to lust after her," though she was guilty of no deliberate provocation.

In September 1913 Jack received a classical scholarship and entered Malvern College. Around this time he was working on one of many writings, "Loki Bound," a poetic tragedy about the Norse gods. Then, in April 1914, he got to know someone who would become a soul mate—Arthur Greeves (1895–1966), who lived in a large house, "Bernagh," just up from Little Lea. Lewis later said of him that, after his brother Warren, Arthur was his oldest and closest friend.

A second life-changing event occurred soon after. On September 19, 1914, Jack began private study with William T. Kirkpatrick (1848–1921), "The Great Knock," in Great Bookham, near Leatherhead, Surrey, with whom he was to remain until April 1917. His private tutorage under the retired headteacher was one of the happiest periods of his life. He blossomed under the stringent rationality and formidable classical discipline of this scholar. At the same time, in a kind of parallel life, he discovered the beauty of the English countryside and fantasy writers such as William Morris. Kirkpatrick allowed him rapidly to catch up on the wasted years of education and then to outspeed his contemporaries at the best schools. He also prepared Jack for the Oxford entrance examinations, the boy's only weak area being in mathematics.

1909

W. H. Taft becomes president of the United States. The Girl Guides movement is founded. Henry Ford's "Model T" car is produced.

Eric Ambler, Isaiah Berlin, Ernst Gombrich, Malcolm Lowry, James Reeves, and Stephen Spender are born.

Arthur William à Beckett, Rosa Nouchette Carey, John Davidson, George Manville Fenn, Frederick Greenwood, Sir Theodore Martin, George Meredith, Algernon Charles Swinburne, and John Millington Synge die.

FEBRUARY 21 (Sun)

Jack writes to Albert from Wynyard School thanking him for sending H. G. Wells's *The First Men in the Moon*.

APRIL 9 (Fri)

The town of Widnes in England introduces the first closed-top double-decker buses.

[*Twenty years later Lewis becomes convinced of God's existence while travelling in such a bus up Headington hill in Oxford.*]

SUMMER

Jack composes a historical novel, a fragment of which has survived, called "The Ajimywanian War."

— *Unpublished Writings in Early Life* —

The Ajimywanian War

Childhood of Medea

The "Easley Fragment"

Foster

Hegemony of Moral Values

Helen

Hippolytus

King of Drum

Loki Bound

Metrical Meditations of a Cod

Moving Image

My Life During the Exmas Holadys of 1907

Nimue

Optimism

Pudaita Pie

The Quest of Bleheris

Some Problems of Metaphor

Tristram and King Mark

Way's the Way (with Leo Baker)

Wild Hunt

JULY 25 (Sun)

Frenchman Louis Blériot flies across the English Channel in a monoplane, winning a £1,000 prize offered by the Daily Mail.

SEPTEMBER

Warren becomes a student at Malvern College, Malvern, England.

NOVEMBER 29 (Mon)

Jack's eleventh birthday.

DECEMBER 15 (Wed)

Jack and another Wynyard pupil, Mears, take part in a paper chase, as the hares. Jack considers this absurd, as he and Mears are the two worst runners in the school. They keep up, however, and run a good long way before getting caught by the chasing boys.

1910

The reign of George V begins. Japan annexes Korea. The Union of South Africa becomes a dominion. Arthur Evans excavates Knossos. One of the most influential books of the early twentieth century, The Great Illusion, *by Sir Norman Angell, is published. It will sell more than a million copies.*

A. J. Ayer, William Cooper (Harry Summerfield Hoff), Norman MacCaig, Wilfred Thesiger, Jean Anouilh, and C. V. Wedgwood are born.

F. J. Furnivall, A. J. Munby, Leo Tolstoy, Anna Laetitia Waring, William Holman Hunt, William James, and Florence Nightingale die.

JANUARY

On his way back to Wynyard School Jack's second cousin on his mother's side, Hope Ewart, takes him to see *Peter Pan* in London, which makes a lasting impression on the eleven-year old boy. [*In contrast, theater visits to the Belfast Hippodrome tended to follow Albert's tastes for musical comedies and vaudeville.*]

MARCH 10 (Thu)

The first Hollywood film, D. W. Griffith's In Old California, *is released.*

APRIL 27 (Wed)

Wynyard's Capron writes to Albert, informing him that he is "giving up school work." [*In fact the school had been in terminal decline a long time, and Capron is now unable to sustain his façade.*]

MAY 6 (Fri)

King Edward VII dies from pneumonia. George V—cousin of Kaiser Wilhelm II of Germany—takes the British throne.

JULY 12 (Tue)

Today is Jack's last day as a student at Wynyard.

SUMMER

Wynyard School closes in ignominy.

AUGUST 19 (Fri)

Albert, Warren, and Jack set off to visit William Lewis (Albert's brother) in Scotland.

SEPTEMBER

Jack is enrolled as a boarding student at Campbell College, Belfast, "which had been founded with the express purpose of giving Ulster boys all the advantages of a public [i.e., private] school education without the trouble of crossing the Irish Sea." Campbell is near Little Lea; however, it is arranged that Jack should go as a boarder, but able to come home every Sunday. [*Because of its noise and constant movement Lewis later described it as "very like living permanently in a large railway station."*]

NOVEMBER 13 (Sun)

Albert writes to Warren at Malvern College: "When Jacks came home this morning he had such a frightful cough that I had Dr. Leslie up to examine him. As a result, Leslie has advised me not to send him back to school for some days.... I am strongly inclined to send Jacks [to Cherbourg, a preparatory school at Malvern] until he's old enough to go to the College." [*Later in the month, Jack is withdrawn from Campbell College.*]

NOVEMBER 29 (Tue)

Jack's twelfth birthday.

1911

The Chinese Republic is proclaimed. There is a crisis in Agadir. Suffragettes riot in Whitehall, London. Roald Amundsen reaches the South Pole on December 14, one month before Robert F. Scott. The British Copyright Act is passed.

Walter Allen, Sybille Bedford, William Golding, Flann O'Brien (Brian O'Nolan), Mervyn Peake, Tennessee Williams, and Terence Rattigan are born.

Sir Charles Wentworth Dilke, Sir Francis Galton, Sir William Schwenck Gilbert, and Gustav Mahler die.

JANUARY

Warren continues as student at Malvern College, and Jack is enrolled at the neighboring Cherbourg Preparatory School (which he refers to as "Chartres"). This is made up of around twenty boys between the ages of eight and twelve. He is pleased to discover that they have hot water in the mornings, unlike at Wynyard and Campbell College.

At the end of the month Jack goes with his school to hear a performance of Handel's *Messiah*, which he enjoys immensely. A favorite piece, "Comfort ye," is sung by "a stout and hideous gentleman" whose voice, however, is excellent. [*"Here indeed," Lewis later wrote, "my education really began." Malvern at this time is famous as a health resort, especially for those with lung problems. Lewis is to remain at Cherbourg until June 1913. It is during this period that he abandons his childhood Christian faith. He also rapidly finds his footing in English and Latin.*]

APRIL 7 (Fri)

The British Parliament passes a bill providing authors and musicians with copyright protection, lasting for fifty years after death.

—— *Essays Written at Cherbourg* ——

Jack compiles a "book" of thirty-five essays written at Cherbourg, including:

"Party Government"

"Richard Wagner"

"Perseverance"

Si vis pacem, para bellum

"Are athletes better than scholars?"

"All is not gold that glitters."

JUNE 15 (Thu)

Annie Strahan arrives as housekeeper at Little Lea. According to the *Lewis Papers*, she turns out to be the "best & longest lived of Albert's succession of housekeepers."

JULY 23 (Sun)

School term is over. Jack gets home early in the morning from the overnight ferry across the Irish Sea, travelling from Malvern, following a train route which means a change at Hereford, where he catches the West and North Express, which stops at Shrewsbury, Chester, and Lime Street, Liverpool. To Albert's satisfaction, Jack looks in fine health, and he is glad to find him in good spirits. He feels that his son will be rather lonely until Warren arrives back home. Jack, however, immediately sets about reading, drawing, and writing, and going off with his bike across the Holywood Hills.

AUGUST

During this month there is a record heat wave, with temperatures up to ninety-seven degrees Fahrenheit at times, leading to thousands of deaths. In one week 855 children below the age of two die.

Albert, Warren, and Jack visit Dunbar, in Scotland, for a joint vacation with Uncle Richard (Albert's brother), Aunt Agnes, and his cousins Eileen and Leonard.

NOVEMBER 18 (Sat)

Robert Capron, Jack's and Warren's brutal ex-headmaster at Wynyard, dies in Camberwell House Asylum.

NOVEMBER 29 (Wed)

Jack's thirteenth birthday.

DECEMBER

Jack is suddenly overwhelmed by the return of the experience he calls "Joy," or a sweet, inconsolable longing. He glimpses the Christmas issue of *The Bookman*. It has a colored supplement reproducing several of Arthur Rackham's illustrations to *Siegfried and the Twilight of the Gods*. This soon leads him to begin composing "Loki Bound," inspired by Norse myth but Greek in form.

1912

Robert F. Scott reaches the South Pole on January 17. The faked "Piltdown Man" remains are produced. The First Balkan War takes place. The Titanic sinks on her maiden voyage. Charles Williams publishes a volume of poetry, The Silver Stair.

Kenneth Allott, John Cage, R. F. Delderfield, Nigel Dennis, Lawrence Durrell, Roy Fuller, William Douglas Home, Pamela Hansford Johnson, Mary Lavin, Anne Ridler, William Sansom, R. W. Southern, Julian Symons, and the novelist Elizabeth Taylor are born.

Robert Barr, William Booth, George Grossmith, Andrew Lang, Justin McCarthy, Robert F. Scott, W. W. Skeat, Bram Stoker, and Henry Sweet die.

JANUARY

Warren begins to keep a diary. [*By the end of his life he will have written more than a million and a quarter words, filling twenty-three handwritten volumes, much of their accounts concerning his brother.*]

FEBRUARY 3 (Sat)

Warren records in his diary skating on Newpool in Malvern. It is his first attempt, and not nearly so hard as he has expected. Jack is with him, and, according to

Warren, also skates, picking it up "quite well." The two of them skate together most of the time that day at the pool.

MARCH

Warren's confirmation at Malvern College, in an Anglican ceremony.

APRIL 15 (Mon)

The Belfast-built Titanic sinks—more than 1,500 of the 2,340 passengers and crew die in the freezing waters of the north Atlantic.

[Jack and Warren would have been able to see the ship under construction in the Belfast docks.]

SUMMER

Jack visits his cousin Hope Ewart (now Mrs. George Harding) in Dundrum, near Dublin. Here he finds the actual illustrated edition of *Siegfried and the Twilight of the Gods* that the 1911 Christmas edition of *The Bookman* had featured.

NOVEMBER 29 (Fri)

Jack's fourteenth birthday.

DECEMBER

Warren asks his father for permission to smoke [*though, as early as spring of 1911, Warren records that both he and Jack were already "confirmed smokers"*].

1913

The Second and Third Balkan Wars take place. Woodrow Wilson becomes president of the United States. A Society for Pure English is founded by Robert Bridges, and he is appointed Britain's Poet Laureate. The New Statesman *is established.*

Benjamin Britten, Albert Camus, Barbara Pym, R. S. Thomas, and Angus Wilson are born.

Alfred Austin, Edward Dowden, Emily Lawless, Frederick Rolfe, Alfred Russel Wallace, and Mark Rutherford (William Hale White) die.

JANUARY 31 (Fri)

At just one minute past midnight the British House of Lords rejects Home Rule for Ireland.

MAY 24 (Sat)

Warren decides to join the Royal Army Service Corps (RASC) as a career.

JUNE 3 (Tue)

This evening, Jack begins his scholarship examination to enter Malvern College. His first scholarship paper is on Latin and Greek grammar and Latin prose. [*He takes the examination over several days while ill in bed at school with a high temperature. Many years later, after Lewis's death, Warren observed, "I am inclined to rate his winning of a scholarship under these circumstances as the greatest academic triumph of his career."*]

JUNE 4 (Wed)

This morning, he takes his second paper, on Latin translation and verses. Then in the afternoon comes the Essay paper, which he relishes.

JUNE 5 (Thu)

Jack takes a "general" paper, which includes history and geography, scripture, and English, in which time runs out

—— Lewis's Scholarship Examination ——

Examination questions for the Essay paper (the candidate chooses one):

1. The qualities of a successful soldier.

2. The possibility of a universal language.

3. West is West, and East is East, and never the twain shall meet.

Jack chose No. 3, applying it mainly to "the Indian question."

---

before he finishes. Later he does a French paper, which he finds difficult. Finally comes the paper on arithmetic and algebra.

JULY

Warren completes his education at Malvern College on a sour note, as he is expelled for smoking and other pranks. He is to go to Great Bookham in Surrey to be tutored by William T. Kirkpatrick, his father's former teacher.

JULY 29 (Tue)

Cherbourg School breaks up for the summer vacation. Jack's parting shot is his first published poem, which appears in the school magazine: "Quam Bene Saturno," in the style of Tibullus, a minor Latin poet.

AUGUST

Jack and Warren holiday at Dundrum, near Dublin, staying with Hope and George Harding. As Jack cycles with Warren through the Wicklow Mountains he finds himself seeing them through Wagner's eyes—getting glimpses of a Wagnerian world of Nordic romance—and gaining a new appreciation for the natural world. [*Throughout his life Lewis was enraptured by the romantic world of Wagner's music, as based on*

German and Scandinavian mythology. His cousin Hope had written earlier in the year to Albert, delighted at the news of Jack's scholarship. She added, "I can't say I'm surprised, however, for I always knew he was a remarkable boy, besides being one of the most lovable I ever came across. George and I are looking forward to the boys' visit in the summer holidays very much."]

SEPTEMBER 10 (Wed)

Warren begins private studies with William T. Kirkpatrick, in "Gastons" cottage, Great Bookham, Surrey, to cram for the entrance exam to the Royal Military Academy at Sandhurst.

SEPTEMBER 18 (Thu)

Jack is enrolled at Malvern College (which he later dubs "Wyvern") and stays until the following June. [*He finds life there uncongenial but receives some satisfaction working on "Loki Bound," his tragedy about Norse gods. The main contrast in his play is between Loki's sad wisdom and Thor's brutal orthodoxy. Thor, in reality, symbolizes "the Bloods" of Malvern College—the ruling older boys. Loki is a projection of Lewis's own self.*]

NOVEMBER

Warren takes the army entrance exam. Jack spends more than two weeks in the sanatorium at Malvern College recovering from a chest infection.

NOVEMBER 29 (Sat)

Jack's fifteenth birthday.

DECEMBER

Warren completes his intensive studies with Kirkpatrick and travels back to Ireland via Malvern, so that he can attend a House Supper there (the boys were divided into several Houses) and accompany his brother for the return home to Little Lea for Christmas. At Malvern he notices his brother's deep unhappiness. That House Supper, he records, is "a noisy, cheerful function, of which all I remember is Jacks's gloom and boredom glaringly obvious to all, and not tending to increase his popularity with the House." [It was not gloom all the time, however. A fellow student, Hardman (later Air Chief Marshal Sir Donald Hardman) recalled a not-so-dreary Lewis: "I can remember going with him for long walks on Sundays when he was in the gayest of moods—story telling and mimicking people."]

CHRISTMAS

Albert gives Jack a copy of The Rhinegold and the Valkyries, to match Siegfried and the Twilight of the Gods. [This is a good move on Albert's part. Jack is deep into "Northernness," looking deeper than Wagner's versions, and discovering the Norse and Icelandic originals of northern myth.]

1914

Suffragettes damage Velasquez's Rokeby Venus in the National Gallery, London. Austria's Archduke Francis (Franz) Ferdinand is assassinated at Sarajevo. Germany declares war on Russia, then France, and invades Belgium; Britain declares war on Germany. World War I begins: the battles of Namur and Mons are fought, the German invasion of France is halted at the Battle of the Marne, and the First Battle of Ypres takes place. The Panama Canal opens.

Patric Dickinson, Ronald Duncan, Laurie Lee, Gavin Maxwell, Patrick O'Brian, Henry Reed, C. H. Sisson, and Dylan Thomas are born.

Robert Hugh Benson, S. R. Crockett, Theodore Watts-Dunton, and Sir Alain-Fournier die.

JANUARY 9 (Fri)

Warren's results for the army examination are published, and the family is relieved and overjoyed to discover that he has passed 21st out of 201 successful candidates for the Royal Military Academy at Sandhurst.

FEBRUARY 3 (Tue)

Warren enters Sandhurst.

FEBRUARY 16 (Mon)

Jack reports to his father that "Smugy" (Harry Wakelyn Smith, a popular teacher of Classics and English at Malvern) has set the English class a task which has three alternatives: (a) a poem in imitation of Horace asking a friend to stay with you at the most beautiful place you know; (b) a picture of a specified scene from Sophocles; (c) an original ghost story. He chooses the first, inviting the imaginary friend to stay at Castlerock (though the place name is changed to nearby Moville, to suit the verse). Jack treats the cliffs, sea, and other features of Castlerock with considerable care.

MARCH 18 (Wed)

Jack writes to his father that school life, with its attendant bullying and teasing, gets harder to bear and more severe as the term progresses. He begs him to take him out of the school as soon as possible. [In Surprised by Joy *Lewis will sum up his state at the time*: "I was tired, dog-tired, cab-horse tired, tired (almost) like a child in a factory." *Albert this time takes Jack seriously—he constantly worries about his son. He confides in Warren, in a letter:* "He is very uncomfortable at Malvern. He is not popular with the prefects apparently, and gets more than a fair share of the [teasing] and bullying. In a word, the thing is a failure and must be ended. His letters make me

unhappy. . . . *I suppose the best thing I can do is to send him to 'Kirk' after*
next term." Warren will observe many years later, in his preface to the
Letters of C. S. Lewis: *"The fact is that he should never have been*
sent to a public school at all. Already, at fourteen, his intelligence was such
that he would have fitted in better among undergraduates than among
schoolboys; and by his temperament he was bound to be a misfit, a heretic,
an object of suspicion within the collective-minded and standardizing
Public School system. He was, indeed, lucky to leave Malvern before the
power of this system had done him any lasting damage."]

MARCH 25 (Wed)

Jack arrives at Little Lea for the Easter vacation, full of
unhappiness over Malvern. Albert continues to correspond
with Warren about what to do, and about the possibility
of Jack going to Kirkpatrick (as Warren did) for tutoring.

MARCH 29 (Sun)

Albert writes to Warren that "knowing Jacks's mind and
character, I am not greatly surprised to find him and a Public
School unsuited to one another. . . . In saying that I blame
neither the one nor the other. He is simply out of his proper environment, and would possibly wither and decay
rather than grow if kept in such surroundings. . . . What is
to be done? For a boy like Jacks to spend the next three or
four years alone with an old man like Kirk is almost certain
to strengthen the very faults that are strongest in his dispo-
sition. He will make no acquaintances. He will see few people and he will grow more into a hermit than ever. The position is a difficult one and gives me many anxious hours."

APRIL

Jack becomes close friends with his Belfast acquaintance
and neighbor Arthur Greeves. [In 1933 he will say that Arthur
was, "[a]fter my brother, my oldest and most intimate friend." Owen

Barfield, reflecting after Lewis's death, remarks: "His friendship with Arthur Greeves . . . was based entirely on their seeing things from the same angle rather than on their having the same sort of minds." In his fifties Lewis confesses in Surprised by Joy: *"Many thousands of people have had the experience of finding the first friend, and it is none the less a wonder; as great a wonder . . . as first love, or even a greater."*]

JUNE 2 (Tue)

This term Jack discovers the poems and plays of W. B. Yeats in the Malvern College library (the "Grundy"). He reports today to Arthur Greeves in a letter that Yeats writes with "rare spirit and beauty" of their Irish mythology. His works have the eerie and strange quality that he and Arthur love; what he would later call "romance" in literature, providing a glimpse of other worlds. In the same letter Jack lyrically recalls shared memories of County Down, which he is missing: he pictures the prospect of Belfast Lough and the distant Cave Hill from beside the Shepherd's Hut, the sun's rise over the Holywood Hills, and the refreshing tranquility of early morning. [*Other memories he cherishes at different times are the "distant murmurings" of the dockyards and the fragrance of the small glens and windswept meadows of the nearby hills.*]

JUNE 23 (Tue)

Jack and another boy by the name of Cooper unexpectedly are asked by "Smugy" (his teacher Harry Wakelyn Smith) to accompany him for an excursion. They are driven to the village of Birchwood, to the northwest, where they have tea in an inn, and then walk through sunny cornfields and woods under a cloudless sky. Jack finds the countryside enchanting, with the Malvern Hills a dark and unreal mass close by the horizon, striking in their weird beauty. During their walk they come across a small cottage favored by the composer Sir Edward Elgar as a summer retreat. Jack learns that Elgar and "Smugy" had been on close terms in their younger days.

JUNE 28 (Sun)

The heir to the Austro-Hungarian throne, Archduke Francis Ferdinand, visits Sarajevo, in the Balkans. There he is assassinated, along with his wife, the duchess of Hohenberg. The event precipitates a crisis that will lead to World War I.

JULY 23 (Thu)

Austria makes war almost inevitable by issuing impossible demands upon Serbia in the wake of the assassination. British attempts to mediate are dismissed as insolent by the German kaiser.

AUGUST 4 (Tue)

Germany invades Belgium this morning, and Britain declares war, as its people return to work after the Monday bank holiday. Within hours five superpowers are at war—the Austro-Hungarians, the Germans, the Russians, the French, and the British.

AUGUST 5 (Wed)

While home in Ireland on leave, Warren is recalled to Sandhurst.

AUGUST 17 (Mon)

The British Expeditionary Force lands in France to defend it.

SEPTEMBER 19 (Sat)

Jack is met at Bookham station by William T. Kirkpatrick. Within two days he is presented with Homer, whom he has not previously read. Kirkpatrick reads aloud about twenty lines of the Greek, and translates. This goes on with a few explanations for another hundred lines or so. Then he leaves Jack to go over it with the aid of a dictionary, and to make as much sense of it as he can. The lad has no difficulty in memorizing every word as he looks up its meaning. [*Soon Jack is able to understand what he reads without translating it, actually starting to think in Greek; what he will call the music of Homer becomes a very part of him. Mrs. Kirkpatrick often plays piano music to Jack in the evenings, much to his delight—Chopin, Beethoven, Grieg, and many other old favorites, helping him to feel at home.*]

—A Typical Day in Great Bookham—

Breakfast at 8.00 a.m.

A walk until 9.15

9.15–11.00—reading *The Iliad* in the original language, or similar

11.00—a little break

11.15–1.00—return to Latin

Luncheon at 1.00 p.m.

Afternoon, until 5.00 p.m.—time at his own disposal to read or write or wander the surrounding countryside

5–7—more study with Kirkpatrick

7.30 p.m.—dinner

Evening—after dinner Jack pursues a more relaxed course of English literature, mapped out by Kirkpatrick, excluding novels (felt to be more suitable for leisure reading).

This routine became for him the pattern of a "normal day." Lewis later wrote that "if I could please myself I would always live as I lived there."

SEPTEMBER 26 (Sat)

Recording his new experiences of life with the Kirkpatricks, Jack writes to Arthur Greeves that, now he's tried it for a week, he is already convinced that he is going to have the time of his life—and so it turns out to be for the next two and a half years.

SEPTEMBER 29 (Tue)

A short story, The Bowmen, *by horror writer Arthur Machen, is published in the London* Evening News. *The story tells of the bowmen of Agincourt—from the distant past of King Arthur's Britain—supernaturally appearing above the war trenches at Ypres and using their ghostly arrows against the formidable mechanical weapons of the Germans. German victory seems assured at this time, but the short story kindles tales from the British front lines of supernatural help, culminating in accounts of the angel or angels of Mons. Machen's work of fiction is perceived by many as factual, just as years later Orson Welles's radio theater of H. G. Wells's* War of the Worlds *will be believed—especially around Grover's Mills, New Jersey (identified as the alien invasion point in the broadcast).*

SEPTEMBER 30 (Wed)

Warren is appointed to a commission as a second lieutenant in the Royal Army Service Corps (RASC). Jack notes in a letter to Arthur that "war fever" is raging around the Bookham neighborhood. [*Wartime pressures mean that Warren's officer training is speeded to nine months instead of two years.*]

OCTOBER 6 (Tue)

Jack writes to Arthur enclosing the plot outline of the poetic tragedy he is writing, "Loki Bound," hoping for Arthur to collaborate by composing music for it.

OCTOBER 13 (Tue)

Jack reports to his father in a letter that the village is fussing about with a scheme to prepare a cottage for Belgian refugees. [*With the rapid German push into Belgium, tens of thousands of refugees have poured into England.*]

OCTOBER 17 (Sat)

Jack goes with Mrs. Kirkpatrick to visit the family of seven Belgian refugees now installed in the cottage the village has prepared. Jack tries out his French, with the help of a stilted phrasebook. He is able to tell the Belgian mother that he is well, asks her if she is, remarks on the wetness or fineness of the weather, and asks if her child is well. [*Amongst the family is a teenage girl on whom he is to develop a crush, the development of which he shares with Arthur in sometimes embroidered detail. The "brown girl" of his story* The Pilgrim's Regress *may owe something to his sexual fantasies about the refugee girl at this time.*]

NOVEMBER 4 (Wed)

Warren is deployed to France, where he serves with the 4th Company 7th Divisional Train BEF (British Expeditionary Force), based at Le Havre.

MID-NOVEMBER

Bookham is coated with a deep fall of snow. [*Jack, in his simple delight, sees it in terms almost of what we, from our hindsight, recognize as being like the future winter-world of Narnia.*] The nearby pine wood, particularly, has white snow masses on trees and ground, forming a "beautiful sight." He almost expects a hasty "march of dwarfs" to pass. [*Many years later, Lewis will remember about the origin of Narnia:* "The Lion, [the Witch and the Wardrobe] *all began with a picture of a Faun carrying an umbrella and parcels in a snowy wood. This picture had been in my mind since I was about sixteen. Then one day, when I was about forty, I said to myself: 'Let's try to make a story about it.'*"]

NOVEMBER 28 (Sat)

In deference to Albert, Jack returns to Belfast for his confirmation, in Anglican practice, at St. Mark's Church.

NOVEMBER 29 (Sun)

Jack's sixteenth birthday.

DECEMBER 6 (Sun)

To his later shame, Jack goes through the rites of confirmation disbelieving in the Christian faith. [In Surprised by Joy *he confesses: "My relations to my father help to explain (I am not suggesting they excuse) one of the worst acts of my life. I allowed myself to be prepared for confirmation, and confirmed, and to make my first Communion, in total disbelief, acting a part, eating and drinking my own condemnation." While at Bookham, ironically, he has been attending church under the eye of his atheist teacher.*]

CHRISTMAS VACATION

Over these "holydays" (as Jack likes to call the holidays) it is likely that he confides in Arthur his secret feelings for the pretty Belgian refugee girl.

1915

The Second Battle of Ypres is fought; the Germans use poison gas on the western front; Anglo-French forces land at Gallipoli; Italy declares war on Germany and Austria-Hungary; there is the first zeppelin attack on London; and nurse Edith Cavell is executed by the Germans in Brussels.

Saul Bellow, Monica Dickens, Patrick Leigh Fermor, Marghanita Laski, Alun Lewis, Olivia Manning, and Arthur Miller are born.

Rolf Boldrewood (Thomas Alexander Browne), Mary Elizabeth Braddon, Rupert Brooke, James Elroy Flecker, Stephen Phillips, and W. G. Grace die.

Important People in Lewis's _____
School Days

Annie Strahan—cook-cum-housekeeper at Little Lea from 1911 to 1917.

Arthur Greeves—a close friend of Lewis from teenage years who shared the secret of joy and a similar taste in reading and all things "northern," such as Old Norse mythology. Arthur's skill was in visual art rather than words, though he was an appreciative reader of an extensive life-long correspondence from Lewis. Arthur lived at a house called Bernagh, nearly opposite Little Lea in Belfast. Lewis continued to meet up with Arthur until his death. Between 1921 and 1923 Arthur Greeves studied at the prestigious Slade School of Fine Art in London. Later he exhibited with the Royal Hibernian Academy in Dublin. Lewis did not share Arthur's faith (Arthur came from a Christian Brethren background) until 1931, and later Arthur explored varieties of faith, concluding his life as a Quaker.

"Pogo"—nickname for Percy Gerald Kelsal Harris, a young teacher at Cherbourg School, Malvern, fresh from Oxford University. He was to the youthful C. S. Lewis an attractively worldly-wise figure. He instilled in Lewis a desire for swagger, glitter, and to be part of what he later was to call "the inner ring." Lewis was to meet him in the war trenches. Harris was then a different man—a seasoned officer whose courage was to win him the Military Cross and a place in the history of World War I.

Miss G. E. Cowie—Matron at Cherbourg School, whom Lewis found a comfort during illness and cheering and companionable when he was well. Having lost his mother, he particularly was drawn to her. She also had infectious esoteric and spiritualist beliefs, a vague kind of Theosophy that helped to undermine Lewis's adherence to what seemed harsh Christian creeds.

Belgian girl—a young refugee from the war with whom Lewis fell in love while at Bookham and tried awkwardly to meet up with.

Janie McNeill (1889–1959)—a Belfast friend who as a callow youth Lewis often regarded as a nuisance. As he got older, and the friendship endured, he came to appreciate her qualities and strength of character. Jane was the daughter of the headteacher of Campbell College, James Adams McNeill. _That Hideous Strength_ was dedicated to her.

Cont.

"Smugy" or *"Smewgy"*—nickname for Harry Wakelyn Smith, a favorite teacher of Classics and English at Malvern College, and friend of composer Edward Elgar. He died as a result of the deadly influenza that spread across Europe at the end of World War I.

William T. Kirkpatrick (1848–1921)—Lewis's tutor from 1914 to 1917 and nicknamed by him "the Great Knock" because of the impact of his stringent logical mind on the teenager. Kirkpatrick was then retired as headmaster of Lurgan College, in Northern Ireland, which Albert had attended. He lived in Gastons, Great Bookham, Surrey, where Lewis lodged happily during the tutorage. Lewis held a great affection for Kirkpatrick, describing him as the person who came closer to being "a purely logical entity" than anyone else he had ever met. Kirkpatrick's method was to combine language study with firsthand experience of major works; he guided Lewis in German, French, Italian, Latin, and classical Greek. His rationalism and atheism reinforced Lewis's own beliefs at that time. Kirkpatrick made his mark on Lewis's fiction, to be seen in some characteristics of the learned Professor Digory Kirke in the Narnian Chronicles and in the skeptical Ulsterman Andrew MacPhee in *That Hideous Strength*.

JANUARY 7 (Thu)

Kirkpatrick writes to Albert about Jack: "He was born with the literary temperament and we have to face that fact with all it implies. This is not a case of early precocity showing itself in rapid assimilation of knowledge and followed by subsequent indifference or torpor. As I said before, it is the maturity and originality of his literary judgements which is so unusual and surprising. By an unerring instinct he detects first rate quality in literary workmanship, and the second rate does not interest him in any way." [*Jack continues to read voraciously, one of his latest discoveries being Thomas Malory's* Morte D'Arthur, *opening up a new world to him.*]

JANUARY 23? (Sat?)

The unfortunate village curate, unwary of Kirkpatrick's fierce and uncompromising logic, stops by at Gastons at afternoon teatime. He tells several "patriotic lies" about the Germans and Germany. Allowing him to finish, Kirkpatrick calmly proves point by point that the statements the curate made are not only fallacious and impossible, but also ridiculous. Jack and the rest of the tea-drinkers enjoy Kirkpatrick's procedure "hugeously."

EARLY FEBRUARY

Warren has his first leave from France—one week; Jack is allowed by Kirkpatrick to travel home to Little Lea with him, returning to Bookham on February 9 (Tuesday).

MARCH 7 (Sun)

Jack reports that a serviceman, Gerald Smythe, who has recently lost an arm in battle, stayed at Gastons the previous week. He has only been up from his bed for a week, yet will be returning to the front the next week. Gerald has even learned to light his pipe with one hand, Jack notes. [*Gerald's example is likely to have been one of many factors that steeled Jack's resolve to enlist and fight.*]

MARCH 28 (Sun)

Kirkpatrick fills in Albert about his son's astonishing learning. While, in his opinion, still rather behind with Greek grammar, Jack "has a sort of genius for translating. . . . He has read more classics in the time than any boy I ever had, and that too very carefully and exactly. In Homer his achievement is unique—53 books or more of the *Iliad* and 9 of the *Odyssey*. It will not surprise you to learn that in the Sophoclean drama, which attains a high level in poetic expression, especially in the lyric portions, he could beat me easily in the happy choice of words and phrases. . . . He is the most brilliant translator of Greek plays I have ever met."

MARCH 30 (Tue)

Jack reports to Arthur that he has received a letter from the Belgian girl, which had pleased him very much.

APRIL 18 (Sun)

Helen Joy Davidman is born in the Woodlawn neighborhood of the Bronx, New York City. [*Joy Davidman is to be Lewis's wife late in his life.*]

JUNE

German zeppelins bomb London.

JUNE 29 (Tue)

Writing to Arthur, Jack describes himself as liking "sleeping late, good food & clothes etc as well as sonnets & thunderstorms."

JULY

Jack continues his astonishingly wide reading. This month he is reading *Prometheus Bound* (in Greek, "a red letter day in my life"), Aristotle, Horace, Keats, Ruskin, and Virginia Woolf.

JULY 4 (Sun)

Warren arrives in Bookham on his way home to Belfast on leave from the front. Jack accompanies him and returns to Bookham on July 9.

─────── *Lewis's Reading at the Time* ───────

Agricola, by Tacitus

Anatomy of Melancholy, by Robert Burton

Arcadia, by Sir Philip Sidney

The *Argonautica* of Apollonius Rhodius (in Greek)

Aristotle

Beowulf

Jane Eyre, Villette, and *The Professor,* by Charlotte Brontë

The Canterbury Tales, by Geoffrey Chaucer

Samuel Taylor Coleridge

Comus, by John Milton

Confessions of an Opium Eater, by Thomas De Quincey

Corpus Poeticum Boreale, by F. York Powell (edition of all the mythological
    poems in the *Elder Edda*)

The Essays of Elia

The Faerie Queene, by Edmund Spenser

The Grettir Saga: The Story of Grettir the Strong

Headlong Hall, by Thomas Love Peacock

Henry Osmond and *Pendennis,* by William Makepeace Thackeray

Histories, by Herodotus

A History of Ancient Greek Literature, by Gilbert Murray

History of English Literature, by Andrew Lang

Horace

The House of the Seven Gables, by Nathaniel Hawthorne

John Keats

Rudyard Kipling

Laxdaela Saga, translated by M. A. C. Press

Letters from Hell, by Valdemar Adolph Thisted (with an introduction
    by George MacDonald)

Life of Dr. Johnson, by James Boswell

Cont.

Mallet's *Northern Antiquities* (including most of the prose *Edda*)

Mansfield Park, by Jane Austen

The poems and the prose romances of William Morris

Morte D'Arthur, by Thomas Malory

Myths of the Norsemen, by H. A. Guerber

Oiseau Bleu, by Count Maurice Maeterlinck

Othello, by Shakespeare

Paradise Lost, by John Milton

Pericles and Aspasia, by Walter Savage Landor

Phantastes and *The Golden Key*, by George MacDonald

The Pilgrim's Progress, by John Bunyan

Plato

Prometheus Bound (in the original Greek)

Prometheus Bound, by Percy Bysshe Shelley

John Ruskin

Rob Roy and other novels by Walter Scott

Shakespeare's fairy and romantic plays

Love among the Artists, by George Bernard Shaw

Sir Gawain and the Green Knight

The Song of Roland

A Study in Shakespeare, by Algernon Charles Swinburne

Teutonic Myth and Legend, by Donald A. Mackenzie

Tristan (in medieval French)

Tristram Shandy by Laurence Sterne

The Upton Letters by A. C. Benson

Verses on Various Occasions (including "Dream of Gerontius"), by John
  Henry Newman

Virginia Woolf

Wuthering Heights, by Emily Brontë

W. B. Yeats

JULY 28 (Wed)

Jack spends an uncomfortable evening. A "theatrical lady," a young woman by the name of Miss McMullen, is staying with the Kirkpatricks at that time. [*She also stayed the previous October, and is tolerated by the often solitary Jack.*] Tonight, he is employed by her as a dummy for bandage practice, in view of the likely demands of war. He is, in turn, treated for a broken arm, sprained ankle, and head wound. With the accompanying abundant use of pins and small talk this takes up the whole evening.

SEPTEMBER

In France, Warren is transferred to the 3rd Company 7th Divisional Train.

OCTOBER 12 (Tue)

Jack writes to Arthur that, though he has no experience of love, he has something better—acquaintance with great authors writing on love: "We see through their eyes."

OCTOBER 22 (Fri)

In a letter to his father Jack refers to the threat of the German zeppelins. The last time they were here, he recalls, they bombed Waterloo Station in London. From Bookham they saw electric flashes in the skies as a result of the bomb explosions.

NOVEMBER 15? (Mon?)

Jack writes that Kirkpatrick is easily roused on the topical subject of the alleged angels of Mons supporting the British troops. His critical logic comes into action as soon as a visitor mentions that he has met someone who claims to have seen the angels with their own eyes.

NOVEMBER 29 (Mon)

Jack's seventeenth birthday.

DECEMBER 21 (Tue)

Lewis arrives home for the Christmas vacation, where he and Albert are joined by Warren, who is on leave from France.

1916

The Battle of Verdun begins. The Easter Rising in Dublin. The Battle of Jutland is fought; the Battle of the Somme begins; tanks are used for the first time. Roger Casement is executed by the British. There are mutinies and strikes in Russia. David Lloyd George becomes British prime minister. Carl Gustav Jung publishes his Psychology of the Unconscious.

Jack Clemo, Gavin Ewart, and Penelope Fitzgerald are born.

Stopford Brooke, Julia Frankau, Henry James, and "Saki" (Hector Hugh Munro) die.

JANUARY 21 (Fri)

Jack returns to Bookham to continue his tutorage under Kirkpatrick.

FEBRUARY 10 (Thu)

The Military Service Act comes into force (bringing in conscription). Among those obligated to serve are "Every male British subject who, on the fifteenth day of August nineteen hundred and fifteen – (a) was ordinarily resident in Great Britain; and (b) had attained the age of eighteen years and had not attained the age of forty-one years; and (c) was unmarried or was a widower without children dependent on him."

[*Because he is an Irish resident, Jack seems to be excluded from the obligation as being among those who are "resident in Great Britain for the purpose only of their education or for some other purpose." However, as the issue of exemptions for Irishmen is debated over many months, he determines that he will enlist even if exempt from conscription. If he manages to enter Oxford University he will be able to join the Officers' Training Corps and get a commission as soon as his papers come through.*]

FEBRUARY 13 (Sun)

The British Government announces that it plans to recruit four hundred thousand women to till fields.

MARCH 4 (Sat)

Jack finds a weathered copy of George MacDonald's *Phantastes* on the Leatherhead train station bookstall, which powerfully "baptizes his imagination" and impresses him with a deep sense of the holy. It is in the popular Everyman edition. [*Years later he will acknowledge about MacDonald: "I have never concealed the fact that I regard him as my master; indeed, I fancy I have never written a book in which I did not quote from him."*]

APRIL 5 (Wed)–MAY 11 (Thu)

Jack is in Belfast for the Easter vacation. He starts writing poems into a notebook, which he entitles "Metrical Mediations of a Cod," i.e, "a nonsensical fellow." [*Some of the poems will be included in his first publication,* Spirits in Bondage (1919).]

APRIL 7 (Fri)

Kirkpatrick writes to Albert about preparation for the Oxford University entrance examinations. He has no doubts about Jack's abilities. Indeed, "He hardly realizes—

how could he at his age—with what a liberal hand nature has bestowed her bounties on him. . . . He has read more classics that any boy I ever had—or indeed I might add than any I ever heard of, unless it be an Addison or Landor or Macaulay. These are people we read of, but I have never met any."

APRIL 25 (Tue)

The Easter Rising in Dublin.

───── *MacDonald's "Phantastes"* ─────

This is one of ten books Lewis once listed as particularly influencing his thinking and vocational attitude. *Phantastes* was George MacDonald's first work of prose fiction. It begins:

"I awoke one morning with the usual perplexity of mind which accompanies the return of consciousness. As I lay and looked through the eastern window of my room, a faint streak of peach-colour, dividing a cloud that just rose above the low swell of the horizon, announced the approach of the sun. As my thoughts, which a deep and apparently dreamless sleep had dissolved, began again to assume crystalline forms, the strange events of the foregoing night presented themselves anew to my wondering consciousness."

Anodos, the narrator, then recounts how his bedroom had metamorphosed into a woodland scene. He continues:

"After washing as well as I could in the clear stream, I rose and looked around me. The tree under which I seemed to have lain all night was one of the advanced guard of a dense forest, towards which the rivulet ran. Faint traces of a footpath, much overgrown with grass and moss, and with here and there a pimpernel even, were discernible along the right bank. 'This,' thought I, 'must surely be the path into Fairy Land, which the lady of last night promised I should so soon find.' I crossed the rivulet, and accompanied it, keeping the footpath on its right bank, until it led me, as I expected, into the wood."

MAY 16 (Tue)

Jack sends Arthur the first installment of a new piece of writing, a prose romance entitled "The Quest of Bleheris."

MAY 17 (Wed)

Jack goes to London with Mrs. Kirkpatrick to see that year's exhibition of new art at the Royal Academy of Art. He enjoys it very much, though missing Arthur's company (Arthur is on his way to becoming an accomplished artist);

Anodos, whose name means "aimless" or "pathless," has many encounters and adventures, the narrative unfolding with a dreamlike logic rather than the normal pattern of a story. The effect is to convey a mood and new emotional experience that instantly captivated Lewis. It is in this book that he encounters another magical wardrobe of sorts (the first was in Edith Nesbit's story *The Aunt and Amabel*). This time it is a cupboard in the wall inside a mysterious hut in a forest clearing:

"It seemed a common closet, with shelves on each hand, on which stood various little necessaries for the humble uses of a cottage. In one corner stood one or two brooms, in another a hatchet and other common tools; showing that it was in use every hour of the day for household purposes. But, as I looked, I saw that there were no shelves at the back, and that an empty space went in further; its termination appearing to be a faintly glimmering wall or curtain, somewhat less, however, than the width and height of the doorway where I stood. But, as I continued looking, for a few seconds, towards this faintly luminous limit, my eyes came into true relation with their object. All at once, with such a shiver as when one is suddenly conscious of the presence of another in a room where he has, for hours, considered himself alone, I saw that the seemingly luminous extremity was a sky, as of night, beheld through the long perspective of a narrow, dark passage, through what, or built of what, I could not tell. As I gazed, I clearly discerned two or three stars glimmering faintly in the distant blue."

one painting in particular reminds Jack of a walk that he and Arthur had taken through a wood in fierce rain.

SPRING AND SUMMER

Jack is composing "The Quest of Bleheris." He tries to write one chapter every Sunday afternoon. He confesses to Arthur, who receives it in installments, that the meaning is quite anti-Christian, though the story is more important than the "allegory." [*One character, a youth called Wan Jadis, is caught in the Grey Marish (Marsh) on his way to the country of the past. The story is eventually abandoned, but Lewis will use the name "Jadis" for the White Witch in his Narnian Chronicles.*]

JUNE 5 (Mon)

Lord Kitchener, secretary of state for war, dies with all the crew of the British Cruiser Hampshire *when it is sunk by a German submarine off the Orkney Isles.*

[*After he hears the news, Jack wonders, in a later letter to Albert, what the great loss will mean for the war.*]

JUNE 20 (Tue)

Jack shares with Arthur a description of Lyonesse from a French text, *Tristan*, that might have been describing the land of Narnia: "Climbing to the top of the cliff he saw a land full of vallies [*sic*] where forest stretched itself without end."

AUGUST 1 (Tue)

Jack arrives back at Little Lea, and sometime after goes on holiday with Arthur to Portsalon in County Donegal, before returning to Belfast.

SUMMER, BATTLE OF THE SOMME

Henry "Hugo" Victor Dyson Dyson (1896–1975)—later a member of the Inklings, and close friend of Lewis and J. R. R. Tolkien—is twenty, and fighting with the Queen's Own Royal West Kent Regiment. He is severely wounded and has an out-of-body experience. He seems to be looking from above at his shell-ripped body lying face down in the mud. [*Many years afterwards, in answer to a BBC radio interviewer's question, "What was your very first impression of death?" Dyson recalls: "I think abhorrence. Failure to comprehend, and then abhorrence. Rather than sorrow, I was always more afraid—this is personal in the business of the war—of corpses, especially if they were very mutilated, than of shells. Heavens, I was afraid enough of shells, but corpses . . . the appearance of that which was once a source and a centre of subjectivity, become pure distorted object, filled me with abhorrence."*]

John Ronald Reuel Tolkien (1892–1973) arrives at the Somme on June 27 (Tuesday), two days before the British offensive begins. British casualties for August alone are 127,000. Two and a half months into the battle, tanks are used for the first time. [*Soon after, Tolkien begins writing "The Fall of Gondolin," in which a great city is lost in a bitter battle against the evil forces of Melko (Morgoth). These forces use machines, great iron dragons, their hollow bellies filled with orcs. These machines echo the tanks Tolkien sees at the Somme, and prefigure the link he was to grasp between the technological and satanic magic; for him, the machine becomes the modern form of magic, a belief he will share in future years with Lewis.*]

SEPTEMBER 24 (Sun)

Warren is promoted to lieutenant.

OCTOBER 1 (Sun)

Warren is promoted to the rank of temporary captain.

OCTOBER 10 (Tue)

Irish nationalists resolve unanimously to oppose conscription.

OCTOBER 12? (Thu?)

Arthur has asked Jack about his religious views. Jack replies that he believes in no religion, as there is no proof for any of them, and Christianity, philosophically speaking, is not even the best of them. Mythologies are simply human invention, whether of Loki or Christ, and belong to the primitive stages of human development. He regards himself as being emancipated from superstition. We must try to be truthful, chaste, kindly, honest, and so on, but we owe these qualities to our dignity and humanity, not to imagined gods, he explains. [*A week or so later he admits to a more or less agnostic position over the immortality of the soul.*]

NOVEMBER 13 (Mon)

Warren is appointed officer commanding 4th Company 7th Divisional Train, France.

NOVEMBER 21 (Tue)

Warren is transferred to the 32nd Divisional Train, France.

NOVEMBER 29 (Wed)

Jack's eighteenth birthday.

DECEMBER 3 (Sun)

Geoffrey Bach Smith, a close friend of Tolkien from school days, is injured by shell fire. [*He dies a few days later from gangrene. The loss of two of his three closest friends in the conflict motivates Tolkien to write down his mythology, which is already concerned about the struggle of good against seemingly invincible evil.*]

DECEMBER 4 (Mon)

Jack makes his first trip to Oxford to take an initial scholarship examination. [*This takes place from December 5 to 9, after which Jack makes his way to Belfast. Passed over by New College, Oxford, he receives a classical scholarship to University College, Oxford. Now only his university-wide entrance examinations ("Responsions") remain to be taken.*]

DECEMBER 14 (Thu)

The *Times* lists amongst the successful scholarship candidates, besides "Clive S. Lewis, University College," two who one day are to be among his closest friends, "Alfred C. Harwood, Christ Church College," and "Arthur Owen Barfield, Wadham College."

CHAPTER THREE

Oxford and France: World War I

(1917–1918)

Britain had been at war with Germany for nearly two and a half years.

C. S. Lewis had passed the scholarship examination and received a classical scholarship for University College, Oxford. In spite of failing the initial university entrance examinations ("Responsions") in the spring of 1917, he was allowed to come into residence in the Trinity (or Summer) Term of 1917. This enabled him to pass into the army by way of the University Officers' Training Corps. (Though he went for algebra lessons to John E. Campbell of Hertford College—his poor grasp of mathematics was the cause of his failure—he never did pass Responsions. By a bizarre irony Lewis—one of the most brilliant minds ever at Oxford—would have been barred from entering the university if it had not been for his war service— ex-servicemen were exempted from having to pass the examinations.)

He was a student at Oxford from April 26 until September 1917. Despite evidence of the impact of war everywhere, Lewis spent a pleasant few months. He enjoyed the library of the Oxford Union, punting on the River Cherwell, or swimming in it at "Parson's Pleasure." Most of his college building was taken up with serving as an army hospital. In all of the Oxford colleges there were merely 315 students in residence at the time. Among these about 120 were members of the Officers' Training Corps.

As there was no conscription for people born in Ireland, Lewis voluntarily enlisted in the army and was billeted in Oxford's Keble College for officer's training. The alphabet dictated that his roommate was fellow Irishman Edward Courtnay Francis ("Paddy") Moore (1898–1918), a trivial-seeming fact that was to dictate much of the shape of Lewis's future life. Paddy was the son of Mrs. Janie Moore (1872–1951), who had left an unhappy marriage and Ireland in 1907 to live in Bristol with Paddy and his young sister, Maureen Daisy Helen (1906–1997). With Paddy's commission, Mrs. Moore and Maureen moved to Oxford to be near him. She and Lewis first met in June 1917. Immediately attracted to the Moore family, Lewis increasingly was to be found in their company. Maureen, who was eleven at the time, remembered, "Before my brother went out to the trenches in France he asked C. S. Lewis . . . 'If I don't come back, would you look after my mother and my little sister?'" Lewis became attracted to Paddy's mother, a feeling heightened by Albert Lewis's apparent inattention to his son at that time.

Lewis was commissioned an officer in the 3rd Battalion, Somerset Light Infantry, on September 25, 1917, and reached the front line in northern France in November, about the time of his nineteenth birthday. By January 1918 Lewis had survived his first few weeks in the trenches, and was hospitalized at Le Tréport, France, with "trench fever." He returned to the front at the end of February and had, he says, a pretty quiet time of it until the great German Spring offensive, one of the worst

bloodlettings of the war. Lewis took sixty German prisoners who had surrendered. On April 15, 1918, he was
severely wounded by friendly fire at Mount Bernenchon
(near Lillers). Pieces of shrapnel remained in his chest for
much of his life. He recuperated in England and was able
to return to military duty in October 1918, being assigned
to a camp in southern England. He was discharged in late
December 1918, not long after the end of the war. Lewis
learned that his former roommate and friend, Paddy
Moore, had been killed in battle; he began to fulfill his
promise to look after Mrs. Moore and Maureen.

While serving in France, through times of waiting,
battle, and hospitalization, he carried a pocket notebook
and was able to jot down poems. Writing had become a
necessity long before he enlisted, whether poetry, fiction,
or long letters to Arthur Greeves. Now he focused upon
poetry, with increasing ambitions to make his mark as a literary man. In effect he became a war poet, publishing a
book of poetry in 1919. This was made up of poems written in France and during convalescence afterwards, as well
as poems from the Bookham days with Kirkpatrick and
from his brief sojourn in Oxford. The publication, entitled
Spirits in Bondage, came about as a result of sending the manuscript to William Heinemann.

Through this period, whenever possible, he wrote to
Arthur Greeves once a week. It was an indication of his
isolation and solitary nature that he eagerly anticipated
Arthur's return letters. Lewis confessed that on Tuesday
evenings and Wednesday mornings he hung on for Arthur's
mail "just like a schoolgirl."

1917

*The Russian Revolution takes place, and Nicholas II abdicates. The
United States enters the Great War against Germany, and its forces
land in France. Balfour makes his Declaration on Palestine. Germany*

and Russia sign an armistice at Brest-Litovsk. The Pulitzer Prizes are established.

Anthony Burgess (John Anthony Burgess Wilson), Charles Causley, Arthur C. Clarke, Richard Cobb, Robert Conquest, Eric Hobsbawm, John F. Kennedy, Robert Lowell, Jessica Mitford, and Conor Cruise O'Brien are born.

Jane Barlow, Sir F. C. Burnand, Edgar Degas, Harry Buxton Forman, T. E. Hulme, William de Morgan, François Auguste Rodin, and Edward Thomas die.

JANUARY 2 (Tue)

Lewis is at Little Lea with his father. Warren is away serving in France. In a letter today to Albert, Kirkpatrick tells him that in Responsions mathematics "form an important element" and that his son "could very well usefully employ a good part of the day in working up a subject for which he has not only no taste, but on the contrary a distinct aversion."

JANUARY 8 (Mon)

In a letter to Warren, Lewis describes his impression of his recent visit to Oxford as "absolutely topping"; he is "awfully bucked" with it. He is longing to start his studies there, but apparently he is not to do this until October. In the meantime he is going back to "the Knock" (Kirkpatrick) to prepare for Responsions, expressing ignorance about what these examinations entail.

JANUARY 26 (Fri)

Lewis arrives in Oxford after taking leave of Belfast the evening before. After a cold and rough sea crossing to Fleetwood, it is not an easy rail journey because of the very crowded trains, which stop for long periods at unfamiliar stations. He does not arrive until 6 p.m.

JANUARY 27 (Sat)

He calls on the master of University College (for which he received his scholarship), who lives in a house amassed with books on the college grounds. The master promises that if Lewis passes the Responsions in March he can come up to Oxford at the start of Trinity term in April and join the O.T.C. (Officers' Training Corps). After a pleasant lunch with the master, the master's wife, and his niece, Lewis then takes the train from Oxford to Bookham to prepare for the examinations with Kirkpatrick. He fantasizes about the attractive niece.

JANUARY 28 (Sun)

Lewis shares his fantasies about the master's niece with Arthur in a letter the next day. [*Adolescent fantasies they share at this time often involve sadomasochism, probably a legacy of the brutal whippings the terrified Lewis had seen inflicted at Wynyard School in earlier years.*]

Some Oxford Colleges Associated with Lewis

Oxford University is made up of a number of individual colleges throughout the city, with names like Jesus, Trinity, St. John's, Wadham, Hertford, Worcester, Exeter, Lincoln, Brasenose, Ruskin, and Balliol.

University College—Here Lewis was an undergraduate.

Magdalen College— Here Lewis was a fellow and tutor in English Literature from 1925 to 1954.

Keble College—Lewis was billeted here while undergoing officer training in preparation for service in World War I.

Merton College—This college employed at various times Lewis's friends Nevill Coghill, "Hugo" Dyson, and J. R. R. Tolkien.

FEBRUARY 4 (Sun)

It has been snowing, much to Lewis's delight. He relishes walking in the countryside near Bookham, especially because the sky is a clear blue and the air very dry. He takes a road through the woods, walking towards Wisley. The winding road is snow-covered, as are the branches of the bare trees. He notices the sunlight throwing bars onto the snowy ground as it passes through them. At Wisley is a lake, where he spends the whole day skating.

FEBRUARY 6 (Tue)

Late in the evening after studying, as is usual for him, Lewis spends an hour reading, and tonight he is rereading an old favorite, John Milton's *Paradise Lost*. He finds he loves Milton more every time he comes back to him. [*During World War II, Milton will be the inspiration for his science-fiction story* Perelandra.]

FEBRUARY 8 (Thu)

Lewis reports to Albert that he has dropped the study of German under Kirkpatrick in favor of Italian (the idea is to master it in seven weeks). This is so that he will have another language in case he fails the Oxford entrance examinations and has to try for the Foreign Office for employment instead. [*As with the other languages, Kirkpatrick pays no attention to pronunciation. Lewis invariably in later life speaks in other languages employing his cut-glass British accent.*] Lewis in the same letter asks his father's opinion about the United States coming into the war, which is now a possibility.

MARCH 8 (Thu)

Lewis and the Kirkpatricks increasingly find that food rationing is hurting, and today is no exception. This has much to do with the impact upon shipping by German submarines, a daily topic of conversation at Gastons. Particularly there are shortages of bread and potatoes.

The date of the entrance examinations is looming. Lewis realizes suddenly that he has left behind in Belfast the waistcoat of his new brown suit—which he will need to wear for the exams. He writes a letter asking Albert to send it, identifying it as the one with the blue lining.

MARCH 10 (Sat)

Lewis spends a long morning exploring the secondhand bookshops of Charing Cross Road in nearby London. He is particularly hunting down foreign-language books, made scarce (with the exception of French) by the war.

MARCH 21 (Wed)–23 (Fri)

Lewis takes Responsions but fails in mathematics, particularly algebra. He lodges at a Mrs. Etheridge's, 1 Mansfield Road, Oxford (the first house on one's right after turning into Mansfield Road from Holywell).

MARCH 23/24 (Fri/Sat)

He starts out for home to Belfast for the Easter vacation, crossing the Irish Sea from Fleetwood Friday night and arriving Saturday morning.

APRIL 6 (Fri)

At 1.18 p.m. President Woodrow Wilson signs a declaration of war. The United States is joining the battle for Europe. Four days earlier, before a joint session of Congress, President Wilson had said: "The world must be made safe for democracy."

APRIL 16 (Mon)

In France, the spring offensive begins against Germans manning the Hindenburg Line opposite Arras.

APRIL 26 (Thu)

Lewis arrives at the porter's lodge of University College, Oxford, weighed down with coats, parcels, and suitcase. His hope is eventually to study Classics there. The effect of the war surprises him: there are only twelve students at the all-male University College, of which three, including himself, are freshmen. Everything is adjusted accordingly, creating quite a homely effect. Instead of eating in the Dining Hall, for instance, they use a small lecture room, with none of the dons appearing for the meal. He is also surprised by the size of his college "rooms," his accommodation. Though modest, the rooms are a good size, and are on the other side of the Radcliffe Quad from the college entrance. He is in Set no. 5, on Staircase XII. (It is the custom to locate the college rooms by staircase number.) [*He is particularly drawn to the sight of the quad in moonlight, long shadows thrown halfway across the perfect lawn, and beyond, spires and towers jutting up, dense black against the dark sky.*]

APRIL 30 (Mon)

Today Lewis joins the Officers' Training Corps and has a physical examination, whereby details of his height and weight are recorded, and it is noted that he lacks sufficient training to be entered to an Officer Cadet Unit before the end of June. His military duties are to include morning parade from 7.00 to 7.45, and an afternoon parade from 2.00 to 4.00, with occasional evening lectures on map reading and similar topics.

MAY 3 (Thu)

Lewis writes one of his frequent letters to his father. He confesses that it is distressing to consider the lonely life that Albert now has to live. He comments on the troublesome Flying Corps cadets in Oxford who, like most peo-

―――― *Lewis's Physical Appearance* ――――

Height: 5 feet 10¾ inches

Weight (in 1917, aged eighteen): 13 stone (180 pounds)

Around 1917: "Rather slim, but nice looking, talkative." (Maureen Moore)

1930s: "Perhaps the first thing you noticed about him, he had an extraordinary red complexion, rather as if he might have a stroke at any time. . . . He had rather solid well-marked features, fine expressive eyes, a very solid physical build, a clear, emphatic voice. . . . He dressed very informally. He always wore a tweed jacket and flannel trousers, which was at the time the uniform of the undergraduate population." (Professor A. G. Dickens)

Mid-1930s and after: "Lewis was a big, full-blown man—overbearing, almost, both in his weight of personality and his physical weight." (Dr. "Humphrey" Havard)

During World War II: "He was not naturally impressive: his clothes were rumpled and invariably creased; he was short and stocky and almost pudgy; his face, which was full, was florid; his eyes had the appearance of being puffy and distended. He spoke easily and fluently, without hesitation, and without gestures." (Stuart Barton Babbage, RAF chaplain)

March 31, 1944: Lewis describes himself, to be recognized at a rendezvous for a meeting: "I am tall, fat, cleanshaven, don't wear glasses, and shall be in corduroy trousers, probably with a walking stick." (to John S. A. Ensor)

1950s: "A slightly stooped, round-shouldered, balding gentleman whose full smiling mouth revealed long, prominent teeth. . . . He was wearing the oddest clothes, too! Baggy grey flannel trousers, dusty with cigarette ash and sagging at the turn-ups (equally full of ash), an old tweed jacket with the elbows worn away, an open soft-collared shirt. . . . His florid and rather large face was lit as if from within with the warmth of his interest and his welcome. I never knew a man whose face was more expressive of the vitality of his person. This, I was told, was Lewis." (Douglas Gresham)

ple caught up in danger, eat, drink, and are merry, for tomorrow they might die.

MAY 6 (Sun)

In his weekly letter to Arthur he tells him he has become acquainted with the College library, and, better still, the Library of the Union Society—the club to which all Oxford students belong. He had spent a happy morning poring over one book discovery after another. [*Lewis often makes it clear in his letters to Arthur that he, like his friend, finds the binding and even smell of books intoxicating, as well as the delights of their content.*]

MAY 12 (Sat)

Lewis asks John Edward Campbell, of Oxford's Hertford College, about his fees for tutoring him in mathematics, for another attempt at Responsions. Campbell tells him he wants none; he feels it is a service of gratitude he can offer to University College. Campbell turns out to be a friend of Janie McNeill.

MAY 13 (Sun)

Lewis begins the day quite typically, by waking at 7 a.m., then reading until 8.30 a.m. (William Morris and also *Le Chanson de Roland*), before taking first a hot, then a cold bath (the habit in college). He has an invitation with the other freshmen to "brekker" (breakfast) with a senior student, Theobald Butler. Butler is a fellow Irishman, and a Sinn Feiner. Fresh on his bookshelves, Lewis notices, is a volume of poems by Joseph Plunckett, executed after the Easter Rising the year before in Dublin. He likes Butler a great deal, and the conversation turns to Ireland, W. B. Yeats, and then books. After breakfast they decide to bicycle to the river to bathe (Lewis is lent a bike). After a quarter of an hour cycling through quiet Oxford streets they arrive at "Parson's Pleasure," an area of riverbank customarily reserved for men, eliminating the need for swimming clothes. Here two branches of the Cherwell come together, forming in the tract between them "Mesopotamia" (a local name, after the biblical lands between the Tigris and Euphrates).

MAY 27 (Sun)

In his weekly letter to Arthur, Lewis tells of being surprised by a visit from his second cousin Gundreda (whose beauty he greatly admires). With her is her aunt, Kittie Robbins, and Kittie's daughter, Lewis's second cousin Cherry. Though Cherry is not, in Lewis's view, "pretty," he clearly is attracted to her, and awkwardly chosen superlatives start to flow in his letter. She is "a really ripping kind of person," indeed "an awfully good sort." Most of all, she is a "lover of books." Cherry is stationed at a military hospital in Oxford, serving with a Voluntary Aid Detachment. [*Cherry and Lewis are able to continue seeing each other during the coming months. Later he writes of her playing the piano (Lewis's favorite instrument at that time) when visiting the college, and of her being plain in a pleasant way. She is the kind of person he very much likes.*]

JUNE 3 (Sun)

In his letter to Arthur, Lewis reminisces about the beauty of Donegal. He thinks, as he often does, about how appropriate it would be to take up Oxford's city and place it by a "northern sea" between Donegal's mountains. Lewis also speaks of his growing interest in the occult and psychic research (an interest evidently that does not reflect a shift away from his materialist philosophy). [*Lewis's—in many ways idyllic—stay at University College ends when he eventually is able to join a cadet battalion.*]

JUNE 7 (Thu)

The battalion Lewis joins today is encamped at Oxford's Keble College, and so he is to remain in Oxford for another four months. This allows him to keep in contact with his friends at University College, and with Cherry Robbins. Lewis, an "L.", is placed in a room with an "M.," an Irishman of his age named Edward (Paddy) Moore. The tiny room is carpetless, with two beds, in sharp contrast to his comfortable rooms at University College. Paddy tells him that his mother, Janie King Moore, has come to Oxford from Bristol with her twelve-year-old daughter, Maureen, to be near him. She and Maureen are staying in rooms in Wellington Square, not far from Keble College. [*Lewis gives his address as No. 738 Cadet C. S. Lewis, "E" company, Keble College, Oxford. Among the cadets are his "set" of six, including*

"Set" of Cadets Billeted at Keble College, 1917

C. S. Lewis—fought with the infantry, seriously wounded north of Arras, France, April 15, 1918.

Paddy Moore—with the Rifle Brigade, died at Pargny, France, March 24, 1918.

Martin Ashworth Somerville—served in Egypt and Palestine with the Rifle Brigade, died in Palestine, September 21, 1918.

Alexander Gordon Sutton—fought with Paddy Moore in the 2nd Battallion of the Rifle Brigade, killed on January 2, 1918.

Thomas Kerrison Davy—with the 1st Battallion of the Rifle Brigade, severely wounded near Arras on March 29, 1918, dying later.

Denis Howard de Pass—served with the 12th Battalion of the Rifle Brigade, reported "wounded and missing" on April 1, 1918. He was captured by the enemy and survived to fight in World War II. Later in life he became a dairy farmer in Sussex.

his billet-mate, Paddy. These are "public school men and varsity men." Only two out of the six will survive the war, and they will be wounded in battle.

Lewis will soon be a frequent guest at the Moore's. Years later Maureen will recall: "Before my brother went out to the trenches in France he asked C. S. Lewis . . . 'If I don't come back, would you look after my mother and my little sister?'"]

JUNE 9 (Sat)

Lewis spends the afternoon on the river in the company of Cherry Robbins. He is pleased to discover that she is a fervent admirer of both Wagner and Arthur Rackham. From comments Cherry lets fall about Christian and Norse mythology, Lewis suspects that she is an agnostic. Though he is sad that she is not beautiful (i.e., pretty, and of the shape that he admires in women) he is finding that she is not nearly so plain as he at first thought. [*He playfully complains to Arthur in his letter the next day of her liking for Browning's poetry and for photography. A couple of weeks later he confesses that she is a "great anodyne" in the life he is living as a cadet.*]

JUNE 18 (Mon)

Writing to Albert, he mentions his roommate Paddy, and the fact that Paddy's mother is staying up in Oxford—he has met her "once or twice." He urges "Papy" to visit Oxford for a week. They could both stay at University College—he is allowed to invite a guest. He tells Albert that he is reading the Irish philosopher Bishop Berkeley. [*In fact, Lewis becomes deeply interested in Berkeley's form of idealism, because of the philosopher's spiritual emphasis when it comes to understanding our perception of natural things. Berkeley denies the self-sufficient existence of material things. Lewis's materialism is becoming much more complex than it has been up to then.*]

AUGUST 8 (Wed)–12 (Sun)

Lewis's battalion is granted a brief leave, much of which he occupies in traveling, in uniform, to and from Belfast in order to see Albert.

AUGUST 22 (Wed)

Warren visits his brother in Oxford, on his way back to France after visiting Albert in Belfast for a week. They have a "most enjoyable" afternoon and evening together, mainly talking in his rooms at University College. [*Throughout this week Lewis is enjoying a stay with Paddy at his mother's digs, and he tells his father when he next writes that he likes her "immensely."*]

SEPTEMBER 13 (Thu)

As part of their officer training, Lewis, Paddy, and the other cadets go to the Wytham Hills to bivouac, and employ model trenches, made more realistic by recent heavy rain. The experience of sleeping out proves to be more pleasant than anticipated, as there is bracken aplenty to make a soft bed, and the rain keeps off.

SEPTEMBER 25 (Tue)

Lewis is given a temporary commission as a second lieutenant in the Somerset Light Infantry. [*Within two months he will be at the front lines in northern France. He begins a month's leave, upsetting Albert by using three weeks of this to stay with Paddy and the Moores at their home in 56 Ravenswood Road, Redlands, Bristol. He claims that he was unwell with a sore throat, and had to remain to rest.*]

OCTOBER

Annie Strahan retires as cook-housekeeper at Little Lea, to be replaced by Mary Cullen (the "Witch of Endor"). Paddy Moore is posted to France with the Rifle Brigade.

OCTOBER 12 (Fri)–18 (Thu)

Lewis arrives in Belfast. He evidently talks with Arthur Greeves about his feelings for Mrs. Moore.

After Lewis leaves, Albert writes to Mrs. Moore thanking her for her hospitality to his son while she was in Oxford, and for caring for him when he was unwell in Bristol. She responds:

"Dear Mr. Lewis,

Thank you for your letter about the small kindnesses I have done to Jacks. . . . One is only too pleased to do anything one can for these boys at present. . . . Your boy of course, being Paddy's room mate, we knew much better than the others, and he was quite the most popular boy of the party; he is very charming and most likeable and won golden opinions from everyone he met here. Paddy is so very much disappointed that they are not both in the Somersets; he would so very much rather have Jacks with him than anyone else. . . . I am sure you, like myself, would rather be in the trenches than have them there.

Yours sincerely, Janie K. Moore"

OCTOBER 18 (Thu)

Lewis leaves Little Lea to join his new regiment at Crownhill, near Plymouth, South Devon. [*Here he becomes friendly with Laurence Johnson, who had been commissioned just a few months before Lewis, and like him had been elected to an Oxford College (in his case, Queens College). He has similar interests to those Lewis shares with Arthur Greeves.*]

OCTOBER 28 (Sun)

Regretting what he confided to Arthur about a "certain person," Lewis writes asking him to try to forget what he said and to regard the subject of Mrs. Moore as now taboo between them. He reiterates that philosophy, particularly metaphysics, is his "great find" at the moment.

NOVEMBER 15 (Thu)–17 (Sat)

The Somerset Light Infantry suddenly is ordered to go to the front after a forty-eight-hour leave. Unable to visit his father in Ireland in that time, Lewis spends it with Mrs. Moore in Bristol, desperately telegramming his father to rush to Bristol to see him. "Have arrived Bristol on 48 hours leave. Report Southampton Saturday. Can you come Bristol. If so meet at Station. . . . Jacks." Albert Lewis simply wires back: "Don't understand telegram. Please write."

NOVEMBER 17 (Sat)

Lewis reports to Southampton at 4 p.m. and crosses to France, to a base camp at Monchy-Le-Preux, a place that later inspires one of his war poems, "French Nocturne."

NOVEMBER 29 (Thu)

Lewis's nineteenth birthday. He finds himself at the front line and introduced to life in the trenches, where infantrymen prepare to engage the enemy but often encounter a burst of anonymous hot bullets, drifting poison gas, or a fragmenting shell. This same day his brother, elsewhere in France, is promoted to substantive rank of captain. Lewis is astonished to discover that his company's captain, P. G. K. Harris, is the "Pogo" who taught and dazzled him at Cherbourg School. But "Pogo," he immediately discovers, has transformed into a somber war hero uninterested in his gaudy schoolmaster past. [*Lewis soon starts to receive letters from Albert, Arthur Greeves, and Janie Moore. He also has a letter from Jane McNeill, his friend from Belfast.*]

—————— "French Nocturne" ——————

Long leagues on either hand the trenches spread
And all is still; now even this gross line
Drinks in the frosty silences divine,
The pale, green moon is riding overhead.

The jaws of a sacked village, stark and grim,
Out on the ridge have swallowed up the sun,
And in one angry streak his blood has run
To left and right along the horizon dim.

There comes a buzzing plane: and now, it seems
Flies straight into the moon. Lo! where he steers
Across the pallid globe and surely nears
In that white land some harbour of dear dreams!

False mocking fancy! Once I too could dream,
Who now can only see with vulgar eye
That he's no nearer to the moon than I
And she's a stone that catches the sun's beam.

What call have I to dream of anything?
I am a wolf. Back to the world again,
And speech of fellow-brutes that once were men
Our throats can bark for slaughter: cannot sing.

C. S. *Lewis* (writing as Clive Hamilton, 1918)

DECEMBER 13 (Thu)

Lewis writes to Albert that he is, at present, billeted in a war-battered town somewhere behind the front line (he is not allowed to reveal his location).

DECEMBER 14 (Fri)

In a letter to Arthur from the same place, Lewis tells his friend that he gets some time for reading here. He thanks Arthur for writing to Mrs. Moore (she has mentioned this in a letter to him). It makes him feel at home, he says, to know that the two people who matter the most to him are in communication.

DECEMBER 23 (Sun)

Warren arrives at St. Omer in northern France for a course at the Mechanical Transport School. [*Lewis is up in the trenches for a few days, attached to an unnamed company for instruction.*]

NEW YEAR'S EVE (Mon)

Today, as usual, many shells sing over the heads of Lewis and his battalion, aimed at the British gun batteries far behind. This is a "quiet" section of the line, where the dugouts are relatively comfortable and very deep. The wire bunks allow a comfortable sleep. He feels grateful that he has only been once in a dangerous situation, when a shell fell close by the latrines as he was using them. Thinking back over an eventful year, Lewis writes to Arthur that his hope is that he has gained the new (meaning Mrs. Moore) without losing the old (that is, Arthur). He is sure that, if the three of them were all together, they could all be very happy, and not have a conflict of interests. [*This and other comments by Lewis about Mrs. Moore increasingly trouble Arthur.*]

1918

The German forces begin a spring offensive on the western front; the British Royal Air Force (RAF) is formed (out of the Royal Flying Corps and the Royal Naval Air Service). Women over thirty are grant-

ed the vote in Britain. The German offensive is halted on the Marne. The Russian imperial family is murdered by Bolsheviks. Germany signs an armistice at Compiègne, and World War I ends. The first Pulitzer Prize for Fiction is awarded (to Ernest Poole for His Family).

A. L. Barker, Richard Ellmann, John Heath-Stubbs, Richard Hoggart, James Kirkup, Nelson Mandela, Penelope Mortimer (née Fletcher), P. H. Newby, Alexander Solzhenitsyn, and Muriel Spark are born.

Guillaume Apollinaire, Claude Debussy, Wilfred Owen, Isaac Rosenberg, Dora Sigerson, and Frank Wedekind die.

LATE JANUARY

Lewis is hospitalized for three weeks at Le Tréport, miles away from the front line, with trench fever, aka PUO (pyrexia, unknown origin). Le Tréport, he soon discovers, is a small fishing village about eighteen miles along the coast from Dieppe. This reminds him of the holiday he and Warren spent with their mother close by the year before she died.

FEBRUARY 2 (Sat)

Lewis, on his hospital bed, is reflecting about how fate has performed extraordinary tricks on him over the last year. He distinctively feels that he has been placed in a new epoch of his life, in which he finds himself strangely helpless over the outcome. Love unexpectedly has come into his life. There is still room, however, for the delights of the older days, like walking and talking with Arthur, and enjoying tea and digestive biscuits with him in his drawing room at Bernagh. With these thoughts in mind he picks up his pad and writes to Arthur to update him on events, in which, as usual, his reading plays an important part.

FEBRUARY 28 (Thu)

Lewis rejoins his battalion at Fampoux, a village to the west of Arras. He is in the direct line of the final German attack on the western front.

MARCH 1? (Fri?)–4? (Mon?)

Lewis begins a four-day tour of the battlefront, during which he is to have only as many hours sleep.

MARCH 4? (Mon?)

When Lewis returns to comparative safety outside the fighting area he spends the whole night digging, in anticipation of the German advance southwards. [*He later remembers, "Through the winter, weariness and water were our chief enemies. I have gone to sleep marching and woken up again and found myself marching still. One walked in the trenches in thigh gumboots with water above the knee; one remembers the icy stream welling up inside the boot when you punctured it on concealed barbed wire."*]

MARCH 4 (Mon)

Warren graduates from Mechanical Transport School (first in his class).

MARCH 21 (Thu)

In the early hours of this morning General Erich Ludendorff launches an offensive designed to sweep the Allied forces off the western front— the French from the Aisne and the British from the Somme—and to open the way for the capture of Paris. The initial softening-up bombardment lasts five hours. In action are more than six thousand heavy German guns, supported by another three thousand mortars. The first of two million poison-gas shells fall; they will descend on British lines over the next two weeks. In one of the battles, as German infantry surge forward, a British regiment fights to the last man and the last round.

Today alone, twenty-one thousand British solders are taken prisoner.
This is the conflict in which Lewis finds himself, though he is out of the
immediate fighting area on this day.

MARCH 23 (Sat)

Three German guns, made for their purpose by Krupp, start to bombard
Paris from Crépy-en-Laonnoise, which is a staggering seventy-five miles
away. Shells from "Big Bertha," as it is nicknamed by the British, take
four minutes to arrive at their destination. Two hundred and fifty-six
Parisians are killed by the more than twenty shells of terror that fall. As
the day progresses British forces retreat to the Somme, and, in Berlin, the
kaiser declares "the battle won, the English utterly defeated." Among the
soldiers who die today is a former schoolteacher, who had written:

> The magpies in Picardy
> Are more than I can tell.
> They flicker down the dusty roads
> And cast a magic spell
> On the men who march through Picardy
> Through Picardy to hell.

MARCH 24 (Sun)

Elsewhere on the front in France, at Pargny, Paddy Moore
is fighting with his 2nd Battalion of the Rifle Brigade,
resisting the great German offensive. He is last seen this
morning. His remains are taken up and buried in the field
just south of Peronne. [Second Lieutenant E. F. C. (Paddy) Moore's
death will not be confirmed officially until September. Meanwhile, he
lies buried in the British Cemetery at Pargny.]

LATE MARCH

During the German offensive, from March 21 to 28, Lewis
is positioned in or near the battle front at different times.

APRIL 3 (Wed)

French Field Marshal Ferdinand Foch takes over supreme command of the Allied (British, French, and American) armies. With difficulty, he slows and halts the German advance within a mere forty miles of Paris. This strategic defeat presages the ultimate end of the war.

APRIL 12 (Fri)–15 (Mon)

Still in the area north of Arras (near Lille), Lewis is caught up in the Battle of Hazebrouck. The action he sees takes place further to the south, around the village of Riez du Vinage. Around this time he takes sixty German prisoners, and is wounded on Monday the fifteenth by friendly fire at nearby Mont Bernenchon. A shell bursts close by, killing a sergeant beside him, and its shards rip into him in three places, including his chest. Lewis then crawls back towards his trench over the cold mud and is picked up by a stretcher-bearer. [*Pieces of shrapnel remain in his chest for much of his life. In middle age, Lewis will recall the German onslaught in* Surprised by Joy: *"Even then they attacked not us but the Canadians on our right, merely 'keeping us quiet' by pouring shells into our line about three a minute all day. . . . I came to know and pity and reverence the ordinary man: particularly dear Sergeant Ayres, who was (I suppose) killed by the same shell that wounded me. I was a futile officer (they gave commissions too easily then), a puppet moved about by him, and he turned this ridiculous and painful relation into something beautiful, became to me almost like a father. But for the rest, the war— the frights, the cold, the smell of H.[igh] E.[xplosive], the horribly smashed men still moving like half crushed beetles, the sitting or standing corpses, the landscape of sheer earth without a blade of grass, the boots worn day and night until they seemed to grow to your feet—all this shows rarely and faintly in memory. It is too cut off from the rest of my experience and often seems to have happened to someone else."*]

Everard Wyrall, in his official History of the Somerset Light Infantry, *reports the following casualties for the 1st Battalion between April 14 and 16: "2/Lieut. L.B. Johnson died of wounds (15/4/1918) and 2/Lieuts. C. S. Lewis, A. G. Rawlence, J. R. Hill and C. S. Dowding wounded: in other ranks the estimated losses were 210 killed, wounded and missing."*]

APRIL 17? (Wed?)

Albert receives a telegram from the War Office; "2nd. Lt. C. S. Lewis Somerset Light Infantry wounded April fifteenth."

APRIL 24 (Wed)

Warren, stationed at Behucourt near Doullens, hears from Albert that Lewis is wounded and at Etaples (south of Boulogne, on the French coast). He borrows a motorbike and navigates the fifty miles west through Frévent, Hesdin, and Montreuil to the coastal hospital. Racked by anxiety, he is able to force himself to concentrate on nursing his engine over rough stretches of road and coaxing it to maximum thrust over straight sections. His fear turns to joy and thankfulness when he finds Lewis sitting up in bed. Though they are serious, he finds the wounds not to be life-threatening, as Albert had thought.

MAY 4 (Sat)

From the Liverpool Merchants Mobile Hospital at Etaples, Lewis tells his father that he was hit in the back of the left hand, on the left leg a little above the knee, and in the left side under the armpit.

MAY 23 (Thu)

In the mobile hospital in Etaples, Lewis is thinking today about the "lusts of the flesh" which so often buffet him. He

Lewis's War Wounds

From the Army medical records:

"The Board find he was struck by shell fragments which caused 3 wounds. 1st, left chest post-axillary region, this was followed by haemoptysis and epistaxis and complicated with a fracture of the left 4th rib. 2nd wound: left wrist quite superficial. 3rd wound: left leg just above the popliteal space. Present condition: wounds have healed and good entry of air into the lung, but the left upper lobe behind is dull. Foreign body still present in chest, removal not contemplated— there is no danger to nerve or bone in other wounds."

has found himself to become almost monastic about them. This is because, he reasons, fleshly desires increase the mastery of matter over us. On the battlefield, and here among the casualties of war, he sees spirit constantly evading matter: evading bullets, artillery shells, and the sheer animal fears and pains that wrack us. He sees the equation starkly now as "Matter equals Nature, equals Satan." The only nonnatural, nonmaterial thing that he discovers is Beauty. Beauty is the only spiritual thing he can find. Nature is a prison house from which man is only capable of escape through the spiritual side of himself. There is, however, no God to aid him.

MAY 25 (Sat)

Lewis arrives on a stretcher at Endsleigh Palace Hospital, London. He reasons that he has been brought this way because he has no uniform (his was cut off him when he was treated for his wounds). He is pleased to find this a comfortable place, where he has a separate room. He is also happily aware of the fact that he can easily order from the bookshops of London.

───────────── *"Satan Speaks"* ─────────────

I am Nature, the Mighty Mother,
I am the law: ye have none other.

I am the flower and the dewdrop fresh,
I am the lust in your itching flesh.

I am the battle's filth and strain,
I am the widow's empty pain.

I am the sea to smother your breath,
I am the bomb, the falling death.

I am the fact and the crushing reason
To thwart your fantasy's new-born treason.

I am the spider making her net,
I am the beast with jaws blood-wet.

I am a wolf that follows the sun
And I will catch him ere day be done.

C. S. *Lewis* (writing as Clive Hamilton, 1918)

─────────────────◆─◆─────────────────

JUNE 14 (Fri)

Lewis goes to Drury Lane Theatre to hear Wagner's *The Valkyrie*. The conductor is Sir Thomas Beecham. He is thrilled and delighted by the production.

JUNE 16 (Sun)

Lewis takes the train to Bookham, Surrey, to visit the Kirkpatricks.

JUNE 20 (Thu)

Lewis writes one of many pleas to Albert to visit him. "Come and see me. I am homesick, that is the long and short of it." [*Warren comments years later, after his brother's death:*

"One would have thought that it would have been impossible to resist such an appeal as this. But my father was a very peculiar man in some respects; in none more than in an almost pathological hatred of taking any step which involved a break in the dull routine of his daily existence. Jacks remained unvisited, and was deeply hurt at a neglect which he considered inexcusable. Feeling himself to have been rebuffed by his father, he turned to Mrs. Moore for the affection which was apparently denied him at home."

Unlike Albert, Janie Moore is a frequent visitor to London. She has transferred to Lewis the attention she gave to Paddy before his death, even eventually to the extent of moving to be near Lewis as he is moved from camp to camp by the army when he is discharged from hospital.]

JUNE 25 (Tue)

Lewis is sent to Bristol, to convalesce at Ashton Court, Long Ashton. [It proved too difficult to arrange a convalescence in Belfast. It is now much easier for Mrs. Moore to visit. Lewis's recovery is slower than anticipated—he is to be in Bristol until the middle of October.]

JULY 1 (Mon)

An accident at an armaments factory in the English Midlands kills one hundred people and injures a further one hundred fifty in the resulting blast.

SEPTEMBER 12 (Thu)

Lewis writes to Arthur Greeves from Mrs. Moore's home in Bristol with the best of news. After keeping his slim manuscript of poetry for what seems a considerable time, William Heinemann has accepted it for publication. He tells Arthur that it will be called "Spirits in Prison," and that it is weaved around his belief that nature is a prison house and satanic. The spiritual—and God, if he exists—opposes "the cosmic arrangement."

SEPTEMBER

Paddy Moore is officially declared dead.

SEPTEMBER 21 (Sat)

Albert Lewis writes to Mrs. Moore to express his sympathy and sorrow. [*He knows all too well that his sons could have been killed at the front, too.*]

OCTOBER 1 (Tue)

"They tell me he was taken a prisoner," Mrs. Moore writes today to Albert, "overthrew his guards, got back to our lines to be sent over again, was wounded in the leg, and as his man was bandaging him up, was shot through the head and killed instantaneously. . . . I had built such hopes on my only son, and they are buried with so many others in that wretched Somme. . . . Of the five boys who came out to us so often at Oxford, Jacks is the only one left. I feel that I can never do enough for those that are left. Jacks has been so good to me. My poor son asked him to look after me if he did not come back. He possesses for a boy of his age such a wonderful power of understanding and sympathy."

EARLY OCTOBER

Lewis is returned to duty by the army medical board, and is sent to Perham Downs camp, Ludgerhall, near Andover, in southern England, "for further convalescence." The camp is a large complex of wooden huts. Lewis enjoys the landscape of Salisbury Plain, with its "long low hills" and somewhat gray-looking grass, and with Savernake Woods not far away, full of beech and oak trees. Mrs. Moore and Maureen find lodgings nearby in a tiny and isolated cottage that keeps pigs and rabbits. Maureen tells him that he has greatly changed since she first met him, but, when he asks in what way, Maureen will, in her child's way, say no more.

OCTOBER 25 (Fri)

Lewis takes today off to travel to London to see his publisher, William Heinemann, about his poetry collection, which at present still has the title "Spirits in Prison." He finds Heinemann a short, bald man who repeats himself and is wont to get his papers mixed up. Lewis has an agreeable meeting for about three-quarters of an hour and a typed agreement is produced, introducing him to the mysteries of the clauses of the publisher's contract, with their terms like "aforesaid," "hereinafter," and stipulating royalties of "10% of the published price of twelve out of every thirteen copies sold." Heinemann lets drop an interesting piece of information: the poet John Galsworthy, who is on the Heinemann list, has seen Lewis's manuscript and wishes to include one of the poems in a new monthly journal called *Reveille*.

NOVEMBER 9 (Sat)

Kaiser Wilhelm II abdicates, and Germany is declared a republic.

NOVEMBER 11 (Mon)

At 11 a.m., this eleventh hour of the eleventh day of the eleventh month of the year 1918, after four and a quarter years of war in which ten million have died, an armistice is signed in a railway carriage in the forest of Compiègne, north of Paris. Guns fall silent across the war fields of Europe.

Warren records in his diary, in the early hours of November 11: "I was in the office at about 9 p.m., and suddenly there was an outburst of sirens, rockets, Verey

[sic] lights, hooters, searchlights and all sorts of things. Hurried back to the mess and found everyone dancing round the room! Everyone off their heads. Cars with people sitting all over them. Australians firing Very pistols in the square. There were six bonfires going with Belgians dancing and shouting round them with our lads. Cathedral and Church bells pealed most of the night. Got home and to bed about 2.30 am. . . . A very great day indeed. So ends the war." Uppermost in Warren's mind this day is the fact that his beloved brother has come through the war safely; the nightmare of losing him has vanished.

NOVEMBER 29 (Fri)

Lewis's twentieth birthday.

DECEMBER 2 (Mon)

Paddy Moore is posthumously awarded the Military Cross for conspicuous gallantry and initiative.

DECEMBER 23 (Mon)

This morning Warren arrives in Belfast, having come to his father on leave. He believes that he will not see his brother, who is not yet on leave, but still at camp.

DECEMBER 27 (Fri)

From Warren's diary: "A red letter day. We were sitting in the study about eleven o'clock this morning when we saw a cab coming up the avenue. It was Jacks! He has been demobilized thank God. Needless to say there were great doings. He is looking pretty fit. We had lunch and then all three went for a walk. It was as if the evil dream of four years had passed away and we were still in the year 1915. In the evening there was bubbly for dinner in honour of the event. The first time I have ever had champagne at home. Had the usual long conversation with Jacks after going to bed."

CHAPTER FOUR

The Early Oxford Years
(1919–1925)

———— • ————

From January 1919 until June 1923, Lewis resumed his studies at University College, Oxford. One physical reminder of the war were the pieces of shrapnel in his body, which meant that he could not swim as energetically as before.

As a result of his war service, Lewis was "deemed to have passed" Responsions (Oxford's entrance examinations). If he had wished he could have immediately started studying for Literae Humaniores or "Greats," that is, specializing in philosophy and ancient history. His tutor, Arthur B. Poynton, counseled against doing this, as Lewis was intent upon gaining a fellowship in one of the Oxford colleges. He therefore set upon the Classical Honour Moderations, or "Honour Mods," course in Greek and Latin literature before going on to "Greats," and only after this he went for the course in English literature. So he was thoroughly grounded in the Classics and philosophy before studying English. He eventually received a triple distinction in his B.A. degree, gaining the highest category, the First Class: a First in "Honour Mods" (Greek and Latin literature) in 1920, a First in "Greats" (philosophy and ancient history) in 1922, and a First in English in 1923. In Oxford fashion, the B.A. in time became an M.A.

Meanwhile, Warren continued to serve in the British army, first in Belgium in the wake of the war and then in England, at the Aldershot Military Garrison. This meant that he was able to see his brother from time to time. Then in 1921 he was posted to Sierra Leone, in West Africa, for a year. After earning an extended leave in England, he served in Colchester and Woolwich.

The February 1919 issue of *Reveille* contained Lewis's poem "Death in Battle," his first publication other than in school magazines. The issue also included poems by Robert Bridges, Siegfried Sassoon, Robert Graves, and Hilaire Belloc. The next month Lewis's collection of poems *Spirits in Bondage* (originally "Spirits in Prison") was published by Heinemann under the name Clive Hamilton (his mother's maiden name).

Fulfilling the promise made to Paddy Moore, Lewis helped Mrs. Moore and Maureen move permanently to Headington, Oxford, so as to be near him. During his early period of undergraduate studies, Lewis was resident in his college, but nevertheless closely tied his life into that of the Moores. Mornings he worked in the college library or attended lectures. Then he frequently took lunch and had afternoons with Mrs. Moore, returning for dinner in the college hall, after which evenings were employed working in his rooms.

From June 1921 onward Lewis lived with the Moores while pretending to his father (who supported him through this period) that he was still resident in the college. He had by then quasi-adopted Mrs. Moore as his mother, while having deeper feelings for her. Although Janie Moore was likely to have been aware of his infatuation at that time, her own feelings for him remained motherly—Jack Lewis became the replacement for her only and much beloved son Paddy. Her attitude to Lewis was deeply affectionate, but practical rather than sentimental. She expected obedience to her matriarchal rule, and he was forced, like any real son in that situation, either to rebel against the regime or to come up with strategies for living in a way that ensured he would remain intact in himself. Because he had quasi-adopted Mrs. Moore, he took on an attitude of basic contentment which became second nature, even when irritated by the frequent storms of their domestic life. Indeed, his adopted family life taught him about ordinary human living at a time when he could easily have become a scholarly recluse or part of a narrow circle. Around this time Janie Moore became known by her nickname, "Minto," probably after a fondness for a popular mint confectionary, Nuttall's Mintos.

Lewis's remarkable powers of concentration helped him to adapt to a family habitat. Maureen at one time had to practice music around five hours a day, sometimes

Posts and Titles at Oxford and Cambridge

(Some are to be found at other British universities as well; few universities, however, are comprised of a number of colleges.)

Professor—Holder of a chair in a school of the university (such as the English School), and having responsibilities to the whole university even though also a fellow of a particular college

Reader—Higher grade of lecturer to the university (below professor)

Fellow—Senior member associated with a college

Tutor—A college fellow supervising the studies and welfare of the undergraduates assigned to him or her, and taking tutorials (individually or in very small groups)

Don—Head, fellow or tutor of a college

in the same room Lewis was working in—but he remained focused upon his books, shutting out everything else. Janie Moore went out from her home little after Paddy was killed, though she did travel to France to visit his grave. She no longer had the heart for the things she used to do, becoming increasingly preoccupied with running the household, although she liked to entertain visitors.

From October 1924 until May 1925, after a year making do with reviewing and private tutoring, Lewis served as philosophy tutor at University College during E. F. Carritt's absence on study leave in America. Then, on May 20, 1925, Lewis was elected a fellow of Magdalen College, Oxford.

1919

The Irish Free State is established. Alcock and Brown fly across the Atlantic. The Treaty of Versailles is signed.

Doris Lessing, Primo Levi, and Iris Murdoch are born.

Amelia Barr, Matilda Betham-Edwards, Weedon Grossmith, Lady Anne Isabella Ritchie (née Thackeray), William Michael Rossetti, Pierre Auguste Renoir, and Theodore Roosevelt die.

MID-JANUARY

Lewis returns to Oxford as undergraduate. [Until June 1923, he studies at University College, Oxford. His tutors during this time include A. B. Poynton for Honour Mods, E. F. Carritt for philosophy, F. P. Wilson and George Gordon in the English School, and E. E. Wardale for Old English.]

JANUARY 21 (Tue)

The Irish Free State is proclaimed.

JANUARY 22 (Wed)

Warren returns from Christmas leave at home in Belfast to duty in France.

JANUARY 26 (Sun)

In his weekly letter to Arthur Greeves, Lewis recounts his good luck that he is able to attend, twice a week, lectures by Gilbert Murray on Euripides' *Bacchae*. He has read the play before, making the lectures more meaningful. [*Among his other lectures, he is particularly impressed by Cyril Bailey's on Lucretius.*]

JANUARY 27 (Mon)

Writing today to Albert, Lewis speaks of his thankfulness over returning to Oxford, which is greatly different from the shadow he knew before in wartime. University College is still diminished in number—only twenty-eight in college—but they are able to dine in the Hall, and the dust sheets have gone from the Junior Common Room. The familiar pattern of lectures, games, tutorials, and debates has started.

JANUARY 31 (Fri)

This evening, upon invitation, Lewis joins a literary and debating society of the college, the Martlets, as secretary. Membership is limited to twelve.

FEBRUARY

The February issue of *Reveille* contains "Death in Battle," from Lewis's forthcoming book of poems, *Spirits in Bondage*. The issue also includes verses by Robert Bridges, Siegfried Sassoon, Robert Graves, and Hilaire Belloc.

MARCH 12 (Wed)

Lewis gives his first paper to the Martlets, on William Morris. The minute-taker records: "After the interval the

───────────────── *The Martlets* ─────────────────

Literary and other debating societies are common among Oxford under-graduates. The Martlets is unusual in that its minutes are archived in the Bodleian Library. During Lewis's time as an undergraduate they met in each other's college rooms in rotation. Other members were Cyril Hartmann, Rodney Pasley, and E. F. Watling, who became friends of Lewis's. [*There was another but short-lived undergraduate society, called the "Inklings"; in the 1930s its name was transferred to the later famous circle of friends around Lewis and J. R. R. Tolkien. Lewis and Tolkien did attend the original undergraduate "Inklings," but only as invited dons.*]

Papers given by C. S. Lewis to the Martlets:

"William Morris" (March 12, 1919)

"Narrative Poetry" (November 3, 1920)

"Spenser" (February 14, 1923)

"James Stephens" (June 18, 1924)

"Boswell" (May 20, 1925)

"The Personal Heresy in Poetics" (March 3, 1930)—This paper led to his essay "The Personal Heresy in Criticism," which in turn led to *The Personal Heresy: A Controversy* (with E. M. W. Tillyard, 1939).

"Is Literature an Art?" (November 23, 1933)

"William Morris" (November 5, 1937)—This second paper of Lewis on Morris was published in *Rehabilitations* in 1939.

"Psycho-analysis and Literature" (Trinity [Summer] Term, 1940, n.d.)—published in *Selected Literary Essays*

"The Kappa Element in Romance" (November 14, 1940), which devel-oped into his essay "On Stories," and much later the book *An Experiment in Criticism* (1961).

usual informal discussion followed. The general sense of the Society was that rather too high a position had been claimed for William Morris." Lewis claims in his paper, according to the minutes: "As a teller of tales he [Morris] yielded to none except Homer. In his prose works he had endeavoured, with some success, to recall the melody and charm of Malory."

MARCH 17 (Mon)

Hilary (Spring) Term ends. [*Lewis stays up at college working for a week, and then takes the train to Bristol to help Mrs. Moore move house. After this he travels to Belfast.*]

MARCH 20 (Thu)

Spirits in Bondage: A Cycle of Lyrics, Lewis's first book, is published by William Heinemann, priced three shillings and six pence. The slim hardback appears under the name "Clive Hamilton" (Hamilton being his mother's maiden name).

Oxford Terms

The three terms of the Oxford academic year are short, merely about eight weeks each.

Michaelmas (or Autumn) Term
October 1 to December 17 inclusive.

Hilary (or Spring) Term
January 7 to March 25 (or the Saturday before Palm Sunday) inclusive.

Trinity (or Summer) Term
April 20 (or the Wednesday after Easter, whichever is the later) to July 6 inclusive.

MID-APRIL

Warren is transferred to the 6th Pontoon Park, Namur, Belgium.

END OF APRIL

Lewis moves into a new set of rooms at University College, satisfied with the "nice quiet greyish blue" of the walls he distempered last term in preparation. On the walls his favorite Dürer prints are shown to advantage. He is also pleased with a small piece of good and useful furniture he has obtained, a dark oak bookcase.

MAY 20 (Tue)

His son's mysterious "entanglement" with Mrs. Moore is greatly troubling Albert, and he confides in a letter to Warren: "I confess I do not know what to do or say about Jack's affair. It worries and depresses me greatly. All I know about the lady is that she is old enough to be his mother—that she is separated from her husband and that she is in poor circumstances. I also know that Jacks has frequently drawn cheques in her favour running up to £10— for what I don't know. If Jacks were not an impetuous, kind-hearted creature who could be cajoled by any woman who had been through the mill, I should not be so uneasy."

JUNE 14 (Sat)

Alcock and Brown fly across the Atlantic.

JUNE 20? (Fri?)–28? (Sat?)

Arthur Greeves visits Lewis in Oxford.

JUNE 29 (Sun)

The Treaty of Versailles is signed.

JULY 23 (Wed)

Warren arrives in Oxford to begin a holiday with his brother.

JULY 25 (Fri)

Warren and Lewis visit the Kirkpatricks in Great Bookham.

JULY 26 (Sat)

The brothers cross the Irish Sea to stay with Albert.

AUGUST 6 (Wed)

Albert and Lewis have a serious quarrel. Afterwards Albert writes in his diary: "Sitting in the study after dinner I began to talk to Jacks about money matters and the cost of maintaining himself at the University. I asked him if he had any money to his credit, and he said about £15. I happened to go up to the little end room and lying on his table was a piece of paper. I took it up and it proved to be a letter from Cox and Co stating that his a/c was overdrawn £12 odd. I came down and told him what I had seen. He then admitted that he had told me a lie. As a reason, he said that he had tried to give me his confidence, but I had never given him mine etc., etc. He referred to incidents of his childhood where I had treated them [he and his brother] badly. In further conversation he said he had no respect for me nor confidence in me."

AUGUST 24 (Sun)

Lewis returns to Oxford and helps Mrs. Moore and her daughter Maureen settle into a flat (76 Windmill Road, Headington).

AUTUMN

Lewis and Owen Barfield (1898–1997) first meet as undergraduates. [*Their close friendship will last until Lewis's death. Barfield is one of his most important friends, in a league with Arthur Greeves and (later) J. R. R. Tolkien and Charles Williams.*]

OCTOBER 15 (Wed)

This evening Lewis is elected president of the Martlets.

NOVEMBER 19 (Wed)

Warren is reassigned to service in England.

NOVEMBER 29 (Sat)

Lewis's twenty-first birthday.

1920

Prohibition is established in the United States in January. Marconi opens the first public broadcasting stations in Britain. The League of Nations is established.

Richard Adams, Keith Douglas, D. J. Enright, P. D. James, and Paul Scott are born.

A. H. Bullen, Rhoda Broughton, Ernest Hartley Coleridge, Olive Schreiner, Howard Sturgis, Mrs. Humphry Ward (Mary Augusta Ward), and William Dean Howells die.

J. R. R. Tolkien is appointed Reader in English Language at Leeds. He continues writing "The Book of Lost Tales," an early version of *The Silmarillion*. He reads "The Fall of Gondolin" to an essay club at Oxford's Exeter College where two undergraduates, Hugo Dyson and Nevill Coghill, along with the others warmly appreciate it.

MARCH 1 (Mon)

Warren begins to take training courses at Aldershot Military Garrison, England. [*About this time he purchases a Triumph motorbike with a sidecar.*]

APRIL 4 (Sun)

Lewis writes to Albert with good and bad news. The good is that he has got a First in Honour Moderations. The bad is that he is, he says, fulfilling a promise by taking a holiday in Somerset "with a man who has been asking me for some time to go and 'walk' with him." This would keep him from visiting Little Lea this Easter vacation. [*Lewis is actually on holiday in Somerset with Mrs. Moore and Maureen.*]

JUNE 1 (Tue)

While enrolled in the second of four courses, Warren is assigned to 487th Company (later 15th Company) Army Service Corps.

SUMMER

Mrs. Moore and Maureen settle more permanently in Oxford.

NOVEMBER

Albert still considers himself estranged from Lewis.

NOVEMBER 3 (Wed)

This evening Lewis reads a paper to the Martlets on narrative poetry. The minute-taker notes that Lewis immediately takes up a "fighting attitude." He has "come to defend the epic against the prejudice of contemporaries." The "real objection of the moderns" is "based on the fact that they would not make the effort to read a long poem." Such an effort is "necessary to the true appreciation of the epic: for art demands co-operation between the artist and his audience." Lewis goes on to bring out the "poetic 'fullness' of narrative poetry, illustrating the power for tragedy by a quotation from the Tenth Book of *Paradise Lost*, and men-

The Literary Critic

Later in life, during his long academic career, C. S. Lewis will be acknowledged as an outstanding literary critic. Much of his critical work will be on Spenser, Chaucer, the Arthurian tales, Milton, and Dante, as well as on myth, allegory, world models, meaning, story, metaphor, linguistics, and fairy stories. He also will write key essays on John Bunyan, Jane Austin, Shelley, and William Morris, many of them collected in *Selected Literary Essays*.

His main works of literary criticism include:

The Allegory of Love: A Study in Medieval Tradition (1936)

Rehabilitations and Other Essays (1939)

The Personal Heresy: A Controversy (with E. M. W. Tillyard, 1939)

A Preface to "Paradise Lost" (1942)

Arthurian Torso (with Charles Williams, 1948)

English Literature in the Sixteenth Century, excluding Drama (1954)

Reflections on the Psalms (1958)

Studies in Words (1960)

An Experiment in Criticism (1961)

The Discarded Image: An Introduction to Medieval and Renaissance Literature (1964)

Studies in Medieval and Renaissance Literature (1966)

Spenser's Images of Life (edited by Alistair Fowler, 1967)

Selected Literary Essays (1969)

tioning Masefield's Jane in Reynard the Fox [a classic hunting poem] as an example of the portrayal of character." With quotations from Spenser he shows "to what advantage a great artist could use external surroundings as a background to develop a mood." [*The anonymous minute-taker concludes: "It was as able a vindication of the narrative form as could well be constructed; and it was strengthened by a varied, though certainly not excessive, use of quotation."*]

NOVEMBER 29 (Mon)

Lewis's twenty-second birthday.

1921

Warren G. Harding becomes president of the United States. Lenin introduces the New Economic Policy. The British Legion is founded.

George Mackay Brown, Edmund Crispin (Robert Bruce Montgomery), Geoffrey Elton, Leon Garfield, Brian Moore, and Raymond Williams are born.

Florence Barclay, Christabel Rose Coleridge, Austin Dobson, E. W. Hornung, Mary Louisa Molesworth, Rosa Mulholland (Lady Gilbert), and Hume Nisbet die.

JANUARY 12 (Wed)

At Little Lea, Lewis and Warren uncover some drawings which they made over fifteen years before, around 1905. They happily paste them into their *Boxen* collection of notebooks.

MARCH 9 (Wed)

Warren sails on the *S.S. Appam* for service in Sierra Leone, West Africa.

MARCH 14 (Mon)

Lewis visits the home of W. B. Yeats in Oxford. He and other visitors sit on unyielding antique chairs, the candle-light revealing a room that has been made to appear Oriental, and which has distinctive flame-hued curtains. They listen in silence while the elderly Irish poet speaks of mystics, magic, and apparitions. Lewis inwardly smiles as he imagines how "the Great Knock" of Great Bookham might have reacted had he been there and heard such "mumbo-jumbo." [*Lewis will base the physical appearance of his magician in* Dymer *on Yeats, and his grandeur may have influenced the creation of Merlin in* That Hideous Strength.]

MARCH 22 (Tue)

William T. Kirkpatrick, "the Great Knock," dies.

MAY 24 (Tue)

Lewis's essay "Optimism" wins the University Chancellor's English Essay Prize, the subject of which is set by the prize-giver. [*No copy of the essay has yet been found.*]

JUNE

Lewis sets up a joint establishment with the Moores, his quasi-adopted family, at 28 Warneford Road, Headington. Writing to Arthur, Lewis describes his "usual life" after moving in with Mrs. Moore and Maureen: "I walk and ride out into the country, sometimes with the family, sometimes alone. I work; I wash up and water the peas and beans in our little garden; I try to write; I meet my friends and go to lectures. In other words I combine the life of an Oxford undergraduate with that of a country householder, a feat which I imag-ine is seldom performed. Such energies as I have left for general reading go almost entirely on poetry —and little enough of that." [*This arrangement lasts until Mrs. Moore dies in 1951. As an undergraduate Lewis suffers financial hardship, as the*

Mrs. Janie Moore: Wicked Stepmother?

Owen Barfield and his wife, Maud, came to know Mrs. Janie Moore well. He observed, late in life:

> During those early years I was given no hint at all of that household background. He [Lewis] was simply a fellow undergraduate and later a literary and philosophical friend. I remember him telling me on one occasion that he had to get back in order to clear out the oven in the gas cooker, and I took it to be something that would happen once in a blue moon. It is only from the Diary that I have learnt what a substantial part of his time and energy was being consumed in helping to run Mrs. Moore's household, and also how much of that was due to the shadow of sheer poverty that remained hanging over them both until at last he obtained his fellowship. . . . [The appearance of the diary in print] will do much to rectify the false picture that has been painted of her as a kind of baneful stepmother and inexorable taskmistress. It is a picture that first appeared as early as 1966 in the introductory Memoir to W. H. Lewis's *Letters of C. S. Lewis*, and it has frequently reappeared in the prolific literature on C. S. Lewis which has since been published here and there. If she imposed some burdens on him, she saved him from others by taking them on herself even against his protestations. Moreover she was deeply concerned to further his career.

Warren Lewis wrote of Mrs. Moore:

> The thing most puzzling to myself and to Jack's friends was Mrs. Moore's extreme unsuitability as a companion for him. She was a woman of very limited mind, and notably domineering and possessive by temperament. She cut down to a minimum his visits to his father, interfered constantly with his work, and imposed upon him a heavy burden of minor domestic tasks. In twenty years I never saw a book in her hands; her conversation was chiefly about herself, and was otherwise a matter of ill-informed dogmatism: her mind was of a type that he found barely tolerable elsewhere.

allowance from his father only covers the needs of a single person living in college. He cannot ask for an increase from Albert, as he keeps the arrangement a secret from his father.]

JULY 24 (Sun)

Albert arrives in Oxford to visit his son, accompanied by his brother-in-law and sister-in-law, Augustus (Uncle Gussie) and Anne (Annie) Hamilton. Together the four set off to tour around southern England for a week in Augustus's pale gray four-seater Wolsley convertible. Half an hour south of Oxford, cruising at a little over thirty miles an hour, Albert in the back seat suddenly asks, "Are we in Cornwall yet?" [*When they eventually reach north Cornwall several days later, Lewis finds the landscape uncannily like the County Antrim coastline he so much loves.*]

AUGUST 22 (Mon)

Writing to his father, Lewis apologetically asks for seven pounds, eighteen shillings, and six pence. This is to cover unexpected costs, which include the dentist's fee ("who stopped a tooth"), a new pair of shoes, trousers, two white shirts, and some socks.

OCTOBER 25 (Tue)

In his regular letter to his father, Lewis contrasts the haste of Oxford life (town and university) with "the infinite leisure" of the street in which the Lewis family lives in the Belfast suburbs. Lewis does not recognize the title someone once gave to Oxford—the "adorable dreamer." It is less like dreaming, he writes, than anything he knows.

NOVEMBER 29 (Tue)

Lewis's twenty-third birthday.

1922

Stalin becomes general secretary of the Communist Party. Andrew Bonar Law becomes British prime minister. The British Broadcasting Company (later Corporation) is founded. The Reader's Digest begins. Lord Carnarvon and Howard Carter discover the tomb of Tutankhamen at Luxor in Egypt.

Kingsley Amis, Ronald Blythe, John Braine, Donald Davie, Philip Larkin, Alistair Maclean, Alan Ross, and Vernon Scannell are born.

Wilfrid Scawen Blunt, W. H. Hudson, Alice Meynell, Sir Walter Raleigh, Michael Collins, Ernest Shackleton, and Marcel Proust die. Erskine Childers is executed.

Lewis is sharing a house with Mrs. Moore and Maureen to the north of Oxford. His "Great War" with Owen Barfield sees its early skirmishes as Barfield joins the Anthroposophical Society, associated with the esoteric thinker Rudolf Steiner.

APRIL 2 (Sun)

Lewis seriously begins writing his long narrative poem, *Dymer.*

APRIL 7 (Fri)

Warren arrives back in Liverpool from his service on the west coast of Africa.

MAY 11 (Thu)

Lewis finishes Canto I of *Dymer.* [It is essentially as the published form.]

MAY 18 (Thu)

Lewis writes to his father about his ideas for the future: a tutor has suggested to him that it would be better to hang on in Oxford after "Greats" than to take employment in a hurry. The college would be likely to continue his scholarship for another year. Another tutor had suggested he take a course in English literature—if he were to get a First in that, he would be in a very strong position.

MAY 24 (Wed)

Lewis leaves home around midday and takes the bus into Oxford, where he meets Barfield outside the Old Oak public house. They stroll together to the lovely gardens of Barfield's college, Wadham, and sit under the trees. They argue stubbornly about the dreams of romantic literature. The love dream, insists Lewis, makes someone incapable of real love, while the hero dream makes one a coward. To Lewis's surprise, when the subject turns to his poem *Dymer*, Barfield's verdict is warmly favorable. He says it is "by streets" the best thing Lewis has done, and "Could he keep it up?" Barfield adds that their mutual friend A. C. Harwood had "danced with joy" over it. Later Lewis walks with him as far as Magdalen College, takes a walk in the cloisters, and then goes home for afternoon tea. Afterwards, he goes in again to town and to his college for a tutorial with the philosopher E. F. Carritt at 5.45 p.m., where he reads his prepared essay. A lively discussion follows, where Carritt is on his usual track that "right is unrelated to goodness."

JUNE 11 (Sun)

Lewis goes for a long walk up Hinksey Hill, and rests in the scrap of woodland. Here the pines and ferns, and the landscape before him, seem to be polished in their brightness. He gets the briefest scent of what he already calls "Joy," the tantalizing, inconsolable longing that he associates with the literature of romance (i.e., literature that has at least a glimpse of other worlds).

JUNE

Because Lewis is pressed for money he advertises in the *Oxford Times*: "Undergraduate, Classical Scholar, First-class in Honour Moderations, University Prizeman will give TUITION, Philosophy, Classics to Schoolboy or Undergraduate."

JUNE 28 (Wed)

It is a drizzly day. Arthur Greeves arrives in Oxford, intending to visit his friend until July 19, and to do a lot of drawing and sketching.

JUNE 30 (Fri)

Lewis bicycles into central Oxford down Headington hill. Finding his tutor at college absent, he presses on through wind and rain to Bee Cottage, Beckley, where he is to stay for the weekend, and where he is warmly welcomed by his friends Owen Barfield and A. C. Harwood. Later the three of them get into a conversation about fancy and imagination. After supper they venture out for a stroll, through woods that are darkening with the approaching twilight. Pierrot, their black and white cat, follows them like a dog. Barfield, a skilled and vigorous dancer, unselfconsciously dances around the cat in a field, watched by the amused Harwood and Lewis and three horses nearby. On the way back to Bee Cottage in the dark they compose a nonsensical poem, each taking on a line in turn. [*Arthur is staying in Islip near Oxford for the weekend.*]

AUGUST 1 (Tue)

Lewis and the Moores move again, to "Hillsboro," 14 Western Road, Headington.

————— *C. S. Lewis's Residences* —————

Between 1916 and 1930 Lewis moved to eight houses (for two of which the location is unknown) before settling into "The Kilns" in 1930 for the remainder of his life. He also had residential rooms in his colleges—Magdalen in Oxford and Magdalene in Cambridge. While an undergraduate he resided in University College, Oxford.

"Dundela Villas" (now demolished), Dundela Avenue, Strandtown, Belfast

"Little Lea" (Leeborough House), 76 Circular Road, Strandtown, Belfast

1 Mansfield Road, Oxford

"Anstey Villas," 28 Warneford, Road, Oxford

"Hillview," 76 Windmill Road, Oxford

58 Windmill Road, Oxford

"Courtfield Cottage," 131 Osler Road, Oxford

"Hillsboro," 14 Western Road (later renamed Holyoake Road), Headington, Oxford

"The Kilns," Headington, Oxford

———————— ✦ ————————

AUGUST 4 (Fri)

Lewis is awarded a First in "Greats," and wires his father with the news.

AUGUST 5 (Sat)

Lewis receives his B.A. The vice-chancellor and rector of Oxford's Exeter College, L. R. Farnell, performs the ceremony. Warren is in attendance and meets Maureen and Mrs. Moore for the first time.

SEPTEMBER 11 (Mon)–21 (Thu)

Lewis spends ten days with his father and Warren at Little Lea. The mood seems less strained. Arthur Greeves is at home across the road, and they see each other frequently, though have little to say to each other. Though Lewis continues to write to Arthur regularly for the rest of his life, he increasingly turns to others like Barfield, and later J. R. R. Tolkien, for intellectual friendship.

OCTOBER 4 (Wed)

Warren's six-month leave, which he gained in reward for his service in Sierra Leone, runs out, and he is assigned as assistant to the officer in charge of the RASC at Colchester, England. [*Here he serves as officer in charge of suppliers.*]

OCTOBER 13 (Fri)

Lewis begins studying in the English School with a visit to his new tutor, Frank P. Wilson. It turns out, however, that Wilson is not at college. Lewis eventually finds him at his house in Manor Place. Wilson tells him that he will have his work cut out to complete the course in time, as it normally takes over two years.

OCTOBER 14 (Sat)

Lewis makes his way to St. Hugh's College in search of his designated language tutor, Miss E. E. Wardale, who is to teach him Early English.

OCTOBER 18 (Wed)

He goes for a walk with his friend Hamilton Jenkin. His first reading of Chaucer's *Troilus and Criseyde* sets him arguing on the subject of Christianity. Talking of Troilus leads them to the question of chivalry. Lewis thinks this a mere ideal, even though it is a great advance. Jenkin differs, thinking the whole thing pretty worthless. Features of chivalry that Lewis argues are good results of the knightly standard Jenkin on the other hand attributes to

Christianity. [*After this Christianity becomes the main subject of their discussions.*]

NOVEMBER 14 (Tue)

The first public radio broadcast by the BBC.

NOVEMBER 29 (Wed)

Lewis's twenty-fourth birthday.

DECEMBER 24 (Sun)

Lewis and Warren arrive in Belfast to spend the holiday at Little Lea with their father, who is becoming increasingly dependent upon alcohol.

1923

The Union of Soviet Socialist Republics (USSR) is established. The French occupy the German Ruhr region. Stanley Baldwin forms a Conservative administration in Britain. Adolf Hitler stages a putsch in Munich. The death of U. S. president Harding leads to the succession of Calvin Coolidge.

Dannie Abse, Brendan Behan, Christine Brooke-Rose, Dorothy Dunnett, Elizabeth Jane Howard, Francis King, and John Mortimer are born.

Henry Bradley, Maurice Hewlett, W. P. Ker, W. H. Mallock, Katherine Mansfield, John Morley, and Sarah Bernhardt die.

Because Lewis is reading English in only one year (instead of at least two), he has only two terms left with which to prepare for the June examinations. This coincides with an acute shortage of money with which to support his "family." Owen Barfield marries a dancer considerably older than himself, Maud Douie, and Lewis notices that Barfield has completely abandoned his materialism and has become an anthroposophist, so that, for him, "the night sky is no longer horrible."

JANUARY 13 (Sat)

Lewis arrives back in Oxford. [*Attending lectures for the English course, he is enraptured by Strickland Gibson teaching bibliography and C. T. Onions discoursing on Middle English. His Anglo-Saxon studies are much more comprehensive than he had anticipated, much to his delight. He develops a fervent love for the alliterative meter used in early English verse.*]

JANUARY 26 (Fri)

The first meeting of the English classes organized by George Gordon, the new Merton Professor of English Literature, fails to impress Lewis. His verdict is that Gordon is more sensible than brilliant.

FEBRUARY 2 (Fri)

At the next English class, Lewis makes a lifelong friend. Nevill Coghill (1899–1980), from Exeter College, enthusiastically reads an impressive paper on "realism," ranging from the tragedy of *Gorboduc* to Shakespeare's *King Lear*. To Lewis he seems sensible and no-nonsensical, with an attractive, unusual chivalry. [*The friendship with Coghill quickly develops.*]

FEBRUARY 9 (Fri)

Lewis reads a paper on Edmund Spenser to Professor George Gordon's discussion class. Nevill Coghill is present, and greatly admires it, writing the minutes of the discussion in Chaucerian verse. [*The same paper is read by Lewis to the Martlets on February 14, described as "brilliant" in the minutes.*]

FEBRUARY 11 (Sun)

Coghill and Lewis take the first of many long walks together, fervently talking about literature and life as they skirt the Hinksey Hills. To Lewis's surprise and shock, he discovers that this highly intelligent and well-informed man—the best in the discussion group—is a Christian, and a "thoroughgoing supernaturalist."

A New Friendship

Nevill Coghill writes in 1965:

> We used to foregather in our rooms, or go off for country walks together in endless but excited talk about what we had been reading the week before—for Wilson [whom Lewis and Coghill both had as tutor] kept us pretty well in step with each other—and what we thought about it. So we would stride over Hinksey and Cumnor—we walked almost as fast as we talked—disputing and quoting, as we looked for the dark dingles and the tree-topped hills of Matthew Arnold. This kind of walk must be among the commonest, perhaps among the best, of undergraduate experience. Lewis, with the gusto of a Chesterton or a Belloc, would suddenly roar out a passage of poetry that he had newly discovered and memorized, particularly if it were in Old English, a language novel and enchanting to us both for its heroic attitudes and crashing rhythms. . . . His big voice boomed it out with all the pleasure of tasting a noble wine. . . . His tastes were essentially for what had magnitude and a suggestion of myth: the heroic and romantic never failed to excite his imagination, and although at that time he was something of a professed atheist, the mystically supernatural things in ancient epic and saga always attracted him. . . . We had, of course, thunderous disagreements and agreements, and none more thunderous or agreeing than over Samson Agonistes, which neither of us had read before and which we reached, both together, in the same week; we found we had chosen the same passages as our favourites, and for the same reasons—the epic scale of their emotions and their over-mastering rhythmical patterns. Yet when I tried to share with him my discovery of Restoration comedy he would have none of it.

FEBRUARY 23 (Fri)–MARCH 12 (Mon)

Mrs. Moore's brother, "Doc" Askins, visits the "family" as Lewis prepares for his finals. The result is three weeks of hell. The "Doc" suddenly suffers what Lewis calls "war neurasthenia," in which he endures nightmarish mental torment. [*Finally, he is admitted to hospital at Richmond, where soon his heart stops, releasing him from his terrors. Lewis describes the events in a letter to Arthur Greeves on April 22, concluding: "Isn't it a damned world—and we once thought we could be happy with books and music!"*]

JUNE 1 (Fri)

Lewis attends Gordon's last English class, marking the end of the shortened and concentrated course. It is held in Nevill Coghill's rooms at Exeter College, where they discuss tragedy, then drift into talking of John Masefield's poetry, and then to reminiscences of the war. Coghill at this point produces a bottle of port to celebrate the last meeting, and they drink to Gordon's health.

JUNE 14 (Thu)–19 (Tue)

Lewis sits for his English School examinations.

JULY 10 (Tue)

The *viva* takes place, Lewis's oral defense of his English exams. His oral examiners are W. A. Craigie, a foremost Icelandic scholar, and H. E. B. Brett-Smith, the editor of an edition of Thomas Love Peacock. Lewis comes away after two minutes greatly encouraged, delighted to escape so easily what could have been a lengthy ordeal at the hands of the "language people." [*In the English School at that time there is a conflict between those dons committed to the teaching of English language and those who emphasize literary studies.*]

JULY 16 (Mon)

The English School results appear. Lewis and Coghill are among the six in the University to obtain "First Class Honours in the Honour School of English Language and Literature." [*Despite his brilliant results—his third First Class degree in a little over four years—Lewis will have to wait two years for a permanent position in an Oxford College.*]

SEPTEMBER 12 (Wed)

Worried about the future and suffering from depression and ill health, Lewis takes a walk. He makes his way through "Mesopotamia," between the branches of the River Cherwell, and then on to Marston. Here he has a glass of beer and a packet of cigarettes, an extravagance he has not been able to indulge in for many a day. [*Over the summer period he corrects Higher School Certificate examination papers to earn money.*]

SEPTEMBER 22 (Sat)

Lewis arrives in Ireland to see his father. He stays for nearly three weeks, and Albert generously agrees to continue his allowance while Lewis seeks an academic post.

OCTOBER 11 (Thu)

The day after Lewis has left to return to Oxford, Albert notes in his diary, "I repeated my promise to provide for him at Oxford if I possibly could, for a maximum of three years from this summer. I again pointed out to him the difficulties of getting anything to do at 28 if he had ultimately to leave Oxford."

NOVEMBER

Lewis has his first pupil, an eighteen-year-old, Austin Sandeman, who wishes to enter Oxford. Lewis coaches him in essay writing and English in preparation for the entrance examinations.

NOVEMBER 29 (Thu)

Lewis's twenty-fifth birthday.

DECEMBER

Lewis spends three weeks at Little Lea, which, "though improved by Warnie's presence, were as usual three weeks too long." While there he reads Tolstoy's *Anna Karenina* (probably in the translation by Aylmer and Louise Maude), John Masefield's *Daffodil Fields*, Henry James's *Roderick Hudson*, and James Stephens's new book, *Deidre*.

1924

Ramsay MacDonald forms the first Labour government in Britain in January, and Stanley Baldwin puts together a Conservative administration in November.

Patricia Beer, James Berry, Robert Bolt, James Baldwin, and E. P. Thompson are born.

William Archer, F. H. Bradley, Frances Hodgson Burnett, Joseph Conrad, Marie Corelli, Edith Nesbit, C. V. Stanford, Anatole France, Franz Kafka, Lenin, and Giacomo Puccini die.

Lewis has his brilliant Oxford degree, but as yet no academic appointment. He is reading the works of Henry More, the Cambridge Platonist, with the possibility in mind of doing a doctorate on his ethical thought. J. R. R. Tolkien is made Professor of English Language at Leeds.

JANUARY

Lewis tries for a fellowship at St. John's College, Oxford, still considering an academic life in philosophy.

In support of his application, he submits an essay on "The Promethean Fallacy in Ethics." He is unsuccessful, while Nevill Coghill obtains the English fellowship at Exeter College. (Lewis also contemplates a research fellowship at All Souls College, or registering for a D.Phil. degree. Other options for the time being are reviewing and private tutoring.)

FEBRUARY 28 (Thu)

This evening Lewis dines at High Table in University College as guest of E. F. Carritt, his old tutor. Carritt tells him of a fellowship in philosophy that is to be awarded at Trinity College, worth £500 a year, and advises him to apply for it. As he walks home late that night, Lewis examines the details of the Trinity fellowship as he passes from streetlamp to streetlamp. He is in a strange state of excitement, just based on the very slender chance of getting the fellowship. It would mean, he thinks, the end of the poverty of the last years for his quasi-adopted family. [*This comes of nothing, and other disappointments follow. In the midst of these struggles, the leisure time he has allows him to continue working on his long narrative poem,* Dymer.]

MAY 4 (Sun)

Lewis is still hoping to gain a fellowship when he dines at High Table in University College, meeting many of the other fellows there and in the Senior Common Room afterwards.

MAY 5 (Mon)

Sir Michael Sadler, Master of University College, offers him a temporary post for the coming academic year, to take over E. F. Carritt's work as philosophy tutor while Carritt is absent in America. Lewis accepts.

─────────── *Important Oxford People* ───────────

E. F. *(Edgar Frederick) Carritt*—fellow of philosophy at University College from 1898 to 1941, and author of *Theory of Beauty* (1914) and *Philosophies of Beauty* (1931). Lewis stood in for him as philosophy tutor from 1924 to 1925.

Frank Percy Wilson—tutor in the English School

Professor George Gordon—tutor in the English School

Edith Elizabeth Wardale—tutor for Early English

Arthur Poynton—tutor in Greek

Cyril Bailey—Classical tutor at Balliol College

Gilbert Murray—"the most accomplished Greek scholar of the day" and Regius Professor of Greek at Oxford (1908–1936)

Cyril Hughes Hartmann—friend of Lewis and member of the Martlets

Rodney Pasley—friend and member of the Martlets

E. F. *(Edward Fairchild) Watling*—friend and member of the Martlets, who became an accomplished translator of classical texts.

Leo Kingsley Baker—friend who served in the Royal Flying Corps during World War I. He introduced Lewis to Owen Barfield. He became an actor with the Old Vic Company.

Alfred Kenneth Hamilton Jenkin—Lewis's first lifelong friend made at Oxford. From Cornwall, Jenkin was a student at University College, and member of the Martlets, who became an author and broadcaster.

Nevill Coghill—friend and member of the Inklings, from County Cork, Ireland. He was elected fellow of English at Exeter College in 1925. He became famous for his contemporary English translation of Chaucer's *Canterbury Tales* (1951).

Owen Barfield—a lifelong friend and member of the Inklings with whom Lewis engaged in a "Great War" throughout the 1920s, when he was still a materialist and Barfield had espoused the spiritual teachings of anthroposophy. His book *Poetic Diction* (1928) profoundly influenced Lewis.

SUMMER

Warren is now stationed near Colchester, and Lewis is able to spend some weekends and occasional days with him, thanks to his brother's motorcycle. They explore much of the countryside in the Oxford area, and then venture farther into Wiltshire and the counties north of London.

JULY 4 (Fri)

Lewis and Warren search for and find the building that housed Wynyard School, in Watford. This proves to be cathartic for both, as they still carry the wounds of their experience at that institution.

JULY–AUGUST

Lewis corrects local examination papers to bring in some money, and prepares his lectures on philosophy in preparation for the coming academic year.

OCTOBER 14 (Tue)

Lewis presents his first lecture, "The Good, Its Position among Values." He addresses only four students, due to an error in the lecture list and a competing lecture at the same time.

NOVEMBER 29 (Sat)

Lewis's twenty-sixth birthday.

DECEMBER 23? (Tue?), 1924–JANUARY 10? (Sat?), 1925

Lewis and Warren spend three weeks over Christmas with Albert in Belfast. Afterwards they tour on the motorcycle, taking in Shrewsbury and Ludlow, then Warren

stays at Hillsboro, the house Lewis shares with the
Moores in Headington, for a week.

1925

*David Lloyd George becomes Liberal leader in Britain. Hindenburg
becomes president of Germany.* The New Yorker *is launched.*

*Brian Aldiss, Nina Bawden, John Bayley, Pierre Boulez, Gerald
Durrell, Gore Vidal, and John Wain (a future member of the Inklings)
are born.*

*A. C. Benson, Mary Cholmondeley, Sir Henry Rider Haggard, Rudolph
Steiner, and George Curzon, Marquess Curzon of Kedleston die.*

Lewis is now well into his one-year stint temporarily
teaching philosophy in the absence of E. F. Carritt. J. R. R.
Tolkien is elected to the Chair of Anglo-Saxon at Oxford
University (Rawlinson and Bosworth Professor of Anglo-
Saxon), and he moves down from Leeds.

HILARY (Spring) TERM

Lewis gives around four tutorials a day, three in the morning and one between afternoon tea and dinner, and lectures
twice a week on "Moral Good." Philosophy classes can be
small. When so, Lewis sometimes takes the students to his
college rooms for informal discussion instead. Though living in Headington, north Oxford, he often is at the college
for breakfast.

FEBRUARY 10 (Tue)

This evening Lewis sees the Oxford University Dramatic
Society (OUDS) production of Ibsen's *Peer Gynt.* He is disappointed by Ibsen, but does enjoy the way the troll
scenes are visualized—the "best stage devilment" he has
seen. Peer comes across to him as a mere windbag who

needs a kick up the bottom. Lewis is also coming down with influenza. [*This ailment afflicts him regularly at this time of year, allowing some comfortable reading of his favorite books in a warm bed for a few days.*]

APRIL 7/8 (Tue/Wed)

Lewis takes a couple of days off with Warren, visiting Salisbury, Wells, and Stonehenge on the motorcycle.

APRIL

A fellowship in English is announced at Magdalen College, Oxford, and Lewis applies for it, though without much hope as he knows that more experienced people are applying as well.

MAY 20 (Wed)

Lewis gains the post and is elected a fellow of Magdalen College, to serve as tutor in English language and literature. Initially it is for five years, to start from June 25, but this limitation is a formality. He is relieved, both because the appointment establishes his career, and he is now to be financially independent of Albert. It means, too, that he can now better provide for his "family."

In Belfast, Albert notes in his diary his own reaction to the longed-for news of his son's appointment:

> While I was waiting for dinner Mary [Cullen] came into the study and said "The Post Office is on the phone." I went to it.
>
> "A telegram for you."
>
> "Read it."
>
> "Elected Fellow Magdalen. Jack."
>
> "Thank you."

I went up to his room and burst into tears of joy. I knelt down and thanked God with a full heart. My prayers have been heard and answered.

MAY 22 (Fri)

The *Times* announces, "The President and Fellows of Magdalen College have elected to an official Fellowship in the College as Tutor in English Language and Literature, for five years as from next June 25, Mr. Clive Staples Lewis, MA (University College)."

—— Oxford and Magdalen College ——

City and county town of Oxfordshire, England, Oxford was Lewis's home from his undergraduate days (interrupted by service in World War I) until his death in 1963. Oxford is located at the meeting of the rivers Thames and Cherwell, about fifty miles northwest of London. Its importance as early as the tenth century is evident from its mention in the Anglo-Saxon Chronicle for AD 912.

Before World War I Oxford was known as a university city and market town. Then printing was its only major industry. Between the wars, however, the Oxford motor industry grew rapidly.

University teaching has been carried on at Oxford since the early years of the twelfth century, perhaps as a result of students migrating from Paris. The university's fame quickly grew, until by the fourteenth century it rivaled any in Europe.

University College, where Lewis was an undergraduate, is its oldest college, founded in 1249. Erasmus lectured at Oxford, and Grocyn, Colet, and More were some of its great scholars in the fifteenth and sixteenth centuries. Other Oxford scholars beside Lewis who created worlds of fantasy were Charles Dodgson (Lewis Carroll) and J. R. R. Tolkien.

Lewis taught philosophy for one year at University College during the absence of its tutor; then, in 1925, he was elected fellow and

EARLY SUMMER

Lewis completes some examination marking (correcting) he had taken on, and then visits Owen and Maud Barfield in London.

AUGUST 17 (Mon)–SEPTEMBER 6 (Sun)

Lewis holidays with Mrs. Moore and Maureen for three weeks at Oare, on the Exmoor borders. He enjoys blissful days walking and reading favorite books. As the holiday starts to draw to its end he begins to read the texts that he is likely to be teaching in the new term.

---

tutor in English Language and Literature at Magdalen College. He remained there until his appointment to the Chair of Medieval and Renaissance Literature at Cambridge in 1954. During much of Lewis's life in Oxford he lived at The Kilns, on the outskirts of Oxford, at Headington, sharing his habitation with Mrs. Janie Moore (until her death in 1951), her daughter Maureen (until she married in 1940), and his brother Warren. Eventually, in 1956, Lewis would marry Joy Davidman Gresham, and Joy and her sons came to live at The Kilns. Originally this was an isolated dwelling, but it is now surrounded by a housing estate, where a street is named after Lewis.

Magdalen—the College of St. Mary Magdalen—was founded in 1458, and its name is still pronounced as it was by its founder, William of Waynflete: "Maud-elen." The distinct tower of Magdalen was completed in 1503. During the Reformation the medieval trappings of the chapel were stripped away, but the interior was restored in the nineteenth century.

"Addison's Walk" was the favorite footpath of a famous fellow of Magdalen, the essayist and poet Joseph Addison (1672–1719). In 1998 a stone tablet was erected in Addison's Walk to mark Lewis's birth a hundred years before. Lewis's poem about the Walk, "What the Bird Said Early in the Year," is inscribed on the centenary stone.

OCTOBER 1 (Thu)

Albert Lewis notes in his diary: "Jacks returned. A fortnight and a few days with me. Very pleasant, not a cloud.
Went to the Boat with him. The first time I did not pay
his passage money. I offered, but he did not want it."

EARLY OCTOBER

Lewis moves into his college rooms at Magdalen College:
New Buildings 3.3 (that is, Staircase 3, Rooms 3). He is
delighted with them, though some furnishing is needed.
He is enraptured by the views from his windows at the
front and rear of the building. His big sitting-room looks
north. From its windows the scene is rural—no clue presents itself that he is in a small city. He looks down on man-
icured lawns that slowly transform into a distant woodland. There the trees burn an autumn red. Over the turf a
herd of deer graze slowly and erratically. To his right he
can glimpse the beginnings of his favorite walk, a path
through the college grounds beside the River Cherwell
known as Addison's Walk. To the front of the building his
smaller sitting-room and bedroom provide a view southward, across to the main buildings of the college, with
Magdalen tower looming beyond it.

NOVEMBER 29 (Sun)

Lewis's twenty-seventh birthday.

DECEMBER 21 (Mon)

G. K. Chesterton publishes *The Everlasting Man*.

[*This book will have an enormous impact on Lewis, influencing his
conversion to Christian faith. At this stage, in 1925, he is still a
materialist.*]

Lewis and Warren travel home to Belfast for Christmas.

CHAPTER FIVE

J. R. R. Tolkien and the Inklings: Oxford Life (1926–1938)

Now secure in his tenure at Oxford's Magdalen College, Lewis could divide his time between the rented house he shared with Mrs. Moore and Maureen, and his rooms at the college. During term time he slept over at Magdalen. Lewis's students during the Magdalen years included such figures as critic Kenneth Tynan, poet John Betjeman, literary historian and novelist Harry Blamires, and novelist, academic, and poet John Wain.

In the first year of Lewis's post at Magdalen he met Professor J. R. R. Tolkien, recently come to Oxford from Leeds University, who soon became a lifelong friend. They would criticize one another's poetry, drift into theology and philosophy, and pun or talk English department politics. Tolkien soon shared with Lewis what had been a private world, early tales and poems of his invented mythology of Middle-earth, the background for *The Lord of the Rings*.

Tolkien's deep friendship with Lewis was of great significance to both men. Tolkien found in Lewis an appreciative audience for his burgeoning stories and poems of

Middle-earth, a good deal of which was not published until after Tolkien's death. Without Lewis's encouragement over many years, *The Lord of the Rings* would have never appeared in print. Lewis equally had cause to appreciate Tolkien. His views on myth and imagination, and the relation of both to reality, helped to persuade Lewis (who was then still a materialist) of the truth of the Christian gospel. When Lewis first met Tolkien, the two men had radically opposing worldviews. Tolkien was a traditional supernaturalist who had believed the orthodox doctrines of his faith since childhood. Seeing mind to mind on both imagination and the teachings of Christianity eventually became the enduring foundation of their remarkable friendship.

Lewis's growing knowledge of medieval reality spilled over into a series of brilliant lectures that he continued to develop. These were eventually published after his death as *The Discarded Image*. This rich insight inspired the technical framework of his popular science-fiction trilogy, the first book of which, *Out of the Silent Planet*, was published in 1938. In later years it was to give body to the enchanted world of Narnia.

The Inklings, the group of literary friends that formed in 1933, grew out of the rapport between Lewis and Tolkien. According to Tolkien, the Inklings were an "undetermined and unelected circle of friends who gathered around C. S. L[ewis]., and met in his rooms in Magdalen.... Our habit was to read aloud compositions of various kinds (and lengths!)." Both friends had a penchant for informal clubs. Tolkien remembered how much Lewis felt at home in this kind of company. "C. S. L. had a passion for hearing things read aloud, a power of memory for things received in that way, and also a facility in extempore criticism, none of which were shared (especially not the last) in anything like the same degree by his friends."

1926

A general strike paralyzes Britain. Trotsky is expelled from the Politburo. A Book-of-the-Month Club is started in the United States.

Princess Elizabeth (the future Elizabeth II), John Berger, J. P. Donleavy, John Fowles, Elizabeth Jennings, Christopher Logue, and Peter Shaffer are born.

Gertrude Bell, Emma Frances Brooke, Ada Cambridge, Charles Montagu Doughty, Ronald Firbank, Sir Sidney Lee, Claude Monet, Rudolph Valentino, and Israel Zangwill die.

JANUARY

Warren Lewis is assigned to duty as officer commanding No. 17 M. T. Company, RASC, Woolwich, London.

JANUARY 23 (Sat)

At noon Lewis gives his first lecture in the Oxford English School on "Some Eighteenth-Century Precursors of the Romantic Movement," after frantic preparations. [He had planned to lecture on selected poetry, but discovered in time that a distinguished colleague intended to cover the poets. He therefore had to turn to the relevant prose writings of the period, less familiar to him.]

APRIL 27 (Tue)

Lewis and a visitor, T. D. Weldon, a philosophy don at Magdalen, discuss the historicity of the New Testament gospels sitting by the fire in his larger sitting room in the college. To Lewis's astonishment this hardest-edged of all the atheists he knows suggests that the evidence for the historicity of the gospels is surprisingly good. "Rum thing," Weldon remarks. "All that stuff of [Sir James] Frazer's about the Dying God. Rum thing. It almost looks as if it had really happened once." In his diary tonight

Lewis observes: "We somehow got on the historical truth of the Gospels, and agreed there was a lot that could not be explained away." The entry concludes: "a wasted, tho' interesting evening."

MAY 11 (Tue)

Lewis and Tolkien meet at the four o'clock "English Tea"—a meeting of Oxford English School faculty—at Merton College. In attendance are the Rev. Ronald Fletcher; Margaret Lee, a tutor; George Gordon, Professor of English Literature; and Professor Tolkien. Tolkien, Lewis notes, is a slight man, rather dapper in dress, shorter than he is and not much older. He speaks quickly, and one has to listen carefully to catch all his words. He is, in Lewis's impression, "a smooth, pale, fluent little chap." He seems to favor bringing together language and literature studies more in the school. Tolkien says, however, "language is the real thing in the school." Not only that, Tolkien makes matters worse by expressing his opinion that "all literature is written for the amusement of men between thirty and forty." Lewis records in his diary later that, according to Tolkien, "we (in the English School) ought to vote ourselves out of existence if we are honest." He concludes: "No harm in him: only needs a smack or so."

MAY 12 (Wed)

Lewis conducts a philosophy class at Oxford's Lady Margaret Hall with several female students. He approves of their continued interest in the thought of Bishop Berkeley, who sees all existence as dependent on God's perception, and explains to them a distinction that a contemporary philosopher, Samuel Alexander, makes between contemplation and enjoyment, a difference between looking *at* and looking *with* one's perceptions and sensations. It is a matter of where you place your awareness; whether you are self-conscious (focusing on your own moods, awareness, or experiences) or attending to something or someone other than your self. Lewis is particularly pleased that one student, Joan Colbourne, quickly understands the difference. She responds to another student's comment that she wishes to "know" the self: "It is as if, not content with seeing with your eyes, you wanted to take them out and look at them—and then they wouldn't be eyes." [*Alexander's distinction is becoming more and more important to Lewis, one which is already undermining his materialism. It highlights a major problem with focusing exclusively on the subjective, on human inner states.*]

MAY 27 (Thu)

One of Lewis's earliest students is the future poet laureate John Betjeman. Betjeman appears at Lewis's rooms for a

_____ *Some Notable Students* _____
of Lewis

C. S. Lewis was tutor and fellow in English at Magdalen College, Oxford, for close on thirty years. During that time his main duty was to the undergraduates that he tutored. These included:

Sir John Betjeman (1906–1984)—leading poet and Poet Laureate.

John Wain (1925–1994)—novelist, poet, lecturer, literary critic, broadcaster, and Professor of Poetry at Oxford, 1973–78.

Kenneth Tynan (1927–1980)—leading theater critic and director.

Harry Blamires (b. 1916)—novelist, literary critic, and historian, and writer of popular theology.

George Sayer—biographer of C. S. Lewis and master at Malvern College (where Lewis studied briefly as a teenager).

tutorial in a pair of loud bedroom slippers. He says bright-
ly that he hopes Lewis doesn't mind them, as he has a blis-
ter. Because of his evident self-satisfaction, Lewis can't
help replying that he would mind them very much himself,
but that he has no objection to Betjeman wearing them.
This response seems to surprise the overly laid-back student.

SEPTEMBER 18 (Sat)

Lewis publishes his long narrative poem, *Dymer*, under his
pseudonym Clive Hamilton. In *Dymer* Lewis attacks
Christianity bitterly, regarding it as a tempting illusion
that must be overcome and destroyed in one's life.
Christianity is lumped together with all forms of super-
naturalism, including spiritism. [*The story had come to his mind,
complete, when he was about seventeen, but he had abandoned the writing
for some years. By the time Lewis finishes writing* Dymer, *he has serious doubts about orthodox atheism and naturalism and has begun to
favor a rather battered idealism. At this time the "Great War" is still
raging with Owen Barfield, whose spiritual views, associated with
Rudolf Steiner's anthroposophy, Lewis opposes.*]

MICHAELMAS (Autumn) TERM

Lewis presents a twice-weekly course of lectures on the
subject "Some English Thinkers of the Renaissance (Elyot,
Ascham, Hooker, Bacon)." His chosen approach to giving
lectures is not to write them out in full, but only in note
form. Lectures that are read out, he believes, simply send
students to sleep. He has decided to make the plunge from
the very beginning of his lecturing career, forcing himself
to talk rather than recite.

OCTOBER 4 (Mon)

Warren begins a six-month economics course at London
University.

NOVEMBER 29 (Mon)

Lewis's twenty-eight birthday.

DECEMBER 21 (Tue)

Lewis and Warren travel to Belfast. The Christmas holidays of 1926 are the last that Albert, Warren, and Lewis are to spend all together. Relations between Albert and his two sons are very slowly improving.

1927

The economy collapses in Germany. Charles Lindbergh flies from New York to Paris. T. S. Eliot joins the Church of England. In December Werner Heisenberg publishes his "Uncertainty Principle," which further undermines classical physics.

Ruth Prawer Jhabvala, R. D. Laing, Simon Raven, Charles Tomlinson, and Kenneth Tynan are born.

Sir Sidney Colvin, Jerome K. Jerome, William Le Queux, and Mary Webb die.

Albert Lewis begins to experience painful rheumatism. Lewis persists in trying to persuade his father to visit him in Oxford. He begins teaching a series of lectures on "The 'Romance of the Rose' and Its Successors," the substance of which eventually appears in his *The Allegory of Love* (1936).

JANUARY 8 (Sat)

Albert records in his diary: "Warnie and Jacks returned tonight by Fleetwood. As the boat did not sail until 11 o'c. they stayed with me to 9.30. So ended a very pleasant holiday. Roses all the way."

JANUARY 18 (Tue)

After working in the morning on the Norman influence in

Middle English, Lewis has a delightful walk in the afternoon up Shotover Hill, which rises behind The Kilns, and into the countryside beyond. The earlier fog has cleared. While he walks he continues to wrestle with the relation of intellect and imagination, and the "unholy muddle" he is in about them—"undigested scraps of anthroposophy and psychoanalysis jostling with orthodox idealism over a background of good old Kirkian rationalism." His mind feels like a battleground. He feels a constant danger either of regressing into "childish superstitions" or escaping into "dogmatic materialism."

JANUARY 19 (Wed)

His afternoon walking takes him across the fields to Stowe Woods, still puzzling about the imagination and intellect. On his way back he finds himself demanding that he will not give up the notion that "what we get in imagination at its highest is real in some way," even though he doesn't yet know how. His "intellectual conscience" then chides him for not enquiring into what he can know, instead of indulging in such sentimentality.

APRIL 11 (Mon)

Warren sails on the *Derbyshire* for service in China.

JUNE

Warren serves as second in command of the base supply depot, Kowloon, South China (15th Infantry Brigade).

JUNE 26 (Sun)

Writing to Arthur Greeves on this wet morning, Lewis mentions the sorry state of Mrs. Moore's veins—"Minto" may need an operation, he worries. He alludes to translations he has made of *Sir Gawain and the Green Knight* and *Beowulf*, with which Arthur is familiar. Lewis records his joy at attending the Coalbiter Club, organized by J. R. R. Tolkien. The title of the club, he says, comes from an Old Icelandic word which refers to old cronies who sit so close to the fire that it seems as if they are biting the coals. The Oxford Coalbiters are working through Icelandic texts such as the *Younger Edda* and the *Volsung Saga*. He speaks of his delight in seeing the names of gods and giants in an Icelandic dictionary. (Lewis shares with Arthur a love of Wagner and Old Norse sagas.) These mere names, he says, are enough to cast him back fifteen years "into a wild dream of northern skies and Valkyrie music." [*It eventually becomes a regular habit for Tolkien to call into Lewis's college around mid-morning on Mondays (a day when Lewis has no students). They usually cross High Street and go to the nearby Eastgate Hotel or to a pub for a drink.*]

NOVEMBER

Warren is assigned to duty as officer in command of the supply depot, Shanghai, China.

NOVEMBER 29 (Tue)

Lewis's twenty-ninth birthday.

1928

Women's suffrage in Britain is reduced to the age of twenty-one. Alexander Fleming discovers penicillin.

Evelyn Anthony (Evelyn Ward-Thomas), Stan Barstow, Anita Brookner, Jane Gardam, David Mercer, Bernice Rubens, Tom Sharpe, Alan Sillitoe, and William Trevor are born.

Sir Edmund Gosse, Thomas Hardy, Jane Harrison, and Charlotte Mew die.

Lewis begins his twice-weekly lectures on "The Prolegomena to Medieval and Renaissance Studies," which soon makes him one of the most popular lecturers in Oxford. Owen Barfield's *Poetic Diction* is published, the ideas of which have an enormous impact, first on Lewis (who has been exposed to them for several years through his "Great War" with Barfield), then Tolkien.

MAY 2 (Wed)

Albert retires with an annual pension of £550 as Belfast Corporation county solicitor. [*He has held this position since 1889.*]

MAY 27 (Sun)

Lewis has just obtained a copy of Barfield's *Poetic Diction*, and immediately writes to him: "I think in general that I am going to agree with the whole book more than we thought I did. We are really at one about imagination as the source of meanings i.e. almost of *objects*. We both agree that it is the *prius* [antecedent] of truth."

OCTOBER

Warren meets Major H. D. Parkin, officer commanding RASC Shanghai, who becomes a lifelong friend.

OCTOBER 17 (Wed)

Lewis begins lectures on "The 'Romance of the Rose' and Its Successors."

NOVEMBER 29 (Thu)

Lewis's thirtieth birthday.

—— The "Great War" with Barfield ——

In 1922 a "Great War" had begun between Lewis and his closest friend in this period, Owen Barfield, then a fellow undergraduate. The "war" was, for Barfield, "an intense interchange of philosophical opinions" and, for Lewis, "an almost incessant disputation, sometimes by letter and sometimes face to face, which lasted for years." The dialogue ensued soon after Barfield's acceptance of anthroposophy, a "spiritual science" based on a synthesis of Eastern and Christian thought and developed by Rudolf Steiner (1861–1925). It trailed off by the time of Lewis's conversion to the Christian faith in 1931. The dispute centered on the nature of the imagination and the status of poetic insights. It cured Lewis of his "chronological snobbery," making him hostile to the modern period, and provided a rich background of sharpened thought for Barfield's important study, *Poetic Diction* (1928). In this Barfield argued that there is a poetic element in all meaningful language. He was refuting the increasingly popular view that scientific discourse was the only means of true knowledge.

The "war" with Barfield also convinced Lewis that his materialism, if true, in fact made knowledge impossible! It was self-refuting. Barfield jokingly said to his friend after their "war" was over that while Lewis had taught him *how* to think, he had taught Lewis *what* to think.

1929

Trotsky is exiled. Herbert Hoover becomes president of the United States; the Wall Street Crash in October begins the Great Depression. Ramsay MacDonald becomes British prime minister.

Lynne Reid Banks, Brigid Brophy, Len Deighton, U. A. Fanthorpe, Thom Gunn, Martin Luther King Jr., John Osborne, Peter Porter, George Steiner, Keith Waterhouse, and Robert Westall are born.

Edward Carpenter, Lucy Clifford, Henry Arthur Jones, and Flora Annie Steel die.

Tolkien and Lewis are now meeting on a weekly basis, usually on Mondays in Lewis's rooms.

HILARY (Spring) TERM

Lewis begins lecturing on "Elyot, Ascham, Hooker and Bacon."

TRINITY (Summer) TERM

Lewis becomes a theist: "I gave in, and admitted that God was God, and knelt and prayed. . . ."

JULY 25 (Thu)

Albert has his first X-rays in a Belfast nursing home to investigate a recurring complaint.

AUGUST 6 (Tue)

Albert returns to the nursing home for additional X-rays.

AUGUST 13 (Tue)

Albert's illness is serious enough to force Lewis to hasten to Belfast.

Conversion to Theism

After an epiphany on an Oxford bus, traveling up Headington hill, and many other conversations and books that he had encountered, Lewis eventually became a theist. Some kind of God with a definite character, he acknowledged, lay behind the show of reality. He later confessed: "I never had the experience of looking for God. It was the other way round; He was the hunter (or so it seemed to me) and I was the deer. He stalked me like a redskin, took unerring aim, and fired. And I am very thankful that that is how the first (conscious) meeting occurred. It forearms one against subsequent fears that the whole thing was only wish fulfilment. Something one didn't wish for can hardly be that."

SEPTEMBER 25 (Wed)

Albert Lewis dies, succumbing just after his son has returned to Oxford to care for some urgent matters. [*Augustus Hamilton, Albert's brother-in-law, will remember: "Where Allie is such good fun is that he'll always give you an opinion on any subject, whether he knows anything about it or not."*]

SEPTEMBER 27 (Fri)

Warren receives a telegram in Shanghai—"Sorry report father died painless twenty fifth September. Jack." [*With his older brother away, it is left to Lewis to arrange the funeral and settle the estate.*]

NOVEMBER

One Monday evening, after another of many meetings Lewis attends, Tolkien comes back with him to his college rooms and sits "discoursing of the gods & giants & Asgard for three hours" by a bright fire in the larger sitting room. Tolkien leaves at 2.30 in the morning, into the wind and rain. The talk is good.

NOVEMBER 29 (Fri)

Lewis's thirty-first birthday.

EARLY WINTER

Tolkien gives his "Lay of Leithien" to Lewis to read, from his collection of writings about Middle-earth, and draws up his "Sketch of the Mythology" to fill out its background.

DECEMBER 6 (Fri)

Lewis reads Tolkien's poetic version of the tale of Beren and Lúthien during the evening. His response is enthusiastic.

DECEMBER 7 (Sat)

Lewis writes to Tolkien: "I can quite honestly say that it is ages since I have had an evening of such delight: and the personal interest of reading a friend's work had very little to do with it. . . . The two things that came out clearly are the sense of reality in the background and the mythical value: the essence of a myth being that it should have no taint of allegory to the maker and yet should suggest incipient allegories to the reader."

LATE DECEMBER

Lewis stays in London for four days at the Barfields' home. For two of the days Maud and their adopted baby are away, giving Barfield and Lewis an "uninterrupted feast of each other's society."

1930

Gandhi begins a campaign of civil disobedience in India. Hitler's National Socialist German Workers' Party becomes the second-strongest party in the German parliament. Prince Ras Tafari becomes Emperor Haile Selassie of Abyssinia.

John Arden, J. G. Ballard, Elaine Feinstein, Roy Fisher, Ted Hughes, Harold Pinter, Ruth Rendell, Jon Silkin, and Anthony Thwaite are born.

Arthur St. John Adcock, A. J. Balfour, Florence Bell, Robert Bridges, Sir Arthur Conan Doyle, and D. H. Lawrence die.

FEBRUARY 24 (Mon)

Warren sails from Shanghai on the freighter Tai-Yin. [On the voyage home he visits Japan and the United States.]

MARCH 4 (Tue)

Warren's ship is docked at Yokahama, Japan, and he and his friend Leonard H. Barton take a taxi to ancient

Kamakura to see the Dibutsu Buddha. He notes in his diary this evening: "A broad tree lined avenue led up to the Buddha which we had come to see, and there it was, huge and aloof even at two hundred yards distance. . . . Though it is enormous—about 50 to 60 feet high I should say— mere size is not its attraction—or rather that it should have been possible to cast and carve a master piece of such a size is what gives it its fascination: there is something uncanny in staring up into that huge face which looks down under half closed eyes with an expression which seems to say, 'I have always known everything and have always been here, and anything you may do or say in your little life is mere futility.' I would like to stop in this place for a few days and come back and look at this statue at various times—early morning and evening—but not on a moonlight night. I must have looked up, into his face, for nearly ten minutes." [*His encounter with the awesome figure permanently affects him, tied in with his reawakening faith in the historical yet divine Jesus Christ. It provides a numinous experience similar to what his brother finds in literature. The momentous Kamakura Buddha tantalizingly hints at an incarnation of some kind of cosmic presence in this world. Ever after, Warren treasures a souvenir statue of the Dibutsu Buddha he purchases in Kamakura.*]

MARCH 21 (Fri)

Lewis writes to his friend A. K. Hamilton Jenkin, telling him how his outlook is changing. He does not feel that he is moving exactly to Christianity, though, he confesses, it may turn out that way in the end. The best way of explaining the change, he says, is this: Once he would have said "Shall I adopt Christianity"; now he is waiting to see whether it will adopt him. Another party is involved—it is as if he is playing poker, not patience, as he once supposed. [*Around this time Lewis writes in mock alarm to Barfield that terrifying things are happening to him. He says, in the* language of their philosophical concerns, that the "Spirit" or "Real I" is tending to become much more personal and, to his alarm, is taking the offensive. In fact, it is behaving just like God. He concludes: "You'd better come on Monday at the latest or I may have entered a monastery."]

TRINITY (Summer) TERM

Lewis gives his first lectures on Milton.

APRIL 17 (Thu)

Warren arrives in Liverpool after a three-year absence abroad.

APRIL 22 (Tue)–25 (Fri)

Lewis and his brother visit Little Lea and their father's grave. They find that Albert has preserved an immense number of family papers, especially letters and diaries.

MAY 10 (Sat)

Warren decides, upon his retirement from the army, to edit and arrange the Lewis family papers. [He will retire in 1932.]

MAY 15 (Thu)

Warren is assigned as assistant to the officer in charge of supplies and transport at Bulford, England.

MAY 25 (Sun)

Warren decides that he will accept the invitation from his brother and Mrs. Moore to make his home with them upon his retirement.

———— *The Lewis Family Papers* ————

After Warren had settled in Oxford in late 1932, he began the enormous task of arranging the family papers (letters, diaries, photographs, and various documents), typing and arranging the material in what ended up being eleven volumes (everything had been brought over from Belfast and deposited in the room Lewis gave Warren in Magdalen College). Warren drew on Albert's collections, and his and Lewis's diaries and other papers, and arranged the lot in chronological order. During 1933 to 1935 Warren typed the material up with two fingers. The pages were then bound into volumes in stages and entitled *Lewis Papers: Memoirs of the Lewis Family 1850 –1930*. Warren added numerous explanatory notes. It was a feat of editing, arranged with the eye of someone for whom history comes naturally.

The eleven volumes were completed in 1935 and, after Lewis's death, bequeathed by Warren to The Marion E. Wade Center, Wheaton, Illinois, as a result of his friendship with pioneering Lewis scholar Clyde S. Kilby.

JULY 6 (Sun)

Warren and Lewis go to view The Kilns that morning, with a view to its purchase. He records, "The eight-acre garden is such stuff as dreams are made on. . . . The house . . . stands at the entrance to its own grounds at the northern foot of Shotover [Hill] at the end of a narrow lane. . . . To the left of the house are the two brick kilns from which it takes its name—in front, a lawn and hard tennis court— then a large bathing pool, beautifully wooded, and with a delightful circular brick seat overlooking it. After that a steep wilderness broken with ravines and nooks of all kinds runs up to a little cliff topped by a thistly meadow, and then the property ends in a thick belt of fir trees, almost a wood. The view from the cliff over the dim blue distance is simply glorious."

JULY 16 (Wed)

The offer to purchase The Kilns is accepted.

OCTOBER 10/11 (Fri/Sat)

Lewis, Warren, Maureen, and Mrs. Moore engage in the move to The Kilns from nearby Hillsboro, Holyoake Road. [*Around the time of the move into The Kilns Lewis begins reading John's Gospel in Greek; it soon becomes his practice to read some passage of the Bible more or less daily. He also starts attending Magdalen College chapel on weekdays and his parish church, Holy Trinity, on Sundays. Reading John begins to change his picture of the life and person of Jesus.*]

NOVEMBER 29 (Sat)

Lewis's thirty-second birthday.

1931

Ramsay MacDonald is reelected British prime minister for the third time. Spain becomes a republic on the abdication of Alfonso XIII. Britain abandons the gold standard.

Alan Brownjohn, Isabel Colegate, P. J. Kavanagh, John le Carré (David John Moore Cornwell), Peter Levi, Frederic Raphael, and Fay Weldon are born.

Arnold Bennett, Sir Hall Caine, Lucas Malet (Mary St. Leger Harrison), and Katharine Tynan die.

Tolkien's reformed English School syllabus is accepted at Oxford University, backed by Lewis, bringing together "Lang." and "Lit."

JANUARY 1 (Thu)–4 (Sun)

Lewis and Warren take their first annual walking tour (fifty-four miles along the Wye Valley).

MAY 9 (Sat)

Warren returns to belief in Christianity.

MAY 13 (Wed)

Warren explains in his diary: "I started to say my prayers again after having discontinued doing so for more years than I care to remember. . . . This was no sudden impulse, but the result of a conviction of the truth of Christianity which has been growing on me for a considerable time: a conviction for which I admit I should be hard put to find a logical proof, but which rests on the inherent improbability of the whole of existence being fortuitous, and the inability of the materialists to provide any convincing explanation of the origin of life."

MAY 23 (Sat)

Whipsnade Zoo opens to the public after years of planning. It is an ambitious conservation area and the first wildlife habitat zoo in Europe, occupying nearly six hundred acres on the Chilton Downs some distance east of Oxford and north of London.

SEPTEMBER 19/20 (Sat/Sun)

After a long night conversation on Oxford's Addison's Walk with Tolkien and Hugo Dyson, Lewis starts to become convinced of the truth of the Christian faith.

SEPTEMBER 28 (Mon)

Lewis returns to the Christian faith while riding from Oxford to Whipsnade Zoo in the sidecar of Warren's Daudel motorcycle. "When we set out I did not believe that Jesus Christ was the Son of God, and when we reached the zoo I did."

─────── *A Night to Remember* ───────

On the night of September 19, 1931, on Addison's Walk, Tolkien, with support from Hugo Dyson, argued for the Christian gospels on the basis of the universal love of story which, for him, was sacramental. His poem "Mythopoeia" gives a good idea of the flow of the night's conversation: The human heart is not composed of complete falsehood, but has the nourishment of knowledge from the Wise One, and still remembers him. Though the estrangement is ancient, human beings are neither completely abandoned by God nor totally corrupted. Though we are disgraced we still retain vestiges of our mandate to rule. We continue to create according to the "law in which we're made."

Lewis later wrote a powerful essay on the harmony of story and fact in the gospels, remembering that life-changing conversation with Tolkien and Dyson: "This is the marriage of heaven and earth, perfect Myth and Perfect Fact: claiming not only our love and Obedience, but also our wonder and delight, addressed to the savage, the child, and the poet in each one of us no less than to the moralist, the scholar, and the philosopher." He realized that the claims and stories of Christ did demand an imaginative as much as an intellectual response from us. He treated the theme more fully in his book *Miracles* (1947).

For the first time in his life, both sides of Lewis—the analytical and the imaginative—became fully engaged.

─────────────────────●─●─────────────────────

OCTOBER 1 (Thu)

Lewis writes to Arthur Greeves that he now believes in Christ and Christianity.

OCTOBER 9 (Fri)

Warren embarks on the passenger cargo ship *Neuralia* for his second tour of duty in China.

NOVEMBER

Warren serves as officer commanding the RASC in Shanghai.

NOVEMBER 22 (Sun)

Lewis writes to Warren about his meetings with Tolkien as one of the pleasant moments in the week. "Sometimes we talk English school politics: sometimes we criticize one another's poems: other days we drift into theology or 'the state of the nation': rarely we fly no higher than bawdy and 'puns.'"

NOVEMBER 29 (Sun)

Lewis's thirty-third birthday.

1932

The Nazis become the strongest party in the German parliament. Eamon de Valéra is elected president of Ireland. Franklin D. Roosevelt becomes president of the United States. Charles Lindbergh's son is kidnapped. Scrutiny *begins quarterly publication, edited by literary critics F. R. and Q. D. Leavis.*

Malcolm Bradbury, Alice Thomas Ellis, Eva Figes, Penelope Gilliat, Adrian Henri, Geoffrey Hill, George MacBeth, Adrian Mitchell, V. S. Naipaul, Edna O'Brien, Sylvia Plath, and Arnold Wesker are born.

Mona Caird, W. G. Collingwood, Goldsworthy Lowes Dickinson, John Meade Falkner, Kenneth Grahame, Lady Isabella Gregory, Lytton Strachey, and Edgar Wallace die.

Warren Lewis will retire from the army this year and actively settle into his brother's life.

JANUARY 18 (Mon)

Lewis begins lectures on "Prolegomena to Medieval Poetry."

JANUARY 29 (Fri)

The Japanese attack Chinese Shanghai.

[*Warren is based nearby.*]

JULY

Warren applies for retirement from the RASC. [*He will sail for home on October 22.*]

AUGUST 16 (Tue)–29 (Mon)

Lewis writes *The Pilgrim's Regress* while holidaying in Northern Ireland. Now that Little Lea has been sold, he stays at Bernagh with Arthur Greeves. [*He dedicates the book to Arthur Greeves.*]

OCTOBER 22 (Sat)

Warren departs from Shanghai on the cargo liner *Automadon*.

NOVEMBER 29 (Tue)

Lewis's thirty-fourth birthday.

DECEMBER 14 (Wed)

Warren arrives at Liverpool. [*He returns to Oxford where Lewis and Mrs. Moore have added two extra rooms to The Kilns for his benefit. Lewis also gives Warren the use of the smaller of his two sitting-rooms in Magdalen College. He moves permanently into The Kilns.*]

DECEMBER 21 (Wed)

Warren retires from the Royal Army Service Corps after eighteen years, two months, and twenty days of service. He is thirty-seven years old.

WINTER

Tolkien hands Lewis a sheaf of papers to read. It is the incomplete draft of what will become *The Hobbit: or There and Back Again.*

1933

Hitler becomes German chancellor; civil liberties are abolished in Germany, and Hitler is granted dictatorial powers. "New Deal" in the United States. King Kong appears in the cinema.

Michael Frayn, B. S. Johnson, Penelope Lively, Joe Orton, David Storey, and Claire Tomalin are born.

Stella Benson, Annie Besant, Augustine Birrell, Sir John Fortescue, Henry Watson Fowler, John Galsworthy, Anthony Hope (Sir Anthony Hope Hawkins), George A. Moore, and George Saintsbury die.

At this period the daily routines of Lewis and Warren overlap. In his diary Warren outlines a typical day in term-time, when he would share space in Lewis's college rooms during the week. Warren will work in Magdalen College during the morning (he writes a number of volumes on French history), goes home to The Kilns with Lewis for lunch, and then in the afternoon participates in what Lewis dubs "public works"—he and his brother work in the wooded area of the extensive grounds of The Kilns. They are building a footpath made of rubble and sand through the "wilderness and wood which ran up the hill to Shotover." At that time, Warren later observed, "Mrs. King's [Mrs. Moore's] autocracy had not yet degenerated into . . . tyranny." On Sunday evenings Warren plays orchestral and other musical recordings on his gramophone to the assembled "family."

During the Trinity (Summer) Term the original Inklings, an undergraduate group, folds, and the name eventually becomes transferred to a circle of friends around Lewis and Tolkien which begin to meet this autumn. The Inklings will meet at least once a week during term time until near the end of the 1940s, to talk about ideas, to read to each other pieces they have written for pleasure and for criticism, and to have a good time together.

JANUARY 3 (Tue)–6 (Fri)

Lewis and Warren have their second walking tour (continuing their ascent of the Wye Valley).

MARCH 30 (Thu)

Warren purchases a gramophone, which is used to give family "concerts."

APRIL

Warren, Lewis, Maureen, and Mrs. Moore holiday for two weeks at Flint Hall, Hambleden, Buckinghamshire, a farmhouse in the Chiltern hills. They are accompanied by their dog, Mr. Papworth. While here Lewis, with the aid of Warren, corrects the galley proofs of The Pilgrim's Regress. On Good Friday they attend the amateur performance of a Passion Play in a rural church in the village of Frieth. On Easter Sunday Lewis has an idea for a book (probably while in church), which he outlines to Warren, who records it in his diary: "A religious work, based on the opinion of some of the [Church] Fathers, that while punishment for the damned is eternal, it is intermittent: he proposes to do sort of an infernal day excursion to Paradise." [Some years later the idea is realized as The Great Divorce (1945).]

Also in April, Maureen begins to teach the piano to Warren.

MAY 25 (Thu)

Lewis's The Pilgrim's Regress is published.

JUNE 1 (Thu)

The first volume of the Lewis Family Papers returns from the binders.

AUGUST 3 (Thu)–15 (Tue)

Lewis and Warren visit their Uncle Bill and Aunt Minnie Lewis for a weekend in Helensburgh, Scotland. They also see their Uncle Dick and Aunt Agnes Lewis, who live nearby. They then sail for London from Glasgow on the Clyde's Shipping Company tour cruise.

OCTOBER 2 (Mon)

As usual there is what Warren calls the tedious "compulsory daily walk" of the dogs Tykes (Mr. Papworth) and Troddles.

MICHAELMAS (Autumn) TERM

This marks the probable beginning of Lewis's convening of a circle of friends, eventually called "the Inklings." On Thursday evenings they tend to meet in Lewis's college rooms to read from work in progress, while Tuesday mornings in the Eagle and Child pub are more informal. ["*Of course there was no reading on Tuesday, and the talk often veered to college and English School politics; but whatever the topic one could rely upon its being wittily handled.*"]

Maureen has already begun teaching this term in a school in Monmouth, returning at weekends to The Kilns. She is given a lift there and back by the headmistress, on her way to and from London.

OCTOBER 7 (Sat)

The clocks go back an hour, marking the end of British Summer Time. Lewis's autumn term begins, and he sleeps overnight in college, rather than at home in The Kilns. The weather is unpleasant, damp, hot, and overcast.

OCTOBER 8 (Sun)

Lewis is busy with administrative tasks so is not able to get to church at Holy Trinity. Warren and Maureen walk to Headington Quarry to attend the morning service. The sermon is on Matthew 13 (where Jesus speaks of the kingdom of heaven being like a net).

OCTOBER 13 (Fri)

Warren works at Lewis's college rooms in the morning as usual. It is a fine day, and in the afternoon the brothers lay six wheelbarrow loads of rubble on the woodland path, in the grounds of The Kilns. The evening is dark and windy, and they take Mr. Papworth for a walk after supper.

OCTOBER 21 (Sat)

Warren finishes getting volume 3 of the Lewis Family Papers ready for the binders.

NOVEMBER 5 (Sun)

The evening before Mr. Papworth had, notes Warren, been "much alarmed and disgusted" by fireworks (the Guy Fawkes celebrations). He adds in his diary: "In the afternoon J.[ack] and I and the dogs did the Railway walk under conditions which were sheer delight. Everything was still, and a faint blue haze, the merest suggestion of a fog, softened all the colours to a compatible shabbiness—the sort of day when the country seems more intimate, more in undress, than at any other time. J. pointed out to me that one of the best bits of that whole walk is the clump of trees on the [railway] embankment seen from the south side of the level crossing."

About 7 p.m. Maureen is picked up by the school head-mistress to return to Monmouth. Mrs. Moore gives a charac-

—Favorite Public Houses in Oxford—

The Eagle and Child (nicknamed "Bird and Baby"). This was the favored pub for meetings of the Inklings through much of their existence (1933–1963). Meetings here tended to be on Tuesday mornings during term-time, but were switched to Mondays to accommodate Lewis when he began commuting to Cambridge (effectively 1955 to 1963). The Inklings meetings in The Eagle and Child did not feature the reading of manuscripts in progress, unlike the Thursday evening meetings that were usually in Lewis's college rooms. The pub is on St. Giles, a very wide street that leads northwards into the Woodstock Road. The Inklings met at what was then the back of the small and narrow pub, in the Rabbit Room. In 1962 the pub was extended and refurbished.

The King's Arms. This pub is conveniently located near the Bodleian Library, a place much frequented by Lewis as he researched his lectures and books. It is also near the famous Blackwell's Bookshop. The pub is very old, being established in 1609. The Inklings sometimes met here.

The Lamb and Flag is located opposite The Eagle and Child on St. Giles. It was sometimes used by the Inklings, especially after 1962, when The Eagle and Child had lost some of its old charm.

The Six Bells. This was Lewis's "local," the nearest to his home at The Kilns, and located in the Oxford suburb of Headington. Lewis frequented it often.

The Trout. An out-of-town pub favored by Lewis and his friends because of its picturesue location beside the river at Godstow, Wolvercote, on the edge of north Oxford. It was near this pub that Alice disappeared down the rabbit hole, in Lewis Carroll's *Alice in Wonderland*. It is one of Oxford's most well-known and popular pubs.

In a pub Lewis liked nothing better than to drink beer or cider. "Real" cider is called Scrumpy, and can be very strong. At The Eagle and Child he could enjoy a Burton beer, which was brewed in Burton on Trent, in the English Midlands.

---

teristic farewell. Though she has not been off the premises that day, she warns them of the greasiness of the highways, and the perils of the thick fog they would surely encounter. Her parting shot is, "and if I don't hear from you by eleven o'clock tonight, I'll know there has been an accident."

NOVEMBER 9 (Thu)

Lewis undertakes some "public works" for the first time after a period of illness, cutting the ivy on the big oak on the avenue at The Kilns.

NOVEMBER 21 (Tue)

Lewis reads to the Martlets this evening. At this time he has developed a strong aversion to T. S. Eliot's modernist verse. [*The minute book records: "Mr C. S. Lewis read a paper on 'Is Literature an Art?' before ten members and seven visitors. Mr. Lewis's paper was erudite and witty, though distinctly reactionary. He began by defining art as 'a trained habit' and went on to differentiate between the fine arts— music and painting—and literature because the former could always be made to order, which a poem could not. Furthermore, all good literature tells a tale, which good music or pictures, as a rule, do not. He continued, at some length, to emphasize his point of view—that the tale—the thing said—was all-important in literature; that it [the thing said] should not be judged aesthetically. Kipling, he said, often tells his tales perfectly, even though they are often foolish or morally wicked. This led Mr. Lewis to a virulent but not unamusing attack on 'modern' literature, which he sweepingly dismissed because 'it had nothing to say.' Technique has been exalted above matter and the result was 'indeed a waste land.'"*]

NOVEMBER 23 (Thu)

Tolkien comes to tea to The Kilns.

NOVEMBER 29 (Wed)

Lewis's thirty-fifth birthday.

DECEMBER 4 (Mon)

Owen Barfield is up from London and staying at The Kilns. Warren has breakfast with him at 7.45. Barfield borrows ten shillings from him and pockets the banknote. Warren is amused when, a few minutes later, Barfield says, "I find I've no change: could you lend me a shilling?" The two drive into town, where they are joined by Lewis at half past ten. Warren is secretly miffed when he discovers that Lewis has arranged to go for a walk with Tolkien that afternoon. It seems to Warren that he sees less and less of his brother every day.

DECEMBER 10 (Sun)

This afternoon it is so cold that Lewis is able to walk across the frozen pond at The Kilns, though he and Warren do not skate on it.

DECEMBER 21 (Thu)

Warren's diary entry reads, '[Mrs Moore] nags J[ack] about having become a believer, in much the same way that P [Pudaitabird, Albert Lewis] used to nag me in his latter years about my boyish fondness for dress, and with apparently just the same inability to grasp the fact that the development of the mind does not necessarily stop with that of the body." [Mrs. Moore had long ago become an atheist, blaming God for Paddy's death. She would criticize Lewis and his brother for attending Sunday morning "blood feasts" in their local church.]

1934

Hitler becomes "Führer" of Germany, as both head of state and chancellor. He begins to eliminate opponents. Purges start in the USSR. In October the Long March of the Chinese Communists begins. The

Glyndebourne Festival is founded in England. Donald Duck makes his first screen appearance, in The Wise Little Hen.

Fleur Adcock, Beryl Bainbridge, Alan Bennett, Edward Bond, Alan Garner, and Alasdair Gray are born.

F. Anstey (Thomas Anstey Guthrie), Roger Fry, A. R. Orage, Sir Arthur Wing Pinero, Sir Edward Elgar, and Gustav Holst die.

Lewis continues working on *The Allegory of Love*. He suggests, as the book nears completion, that the secret to understanding the Middle Ages, including its concern with allegory and courtly love, is to get to know thoroughly Dante's *The Divine Comedy, The Romance of the Rose*, the Classics, the Bible, and the Apocryphal New Testament.

JANUARY 1 (Mon)-6 (Sat)

Lewis and Warren take their third annual walking tour (continuing along the Wye Valley into Wales). Warren's diary details the holiday. They take a train to Hereford, and from there cross the Wye into Wales, tramping the countryside all day and lodging in small pubs at night.

FEBRUARY 2 (Fri)

In the afternoon Lewis and his brother, between them, shift twelve loads of gravel for the path in the woods by The Kilns, using a wheelbarrow.

MARCH 16 (Fri)

Lewis, Warren, and Maureen travel into Oxford to see a light opera at the Playhouse theater. The libretto of *Tantivy Towers* is by writer A. P. Herbert (1890–1971), and the music by the talented composer Thomas Dunhill (1877–1946).

————— *Walking Tours* —————

Walking tours, preferably in the company of friends, were one of Lewis's great delights. In his science-fiction story *Out of the Silent Planet*, the protagonist, Dr. Elwin Ransom, is on a solitary walking tour during the summer vacation. For a spring walk, Lewis liked a southern tour, perhaps in Dorset, where the season would be remarkably far on, the woodland nearly green, primroses evident in "great cushiony clumps," and the sea glimpsed in the distance. Such a walk would be punctuated by halts, perhaps lying down in barns or on sun-facing hill slopes.

His letters and diaries, together with the diaries of his brother Warren, give details of many walking tours. The plan usually was for friends to make their way to a starting point by train or car and then walk for several days, putting up in small hotels or country pubs, which provided a hot supper, a bed for the night, and break-fast. In April 1927, for instance, Lewis walked with A. C. Harwood and Owen Barfield across the Berkshire Downs. At this period Harwood planned the walks, and in a letter to him in 1931 Lewis called him "Lord of the Walks."

When Warren retired early and joined Lewis's household at The Kilns, an annual walking tour was soon institutionalized. There were eight of them between 1931 and 1939—to the Wye valley, to Wales and Aberystwyth, to the Chiltern Hills, to the Derbyshire Peak District, to Somerset, and to Wiltshire. As Mrs. Janie Moore became infirm it was increasingly difficult for Lewis to take a vacation.

MARCH 26 (Mon)

Lewis, Warren, and Tolkien meet up at Magdalen College to read the script of *The Valkyrie*. Lewis and Tolkien read it in German, and Warren in English. He finds it easy to follow the others' parts. They finish after six o'clock and Tolkien goes home to his family, while the brothers enjoy fried fish and a savory omelet, with beer, at the nearby Eastgate Hotel.

JUNE 3 (Sun)

Warren records that two of Lewis's friends are up in Oxford: Barfield taking his B.C.L. law examination and Dyson examining in the university's English School.

OCTOBER 1 (Mon)

Writing to Arthur Greeves, Lewis remarks how summer weather is lingering unnaturally. The pond in the grounds of The Kilns is below its normal level. The water has not risen despite a reasonable amount of rain.

NOVEMBER 29 (Thu)

Lewis's thirty-sixth birthday.

DECEMBER 26 (BOXING DAY) (Wed)

Replying to a letter from Arthur Greeves, in which Arthur had mentioned David Lindsay's book A Voyage to Arcturus, Lewis wishes Arthur had told him more about this story. [Arthur has, however, said enough to interest Lewis. When he obtains a copy, after much difficulty (it is out of print), it influences the creation of his science-fiction trilogy, beginning with Out of the Silent Planet.]

1935

Hitler repudiates the disarmament clauses of the Treaty of Versailles. Stanley Baldwin is elected British prime minister. Italy invades Abyssinia. Persia changes its name to Iran.

J. G. Farrell, Michael Holroyd, David Lodge, Alan Plater, Dennis Potter, Jon Stallworthy, and D. M. Thomas are born.

Edwin Lester Arnold, Alban Berg, A. C. Bradley, Silas Hocking, Winifred Holtby, T. E. Lawrence, Vernon Lee (Violet Paget), Rosa

Caroline Praed, George William Russell ("Æ"), and Sir William Watson die.

Lewis begins writing his volume of the *Oxford History of English Literature*, after completion of *The Allegory of Love*, at the suggestion of Professor F. P. Wilson, one of the series editors.

JANUARY 3 (Thu)–5 (Sat)

Lewis and Warren take their fourth annual walking tour, in the Chiltern Hills.

SPRING

Dr. Robert Havard—nicknamed "Humphrey" by Hugo Dyson, when he couldn't remember his name on one occasion—is invited to join the Inklings. In the early part of the year Havard attends Lewis, as his general practitioner, for influenza. They are discussing Aquinas within a matter of minutes. The Inklings, he discovers, is made up of friends of Lewis's.

APRIL 28 (Sun)

Writing to his old friend Leo Baker, wrongly thought to be ill with cancer, Lewis fills him in with his news: "My father is dead and my brother has retired from the army and now lives with us. I have deep regrets about all my relations with my father (but thank God they were best at the end). I am going bald. I am a Christian. Professionally I am chiefly a medievalist."

NOVEMBER 29 (Fri)

Lewis's thirty-seventh birthday.

DECEMBER 7 (Sat)

Lewis reports to Arthur Greeves in a letter that guests are still staying at The Kilns. [*These are relations of Mrs. Moore—a widow and her five-year old son, Michael.*] Both Lewis and Warren like the boy, though Warren (who professes to dislike children) gets on better with him. Lewis says that Mrs. Moore reads to the boy every night from the Peter Rabbit stories of Beatrix Potter. This, he says, is a "lovely sight." The boy gazes up into Mrs. Moore's eyes, greatly magnified by her spectacles, as she very slowly reads to him. Lewis expresses pity that she has no grandchildren.

1936

With the death of King George V in Britain, Edward VIII succeeds, but abdicates soon after, and George VI begins his reign. The Popular Front wins a majority in Spanish elections. Germany reoccupies the Rhineland. The Spanish Civil War starts. Allen Lane founds Penguin Books. The BBC begins a regular television service. Franklin D. Roosevelt begins a second term as U. S. president. At the Olympic Games in Berlin, Jesse Owens wins four gold medals.

Hilary Bailey, A. S. Byatt, Nell Dunn, Simon Gray, J. H. Prynne, and David Rudkin are born.

G. K. Chesterton, Edward Garnett, Maxim Gorky, R. B. Cunninghame Graham, A. E. Housman, M. R. James, Rudyard Kipling, and "Houdini" (Erich Weiss) die.

Colin Hardie (1906 – 1998) starts attending the Inklings, after becoming classical tutor at Magdalen College. Warren Lewis has a twenty-foot cabin cruiser built, which has two berths, and is moored on the River Thames. He calls it the *Bosphorus*.

JANUARY 13 (Mon)–16 (Thu)

Lewis and Warren take their fifth annual walking tour, this time in Derbyshire.

MARCH 11 (Wed)

Charles Williams receives his first letter from Lewis, in appreciation of his novel, *The Place of the Lion*. Lewis invites him to attend an Inklings meeting (the first recorded use of the name). Williams, who has been delighted by the proofs of *The Allegory of Love*, replies immediately: "If you had delayed writing another 24 hours our letters would have crossed. It has never before happened to me to be admiring an author of a book while he at the same time was admiring me. My admiration for the staff work of the Omnipotence rises every day. . . . I regard your book as practically the only one that I have ever come across, since Dante, that shows the slightest understanding of what this very peculiar identity of love and religion means. . . ."

SPRING

Lewis and Tolkien discuss writing time and space stories. Tolkien recalls in a letter [no. 294] that Lewis had one day remarked to him that since "there is too little of what we really like in stories" they ought to write some themselves. "We agreed that he should try 'space-travel,' and I should try 'time-travel.' . . . When C. S. Lewis and I tossed up, and he was to write on space-travel and I on time-travel, I began an abortive book of time-travel of which the end was to be the presence of my hero in the drowning of Atlantis."

MAY 21 (Thu)

Publication of Lewis's *The Allegory of Love*. It wins the Hawthornden Prize. In its preface references are made to

A Renaissance
of Religious Writing

The 1930s marked what literary historian Harry Blamires (a former student of Lewis's) has called a "minor renaissance" of Christian themes in English literature. It was not a self-conscious movement as such, as many of the writers were part of smaller groups, such as the Inklings. This resurgence took place in the face of a strong theological liberalism—the latter an impact of a climate of modernism. An indication that something was happening occurred in 1928 when George Bell, then dean of Canterbury Cathedral, decided to bring theater back into the church, picking up a great tradition that had fallen into neglect. He instituted the Canterbury Festival, which soon attracted a following. In 1935 T. S. Eliot's verse drama *Murder in the Cathedral* was first performed there. The next year saw the staging of *Thomas Cranmer of Canterbury*, by Charles Williams. Lewis began writing fiction just at the point when this minor Christian renaissance in literature was taking off.

C. S. Lewis, *Pilgrim's Regress* (1933), *Out of the Silent Planet* (1938)

T. S. Eliot, *Ash Wednesday* (1930), *The Rock* (1934), *Murder in the Cathedral* (1935), *Burnt Norton* (1936), *Family Reunion* (1939)

Charles Williams, *War in Heaven* (1930), *The Place of the Lion* (1931), *The Greater Trumps* (1932), *Thomas Cranmer of Canterbury* (1936), *Taliessin through Logres* (1938), *Descent of the Dove* (1939)

Helen Waddell, *Peter Abelard* (1933)

James Bridie, *Tobias and the Angel* (1930), *Jonah and the Whale* (1932)

Christopher Fry, *The Boy with a Cart* (1937)

Dorothy L. Sayers, *The Zeal of Thy House* (1937), Lord Peter Wimsey stories

David Jones, *In Parenthesis* (1937)

J. R. R. Tolkien, *The Hobbit* (1937)

Graham Greene, *Brighton Rock* (1939), *The Power and the Glory* (1940)

W. H. Auden began composing his "New Year Letter" in 1940, under the influence of Charles Williams's inimitable history of the church, published the year before.

three significant friends, Tolkien, Hugo Dyson, and Owen Barfield—to whom the book is dedicated, and to whom Lewis acknowledges the greatest debt, after his father.

JUNE 28 (Sun)

Lewis writes to Owen Barfield about his children's story: "I lent *The Silver Trumpet* to Tolkien and hear that it is the greatest success among his children that they have ever known." He signs the letter "The Alligator of Love."

NOVEMBER 25 (Wed)

Tolkien gives the Sir Isaac Gollancz Memorial Lecture to the British Academy on "Beowulf: The Monsters and the Critics," early drafts of which have been read by Lewis.

NOVEMBER 29 (Sun)

Lewis's thirty-eighth birthday.

1937

German bombers destroy the town of Guernica in Spain. Neville Chamberlain is elected British prime minister. The Duke of Windsor (formerly Edward VIII) marries Mrs. Wallis Simpson. Japanese forces take Nanking.

Paul Bailey, Steven Berkoff, Jilly Cooper, Anita Desai, Victoria Glendinning, Tony Harrison, David Hockney, Roger McGough, Tom Stoppard, and Jill Paton Walsh are born.

Sir J. M. Barrie, Julian Bell, Ella D'Arcy, John Drinkwater, Ivor Gurney, "Sapper" (Herman Cyril McNeile), Maurice Ravel, and Edith Wharton die.

Lewis is pressing ahead with his story of space travel, *Out of the Silent Planet*, reading it chapter by chapter to the Inklings as it is written.

JANUARY 5 (Tue)-9 (Sat)

Lewis and Warren take their sixth annual walking tour, in Dulverton, Somerset.

FEBRUARY

Writing to Joan Bennett, an English lecturer at Cambridge, Lewis tells her he has had an excellent week in bed with influenza. While thus confined, he had read Jane Austen's *Northanger Abbey*, Wilkie Collins's *The Moonstone*, Lord Byron's *The Vision of Judgment*, volume 3 of John Ruskin's *Modern Painters*, Charles Dickens's *Our Mutual Friend*, and George Meredith's *The Egoist*.

SEPTEMBER 21 (Tue)

The Hobbit is published, complete with Tolkien's own illustrations. [*W. H. Auden writes in a review that* The Hobbit *"in my opinion, is one of the best children's stories of this century."*]

SEPTEMBER 23 (Thu)

Lewis writes to Charles Williams, thanking him for a presentation copy of his latest supernatural novel, *Descent into Hell*, which Lewis says is his best yet. He has found it a "real purgation to read." He invites Williams (who lives in London) to the next Inklings, which, he says, will probably meet on Wednesday, October 20 or 27.

NOVEMBER 29 (Mon)

Lewis's thirty-ninth birthday.

MID-DECEMBER

Tolkien begins writing the "new Hobbit" (*The Lord of the Rings*).

1938

Germany annexes Austria, the Munich agreement gives it the Sudetenland, and the so-called Kristallnacht is a night of widespread violence and rampage against Jews.

Caryl Churchill, Margaret Forster, Frederick Forsyth, Ian Hamilton, and Allan Massie are born.

Lascelles Abercrombie, E. V. Lucas, and Sir Henry Newbolt die.

Adam Fox (1883 – 1977), the new Dean of Divinity at Magdalen College, joins the Inklings this year, and becomes Oxford's latest Professor of Poetry.

JANUARY 10 (MON)–14 (FRI)

Lewis and Warren take their seventh annual walking tour, in Wiltshire, covering nearly fifty-two miles.

FEBRUARY 18 (Fri)

Tolkien writes to Stanley Unwin, his publisher, about a science-fiction story that his friend Lewis has written. It has been, he says, read to the Inklings ("our local club"), which goes in for "reading things short and long aloud." He records that it has proved to be exciting as a serial, and is highly approved by all of them.

JULY 4 (Mon)

Lewis takes the train to London, and meets Charles Williams there. It is an "immortal lunch" which is followed by an "almost Platonic discussion" in St. Paul's churchyard which lasts for about two hours. Williams presents his new friend with a copy of his *He Came Down from Heaven*, hot from the press and published by William Heinemann, who nearly twenty years before brought out Lewis's *Spirits in Bondage*. On the book's flyleaf he inscribes,

"At Shirreffs, 2.10, 4th July 1938." Shirreffs is Williams's favorite restaurant. It is close to his office in the City of London, and located at the bottom of Ludgate Hill, under the railway bridge.

JULY 24 (Sun)

Tolkien writes to Stanley Unwin about his sequel to *The Hobbit*, expressing gratitude to Raynor Unwin (the publisher's young son) for reading earlier chapters. "I am personally immensely amused by hobbits as such, and can contemplate them eating and making their rather fatuous jokes indefinitely; but I find that is not the case with even my most devoted 'fans' (such as Mr. Lewis, and ?Raynor Unwin). Mr. Lewis says hobbits are only amusing when in unhobbitlike situations."

SEPTEMBER 2 (Fri)

Out of the Silent Planet is published. [L. P. Hartley *writes in the* Daily Sketch, *"I warmly recommend this original, interesting and well-written phantasy."*]

MICHAELMAS (Autumn) TERM

Lewis gives his annual lectures on "Prolegomena" to medieval and Renaissance literature. As he never carries a watch himself, he borrows one from undergraduate student Roger Lancelyn Green. Lewis tends to begin his lectures in his booming voice as he strides into the lecture hall, and speaks from notes rather than a script. He engages his considerable rhetorical skill, timing humor with the skill of an actor. Green records: "In describing the various types of men born under the different planetary influences, when he [Lewis] came to Jupiter: 'the Jovial character is cheerful, festive; those born under Jupiter are apt to be loud-voiced and red-faced—it is obvious under which plane I was born!' always produced its laugh." [*Over twenty-five years later Lewis's book based on those lectures,* The Discarded Image: An Introduction to Medieval and Renaissance Literature, *is dedicated to this undergraduate, Roger Lancelyn Green.*]

NOVEMBER 29 (Tue)

Lewis's fortieth birthday.

CHAPTER SIX

World War II
(1939–1945)

W^{ar} with Germany was inevitable. Early in
September 1939, it became a reality in The Kilns
household, when Lewis, Warren, and the "family" (Mrs.
Moore and her daughter Maureen) took in children evacuated from London. Lewis, who had had little experience
with children, took to them, even though baffled by their
inability to amuse themselves. That same month Charles
Williams (1886–1945) was evacuated to Oxford, along
with the rest of the staff of the London branch of Oxford
University Press. He quickly became a regular attendee of
the Inklings meetings, which during university terms usually took place twice-weekly. Williams also met frequently
with Lewis and Tolkien outside of the Inklings gatherings.
Williams spoke with a marked East London accent, which
was unusual to the ears of the mostly private-school-edu-
cated Oxford academics. He brought a freshness to the lives
of Lewis and his friends. Williams had a brilliant though
quirky mind and imagination, and like Lewis and Tolkien
was an orthodox but not tame man of faith.

Williams's move to Oxford, and his admittance into
the Inklings, helped to exert a deep and lasting influence
on Lewis. Tolkien was in later years to describe Lewis as

being under Williams's "spell," and did not entirely approve of this, feeling that Lewis was too impressionable a man. He would also refer to the Inklings as Lewis's "coven," alluding to Williams's fascination with the occult, a taste that disturbed Tolkien. However, Tolkien got much out of his friendship with Williams, and deeply appreciated Williams's attentive listening to episodes of *The Lord of the Rings* as they were written.

Lewis was not required, he discovered, to serve in this war because of his wounds from World War I. Instead, like the older Tolkien, he served in the local Home Guard, or "Dad's Army" as it was nicknamed, fulfilling a variety of duties. Warren, however, was recalled to the British army out of retirement. Two of Tolkien's sons served in the war, and both Lewis and he observed the impact of the war on the undergraduate population in Oxford. It was a period of austerity, with rationing and each household, if possible, growing vegetables and keeping chickens for a supply of eggs.

For Lewis the war years marked his establishment as a major popular communicator of the Christian faith. He published *The Problem of Pain* (1940), *The Weight of Glory* (1942), *Broadcast Talks* (1942), *The Screwtape Letters* (1943), *Christian Behaviour* (1943), and *Beyond Personality* (1944). His popularity was immensely boosted by the four series of talks he gave on BBC radio in 1941, 1942, and 1944. The talks were straightforward and lucid, providing an outstanding example of early media evangelism.

The Inklings continued throughout the war years with their familiar pattern of two types of meetings, the literary gatherings which usually took place in Lewis's rooms in Magdalen, and the more informal meetings in an Oxford public house such as The Eagle and Child.

After Charles Williams's sudden death in 1945, which was a grievous blow to the Inklings, the two most active members became once more Tolkien and Lewis. Novelist and poet John Wain (1925–1994), who joined the group around then, wrote that "While C. S. Lewis attacked [the whole current of contemporary art and life] on a wide front, with broadcasts, popular-theological books, children's stories, romances, and controversial literary criticism, Tolkien concentrated on the writing of his colossal 'Lord of the Rings' trilogy. His readings of each successive instalment were eagerly received, for 'romance' was a pillar of this whole structure."

1939

There is mounting international tension over Hitler's warmongering, as conflict becomes increasingly inevitable. This year marks the beginning of the most savage conflict in human history, in which as many as fifty-five million people may have died.

In January, German physicist Otto Hahn discovers the process of splitting the atom (nuclear fission). In the Spanish Civil War Republican resistance finally collapses. Germany occupies the remainder of Czechoslovakia; Italy invades Albania; the Molotov-Ribbentrop Pact is agreed; Germany invades Poland, and Britain and France declare war on the aggressor.

Alan Ayckbourn, Melvyn Bragg, Shelagh Delaney, Margaret Drabble, Germaine Greer, Seamus Heaney, Clive James, E. A. Markham, Michael Moorcock, Robert Nye, and Colin Thubron are born.

Ethel M. Dell, Charlotte Despard, Havelock Ellis, Ford Madox Ford (Ford Hermann Hueffer), Llewelyn Powys, W. B. Yeats, and Sigmund Freud die.

Warren is called back into active service. Lewis is invited to lecture to Royal Air Force personnel on Christianity. He continues to meet with Tolkien and the Inklings, and publishes *Rehabilitations*, a collection of essays that embody themes and concerns he and Tolkien share.

JANUARY 2 (Mon)–6 (Fri)

Lewis and Warren have their eighth and final walking tour. They cover forty-two miles on and near Wenlock Edge (from Church Stretton to Ludlow) in Shropshire, and include a visit to Malvern, Worcestershire. (Lewis invariably enjoys experiencing local pubs. An ideal one would have a cheering bar, a commercial supplier's calendar on one wall and a stuffed pike in a glass case on another, an emphatically ticking clock, and a board for shove-halfpenny.) After a first day crossing Wenlock Edge in bright sunshine walking on fresh snow, the weather forces them to take to the train. (Lewis likes train travel, having pleasant hours in tiny stations awaiting connections by roaring fires.) One Welsh porter is only four feet tall, and Lewis wonders if he is a leprechaun in disguise. The diminutive porter praises Arthur James Balfour's *Foundations of Belief* (1895). During their visit to Malvern the Lewis brothers watch the new Walt Disney film, *Snow White and the Seven Dwarfs*. Lewis finds it very good and very bad in places. He speculates about how much better *Snow White* would have been had Disney "been educated—or even brought up in a decent society." Lewis enjoys Malvern's unchanging nature, with nearly silent streets after eight in the evening, and its cheerful, bright tranquillity. [*Another of Balfour's books,* Theism and Humanism, *had deeply influenced Lewis in earlier years.*]

JANUARY 22 (Sun)

Lewis begins lecturing to the Cambridge English School on "Prolegomena to Renaissance Literature." [*These introductory lectures are given once a week, every Tuesday between January 11 and March 16. He has been invited to lecture on the sixteenth-century period by H. S. Bennett, an important figure in the Cambridge School. In preparing and giving his lectures Lewis makes a surprising discovery, which he explains to his friend A. K. Hamilton Jenkin in a letter: "I go to Cambridge to lecture once a week this term. Did I tell you I have discovered the Renaissance never occurred? That is what I'm lecturing on. Do you think it reasonable to call the lectures 'The Renaissance' under the circumstances?" Lewis perceives a deep continuity between the medieval period and the Renaissance.*]

JANUARY 28 (Sat)

William Butler Yeats dies, aged seventy-three.

FEBRUARY 8 (Wed)

Writing to Owen Barfield arranging for his friend to visit, Lewis speaks of recovering from an unusually bad bout of influenza. He mentions the continuing bad weather and supposes that war is now certain. [*He has a regular habit of succumbing to flu or colds early in the year during term time, during which period of affliction he reads avidly his old favorites of literature.*]

FEBRUARY 9 (Thu)

The British government announces plans to provide bomb shelters for homes in areas likely to be attacked.

MARCH 8 (Wed)

Tolkien delivers his Andrew Lang lecture, "On Fairy-Stories," at the University of St. Andrews, Scotland. [*This lecture reveals the foundations of Tolkien's fantasy writings, beliefs he shares in large measure with Lewis.*]

MARCH 23 (Thu)

Publication of Lewis's *Rehabilitations and Other Essays* by Oxford University Press. [*Charles Williams sees the text through the press and corresponds with Lewis over the proofs.*]

MARCH 29 (Wed)

The British government decides to double the size of the Territorial Army (the main reserve).

MARCH 31 (Fri)

The prime minister pledges to defend Poland against attack by Hitler.

APRIL 27 (Thu)

Conscription is announced by the British government the day before Hitler is to give a major speech in the Reichstag.

Publication of The Personal Heresy: A Controversy by Lewis and E. M. W. Tillyard, by Oxford University Press.

AUGUST 30 (Wed)

The evacuation of over 1.5 million British children begins from cities in immediate danger of indiscriminate bombing.

SEPTEMBER 1 (Fri)

Nazi forces cross the Polish border, the beginning of Poland's invasion.

SEPTEMBER 2 (Sat)

Evacuee children arrive at The Kilns. [The evacuees at The Kilns take to Mrs. Moore, by then in her late sixties and frail. She is kind to them and they are not put off by the cigarette constantly hanging on her lower lip scattering ash, sometimes on to their food (which they don't care for). They all notice that Mrs. Moore makes a huge fuss of Lewis—he is the center of attention. For her he is the axis around which life revolves. The evacuees make a deep impression on Lewis. Soon after the first children arrive he starts to write a story about some evacuees who stay with an old professor, but soon abandones it. Lewis will pick up the story again ten years later, in 1949, and it becomes the first of the Narnian Chronicles, The Lion, the Witch and the

Wardrobe, *in which evacuee children enter another, magical world through an old wardrobe.*]

SEPTEMBER 3 (Sun)

The British prime minister declares war on Germany. The Commonwealth joins with Britain, and the United States will soon announce its neutrality.

SEPTEMBER 4 (Mon)

Warren Lewis is recalled by the army to active service, and posted to Catterick, Yorkshire.

SEPTEMBER 7 (Thu)

Charles Williams and the London branch of Oxford University Press move to Oxford. [*Later Lewis is able to arrange for Williams to lecture at the university. Lewis remarks that from September 1939 "until his death we met one another about twice a week, sometimes more: nearly always on Thursday evenings in my rooms and on Tuesday mornings in the best of all public-houses for draught cider."*]

OCTOBER

Warren is assigned to serve with No. 3 base supply depot, Le Havre, France.

NOVEMBER 2 (Thu)

At an Inklings gathering attended by Lewis, Williams, Tolkien, and Charles Wrenn, the discussion turns to the issue of God's goodness and the damned.

NOVEMBER 9 (Thu)

After dining at Oxford's Eastgate Hotel, the Inklings listen to Tolkien reading an early part of what will become

———————— *The Inklings* ————————

Henry Victor Dyson "Hugo" Dyson (1896–1975), served in World War I and read English at Exeter College, Oxford. He helped Tolkien to persuade Lewis of the truth of Christianity. He initially lectured in English at Reading University, near enough to Oxford to keep in touch with fellow Inklings. There he pioneered a combined humanities course in 1930. He also encouraged the development of a school of fine arts, and was considered a distinctive and outstanding lecturer. Like Charles Williams, he gave lectures to the Workers' Educational Association. He poured more of himself into teaching than into his writing; he was involved in few publications. He was, in 1945, elected fellow and tutor in English literature at Merton College, Oxford. He retired in 1963.

John Ronald Reuel Tolkien (1892–1973) was born in South Africa to English parents, but from 1895 was raised in Birmingham. He went to Exeter College, Oxford in 1911. He served with the Lancashire Fusiliers from 1915 to 1918, and married Edith Mary Bratt in 1916. They had four children, including Christopher, a member of the Inklings after World War II. Tolkien met Lewis in 1926, and in 1929 they began meeting weekly to read to one another and talk. They were the original Inklings. As well as holding three professorial Chairs, one in Leeds, and two in Oxford, Tolkien was the author of *The Lord of the Rings* (1954–55).

Owen Barfield (1898–1997) was born in London, and after graduating at Oxford in English with a B.A. in 1921 he began a B.Litt., upon which eventually was based his book *Poetic Diction*. In 1925 he published a children's book, *The Silver Trumpet*, which became a success in the Tolkien household. In 1926 his study *History in English Words* appeared. In 1929 Barfield moved back to London, to train in his father's firm of solicitors. Because of this he infrequently attended Inklings meetings. He would visit Oxford once a term, and this sometimes coincided with an Inklings meeting. He always saw himself as a fringe member, but his ideas deeply influenced Lewis and also Tolkien.

Warren Lewis (1895–1973) was one of the very first members of the Inklings. Like his brother he was a gifted writer, producing a number of books on French history. He contributed to *Essays Presented to Charles*

Cont.

Williams, a posthumous tribute. His diaries provide a unique and essential insight into Lewis's life and meetings of the Inklings. A selection has been published as *Brothers and Friends* (1982).

Charles Willams (1886–1945), poet, novelist, biographer, theologian, and literary critic, was born in Islington, London, and gained a place at University College, London, beginning his studies at the age of fifteen. The family unfortunately was not able to keep up paying the fees. Williams eventually joined the Oxford University Press (OUP), first as a proofreader. He married and began giving adult evening classes in literature for the London County Council to supplement the modest family income. He wrote his series of seven supernatural thrillers, including *The Place of the Lion*, for the same reason. When Williams was evacuated with the OUP to Oxford he (in John Wain's words) "gave himself as unreservedly to Oxford as Oxford gave itself to him." Oxford University recognized Charles Williams in 1943 with an honorary M.A., and his writings were admired by T. S. Eliot and W. H. Auden. After Williams's unexpected death, Lewis published a commentary on Williams's unfinished cycle of Arthurian poetry, *Arthurian Torso*. Several of the Inklings—including Lewis, Tolkien, Owen Barfield, and Warren Lewis—contributed to the posthumous tribute *Essays Presented to Charles Williams*.

Dr. Robert E. "Humphrey" Havard (1901–1985) attended many of the Inklings meetings during the war, despite being away for a period on naval service. Affectionately known as the "Useless Quack," he took over a medical practice in 1934 with surgeries in Headington and St. Giles (near The Eagle and Child). He appears briefly as a character in Lewis's *Perelandra*. In 1943 he volunteered for the Royal Navy Reserve and became a naval surgeon. When he returned to Oxford (because of his wife's breast cancer) he was dubbed "the Red Admiral" by Lewis because he now sported a red beard, and turned up to a meeting in uniform. Hugo Dyson called him "Humphrey" because he couldn't remember his name at one point. He had five children; his wife succumbed to the cancer in 1950.

Lord David Cecil (1902–1986) taught English literature and modern history as a fellow at Wadham College, Oxford, before becoming a fellow of English at New College. He was author of many books, writing about William Cowper, Jane Austen, Samuel Palmer, Edward Burne-Jones, and others.

Nevill Coghill (1899–1980), after serving in World War I, read English at Exeter College, Oxford, and in 1924 was elected a fellow there. He was a friend of Lewis's from undergraduate days, and like him hailed from Ireland. He was admired for his theatrical productions and for his translation of Chaucer's *Canterbury Tales* into modern English couplets. He was Professor of English Literature at Oxford from 1957 to 1966. His attendance at Inklings meetings was erratic.

Charles Wrenn (1895–1969) taught at Oxford from 1930, where he assisted Tolkien in the Anglo-Saxon course. From 1939 to 1946 Wrenn was Chair of English Language and Literature at the University of London. When Tolkien transferred to being Merton Professor of English Language and Literature in 1946, Wrenn took over his post. He was Rawlinson and Bosworth Professor of Anglo-Saxon until 1963.

The Lord of the Rings; Williams presenting a nativity play, *The House by the Stable*; and Lewis a chapter from a book he is writing on the problem of pain. Lewis describes the ever-talkative Dyson as "a roaring cataract of nonsense." The piece read by Tolkien may have been a reworked section of Book One of *The Fellowship of the Ring*—he has been making momentous changes relating, amongst other things, to the nature of the ring and the identity of Aragorn. [*Whatever the piece it must have touched upon the nature of evil, as Lewis remarks later in a letter that the subject matter of the readings this evening "formed almost a logical sequence." His own chapter likely enough touched on this theme, just as Williams's play concerned the battle to win over the human soul to evil, effectively presenting the inverse perspective of hell.*]

NOVEMBER 29 (Wed)

Lewis's forty-first birthday.

NOVEMBER 30 (Thu)

There is no Inklings meeting today, as Williams and Gerard Hopkins (also of the Oxford University Press) are both away. Lewis visits Tolkien at home, where they read to each other chapters from *The Problem of Pain* and *The Lord of the Rings*.

1940

Germany invades Norway, Denmark, and the Netherlands; Winston Churchill becomes Britain's prime minister; Germany invades France; the British begin the evacuation of Dunkirk; German forces enter Paris; the French sign an armistice; the Battle of Britain and the London Blitz; the Italians are defeated in North Africa. The Soviet Union annexes Estonia, Latvia, and Lithuania. Franklin D. Roosevelt begins his third term as U. S. president. Trotsky is assassinated. The 1940 Olympic games are cancelled because of the war. Charlie Chaplin's film The Great Dictator *appears.*

Maeve Binchy, Angela Carter, Bruce Chatwin, and Susan Howatch are born.

E. F. Benson, John Buchan, W. H. Davies, Humbert Wolfe, and Eric Gill die.

Lewis begins lecturing on Christianity for the Royal Air Force, which he continues to do until 1941. Joy Davidman's first novel, *Anya*, is published.

JANUARY 25 (Thu)

Writing to Warren, Lewis records that "the usual party assembled on Thursday night, heard a chapter of the new Hobbit [*The Lord of the Rings*], drank rum and hot water, and talked."

JANUARY 27 (Sat)

Warren is granted temporary rank of major.

JANUARY 29 (Mon)

At the Divinity School, Charles Williams celebrates the theme of chastity in Milton's *Comus* in a lecture to Oxford undergraduates.

FEBRUARY 1 (Thu)

Dr. Havard reads a short paper on the clinical experience of pain, prepared as an appendix for Lewis's book *The Problem of Pain*. Lewis writes to his absent brother: "We had an evening almost equally compounded of merriment, piety, and literature."

FEBRUARY 7 (Wed)

James Welch, the director of the BBC's Religious Broadcasting Department, writes to Lewis, saying how impressed he is by the "depth of his conviction" and the "quality of his thinking." He presses him to give a series of radio talks over the BBC.

FEBRUARY 14 (Wed)

T. S. Eliot writes to Charles Williams, commenting that "one of your most important functions in life (which I tried to emulate in *The Family Reunion*) is to instil sound doctrine into people (tinged sometimes with heresy, of course, but the <u>very best</u> heresy) without their knowing it."

FEBRUARY 15 (Thu)

Up from London, Owen Barfield attends an Inklings meeting.

FEBRUARY 29 (Thu)

Hugo Dyson visits the Inklings meeting from Reading, so all are present except for Warren and Owen Barfield. Adam Fox reads a poem on Blenheim Park in winter. On being told of Williams's lectures on Milton and the doctrine of virginity Dyson remarks that he is "becoming a common *chastitute.*"

APRIL 5 (Fri)–8 (Mon)

With his friends Cecil Harwood and Owen Barfield, Lewis has a walking tour on Exmoor, starting out and finishing at Minehead.

APRIL 22/23 (Mon/Tue)

It is the first week of Trinity Term, and these are "quiet days." Consequently, Lewis has evenings to himself, in which he explores what Thomas Aquinas has to say about the Law of Nature, rereads Dr. Johnson's *The History of Rasselas*, and starts Johnson's *Memoirs of Charles Frederick, King of Prussia*.

APRIL 25 (Thu)

In the morning Lewis lectures, and has no students today for tutorial, instead having a visit from his cricketer friend, Brian Hone, who, to Lewis's sorrow, is set to return to Australia to take up a post as headteacher at Cranbrook School, Sydney. [*The two had come to know each other when Hone was an undergraduate, studying English, at the beginning of the 1930s. He then became an assistant master at the prestigious Marlborough College, in Wiltshire.*] In the afternoon, back at The Kilns, the "family" has a visit from its favorite original evacuee, Sheila Morrison, with her mother. One anticipation of Sheila's visit has been her meeting with Bruce, the dog. (Each had been the other's constant companion.)

Disappointment ensues for all, however. In Lewis's words, "The stupid creature had either forgotten her or lost interest in her and with desperate animal sincerity took no notice of her at all!" Later, the first weekly Thursday

—— Dogs, Cats, and other Animals ——

One of the many pet dogs at The Kilns over the years was Mr. Papworth, a mongrel with a predominance of terrier. He died in 1937. In his dotage he developed a peculiarity that led Lewis to develop an "Orpheus-Eurydice" method of feeding him. This meant that Lewis would walk in front of Mr. Papworth down the track to Headington carrying a bowl of food. He would throw some of the food over his shoulder and Mr. Papworth would devour it. If, however, Lewis turned around, Mr. Papworth would assume a fierce look and refuse to eat. (In the Greek myth Orpheus, rescuing Eurydice from the underworld, was forbidden to look back at her or else he would lose her forever.) This peripatetic method of feeding was the only one that worked.

Lewis wondered what might be on his dog's mind whenever the dog would see his master deeply engrossed in a book. He speculated that the dog's thoughts had probably no more value than his master's conjectures about why God does what he does.

Lewis believed that cats and dogs both have consciences. Because a dog is essentially humble and honest she will invariably have a bad one. A cat, however, will always have a good conscience. A cat will outstare you, thanking God that he is not a dog, or a human, or even another cat.

Cats and dogs, Lewis thought, should be brought up together, as this could effectively broaden their minds.

Lewis enjoyed visiting Whipsnade Zoo, which had natural habitats for its animals. He was particularly fond of a bear there whom he called Mr. Bultitude, named after a character (the father of a schoolboy) in F. Anstey's story *Vice Versa* who reminded him of his father Albert. In *That Hideous Strength* Lewis provides an affectionate portrait of a bear called Mr. Bultitude. And he had a love for mice, too—thus the talking mouse Reepicheek in the Narnian Chronicles.

Lewis was strongly opposed to vivisection. He wrote a pamphlet on this subject in 1947 for the New England Anti-Vivisection Society.

evening Inklings meeting of the term takes place. Williams, Tolkien, and Dr. Havard are among those in attendance. Havard reads a hair-raising, straight-talking account he has written of mountain climbing.

MAY 2 (Thu)

Writing to Warren, Lewis recounts an unusually good Inklings meeting this evening at which Charles Williams "read us a Whitsun play, a mixture of very good stuff and some deplorable errors in taste."

MAY 10 (Fri)

German troops invade the neutral countries of Belgium and the Netherlands. The Dutch Queen Wilhelmina, addressing the nation, asks her people to take up arms. "After our country, with scrupulous conscientiousness, had observed strict neutrality . . . Germany made a sudden attack on our territory without warning."

MAY 16 (Thu)

Lewis sits in the north room of his accommodation in Magdalen College, looking out on the hawthorn in the grove, as he awaits the arrival of the Inklings. He much regrets the fact that his brother "had passed from the status of a sense-object to that of a mental picture." Dr. Havard arrives first, then Williams, and then Tolkien. As he goes into the south room with them he notices "the exquisite smell of the wisteria pervading the whole room." Charles Wrenn turns up, and after that they go around the walks in the extensive grounds of the college.

MAY 21 (Tue)

The Germans advance to within sixty miles north of Paris, speeding over the old battlefields of World War I.

MAY 27 (Mon)

German forces take Boulogne, cutting off a vast number of British and French troops. [Warren is among those trapped.]

MAY 30 (Thu)

The first British troops arrive in England in an unprecedented mass evacuation from Dunkirk, employing naval vessels and volunteer civilian boats of all shapes and sizes.

END OF MAY

Warren is evacuated with his unit from Dunkirk to Wenvoe Camp, Cardiff, in south Wales.

JULY 21 (Sun)

During morning service at his local church, Holy Trinity, Headington, Lewis suddenly has the idea of writing a series of letters from a senior to a junior devil. It will employ the inverse perspective of hell on a young man who "unfortunately" comes to believe in Christianity. [*This becomes* The Screwtape Letters.]

AUGUST 16 (Fri)

Warren is transferred to the Reserve of Officers, and, to his brother's relief, sent home to Oxford. [*There he serves as a private soldier with the 6th Oxford City Home Guard Battalion. Throughout the remains of the summer, Warren is part of the "floating" Home Guard, employing his motor boat.*]

AUGUST 27 (Tue)

Maureen Moore marries Leonard J. Blake, Director of Music at Worksop College, Nottinghamshire.

OCTOBER 14 (Mon)

Lewis's *The Problem of Pain* is published. It is dedicated to the Inklings.

NOVEMBER 29 (Fri)

Lewis's forty-second birthday.

WINTER

Around this time Tolkien "discovers" Ents, making notes that use Lewis's concept of *hnau* (the embodiment of personal life in animal or vegetable beings). He speculates, "Are the Tree-folk ("Lone-walkers") *hnau* that have gone tree-like, or trees that have become *hnau*?"

Word Frequency in "The Problem of Pain"

This book is among the best of Lewis's theological writings and a key text in the philosophy of religion. In it he discusses the goodness of God, God's control over all human events including suffering and pain, animal pain, heaven and hell, and more. The words Lewis most frequently used in *The Problem of Pain* are:

act - against - am - animal - bad - between - call - cannot - certain - Christian - come - creatures - desire - divine - doctrine - does - end - even - evil - experience - fact - fall - far - father - feel - find - first - give - God - good - goodness - great - heaven - hell - himself - human - itself - kind - know - law - less - life - love - man - matter - may - mean - men - mere - might - mind - moment - must - natural - nature - need - new - nor - nothing - now - own - pain - people - perhaps - place - possible - power - present - problem - question - real - really - right - said - say - see - seems - self - sense - should - sin - something - soul - spirit - still - suffering - therefore - things - think - though - thus - time - truth - universe - whether - whole - without - words - world - yet

1941

Germany invades Yugoslavia, Greece, Crete, and Russia; Rudolf Hess lands in Scotland; the Siege of Leningrad begins; the Japanese bomb Pearl Harbor; Hitler declares war on the United States.

Derek Mahon, Piers Paul Read, Paul Theroux, and Barbara Trapido are born.

Sherwood Anderson, Robert Byron, Sir J. G. Frazer, James Joyce, A.J.A. Symons, Rabindranath Tagore, Evelyn Underhill, Sir Hugh Walpole, Virginia Woolf, and P. C. Wren die.

JANUARY 7 (Tue)

Dr. Havard drives Tolkien and the Lewis brothers to a pub out at Appleton, some miles west of Oxford. It is a snowy night, and the roads slippery. Tolkien's offer of snuff, a recent gift, is taken up by several locals, and Warren recounts an amusing story about visiting Blackwell's Bookshop in Oxford with the irrepressible Hugo Dyson.

MAY 2 (Fri)

The first installment of what becomes *The Screwtape Letters* appears in a weekly paper. [*From May 2 until November 28, The Guardian (a religious periodical) publishes thirty-one letters from "Screwtape" in weekly installments. Lewis is paid two pounds for each letter and gives the money to charity, unaware that he has to pay income tax on the earnings. One reader, a country clergyman, cancels his subscription because "much of the advice given in these letters seemed to him not only erroneous but positively diabolical."*]

JUNE 8 (Sun)

Lewis preaches a momentous sermon, "The Weight of Glory," at the church of St. Mary the Virgin in Oxford. The church is packed with Oxford students. The sermon is highly quotable, even though it is carefully reasoned:"It is a serious thing to live in a society of possible gods and goddesses, to remember that the dullest and most uninteresting person you talk to may one day be a creature which, if you saw it now, you would be strongly tempted to worship, or else a horror and a corruption such as you now meet, if at all, only in a nightmare."

AUGUST 6 (Wed)

Lewis broadcasts the first of his talks on BBC radio. [*This August, he gives four live radio talks entitled "Right and Wrong" over the BBC on Wednesday evenings from 7.45 to 8.00. An additional fifteen-minute session, answering questions received in the mail, is broadcast on September 6. In total, he will give twenty-five BBC radio talks, divided into four series, between August 1941 and April 1944; the entire collection will eventually be published in book form under the title* Mere Christianity *in 1952.*]

AUGUST 7 (Thu)

Charles Williams refers to Lewis, in a letter to his wife Michal, as the person out of all in Oxford who understands his thinking.

NOVEMBER 29 (Sat)

Lewis's forty-third birthday.

MID-DECEMBER

Stella Aldwinckle, a member of a pastoral team attached to St. Aldate's Church in Oxford, sets up a club for undergraduates to discuss questions about Christian faith raised by atheists, agnostics, and those disillusioned about religion. Lewis helps her to found the "Socratic Club," serving as president. Its committee scours the pages of Who's Who to find intelligent atheists who might have the time

Lewis's Radio Broadcasts
(Series One and Two)

1. Right and Wrong: A Clue to the Meaning of the Universe

BBC Broadcast Talk	*Mere Christianity*, Book 1
1. "Common Decency," Aug. 6, 1941	1. "The Law of Human Nature"
2. "Scientific Law and Moral Law," Aug. 13, 1941	3. "The Reality of the Law"
3. "Materialism or Religion," Aug. 20, 1941	4. "What Lies Behind the Law"
4. "What Can We Do About It?" Aug. 27, 1941	5. "We Have Cause to Be Uneasy"
5. "Answers to Listeners' Questions," Sept. 6, 1941	2. "Some Objections"

2. What Christians Believe

BBC Broadcast Talk	*Mere Christianity*, Book 2
First Talk, Jan. 11, 1942	1. "The Rival Conceptions of God"
Second Talk, Jan. 18, 1942	2. "The Invasion"
Third Talk, Feb. 1, 1942	3. "The Shocking Alternative"
Fourth Talk, Feb. 8, 1942	4. "The Perfect Penitent"
Fifth Talk, Feb. 15, 1942	5. "The Practical Conclusion"

---

or the zeal to come and present their creed. [*Leading Christian thinkers also are main speakers. Lewis himself takes this position on eleven occasions. As president, he usually is expected to provide a rejoinder to the speaker. Lead speakers include Charles Williams, D. M. MacKinnon, Austin Farrer, J. Z. Young, C. E. M. Joad, P. D. Medawar, H. H. Price, C. H. Waddington, A. J. Ayer, J. D. Bernal, A. G. N. Flew, J. Bronowski, Basil Mitchell, R. M. Hare, A. Rendle Short, I. T. Ramsey, Iris Murdoch, Gilbert Ryle, Michael Polanyi, J. L. Austin, H. J. Blackham, Michael Dummett, E. Evans-*

Pritchard, Dorothy L. Sayers, and other outstanding thinkers from different academic disciplines.]

DECEMBER 21 (Sun)

In a letter to Dom Bede Griffiths, the Benedictine monk, Lewis describes Charles Williams and lists the members of the Inklings: "He is an ugly man with rather a cockney voice. But no one ever thinks of this for five minutes after he has begun speaking. His face becomes almost angelic. . . . Charles Williams, Dyson of Reading, & my brother (Anglicans) and Tolkien and my doctor, Havard (your church) are the 'Inklings' to whom my *Problem of Pain* was dedicated."

1942

Singapore surrenders to the Japanese; the British are victorious at El Alamein; Anglo-American landings take place in North Africa.

Howard Brenton, Douglas Dunn, Susan Hill, Howard Jacobson, Bernard MacLaverty, Jonathan Raban, and Hugo Williams are born.

Ernest Bramah (Ernest Bramah Smith) and Violet Hunt die.

Warren writes his first book, *The Splendid Century: Some Aspects of French Life in the Reign of Louis XIV* (not published until 1953). Tolkien, working on *The Lord of the Rings*, bases moon phases and sunsets on this year: "The moons I think finally were the moons and sunset worked out according to what they were in this part of the world in 1942 actually." Lewis publishes *The Screwtape Letters* and *Broadcast Talks*, the first two series of his BBC radio talks (the second series airs in January and February). Charles Williams's *The Forgiveness of Sins* is published, dedicated to the Inklings.

JANUARY 26 (Mon)

The first meeting of the Socratic Club is held in Oxford. [*An early meeting was remembered by Helen Tyrrell Wheeler: "I have*

Oxford University Socratic Club: The War Years

(Lectures involving Inklings and close friends of Lewis.)

1942

Jan. 26: "Won't Mankind Outgrow Christianity in the Face of the Advance of Science and of Modern Ideologies?" (R. E. Havard)

Mar. 2: "Are There Any Valid Objections to Free Love?" (Charles Williams)

May 13: "Did Christ Rise from the Dead?" (Austin Farrer)

Nov. 2: "How Was Jesus Divine?" (Austin Farrer)

Nov. 16: "Christianity and Aesthetics, or 'The Company Accepts No Liabilities'" (C. S. Lewis)

1943

Feb. 8:   "If We Have Christ's Ethics, Does the Rest of the Christian Faith Matter?" (C. S. Lewis)

May 10: "Immortality" (Austin Farrer)

Nov. 1: "Can We Know That God Exists?" (Austin Farrer)

Nov. 15: "Science and Miracles" (C. S. Lewis)

1944

Feb. 7: "Bulverism, or 'The Foundation of 20th-Century Thought'" (C. S. Lewis)

June 5: "Is Institutional Christianity Necessary?" (C. S. Lewis)

Nov. 6: "Is Theology Poetry?" (C. S. Lewis)

1945

May 14: "Resurrection" (C. S. Lewis)

May 28: "Can Myth Be Fact?" (Austin Farrer)

June 4: "Christian and Non-Christian Mysticism" (Gervase Mathew)

Oct. 15: "The Nature of Reason" (C. S. Lewis)

a strong visual memory of these evenings, always associated with lamp-light inside and total blackout without, of a big sprawling comfortable room with as many people sitting on the floor as in the old-fashioned immense armchairs and C. S. Lewis hurrying over Magdalen Bridge from his rooms to preside. He always established an immense, though rather impersonal, geniality and with his bright eyes and ruddy farmer's cheeks looked not unlike a medieval illustration of a fiery seraphim, though dressed in decent academic black." Ian Davie also has memories of Lewis from the Socratic Club. He describes him as like a "jolly farmer . . . a ruddy, back-slapping type."]

FEBRUARY 9 (Mon)

The Screwtape Letters is published by Geoffrey Bles and dedicated to J. R. R. Tolkien.

FEBRUARY 12 (Thu)

Ronald Boswell of the BBC writes to Lewis asking him for the address of the Clergy Widows' Fund, to which (among other beneficiaries) he has asked his fees for the radio broadcasts to be sent. The letter is addressed to "The Rev. C. S. Lewis," an error Lewis emphatically corrects.

MARCH 2 (Mon)

Charles Williams speaks on the topic "Are There Any Valid Objections to Free Love?" to the Socratic Club. The lecture hall is well-filled. Lewis in the chair states, after a wandering discussion, that the meeting must make up its mind whether it wants to discuss the habits of bees or those of humans. Afterwards Lewis invites his student Derek Brewer and two or three others back to his college rooms to meet Williams and partake of a drink. Williams, Brewer notes, is wearing an elderly blue suit, and, while he talks vigorously, flicks cigarette ash all over his waist-coat. During the conversation Lewis and Williams are in agreement that one can no more avoid pleasure than pain in this life. Lewis retrieves his copy of Williams's *Taliessin through Logres* from his shelves and encourages the poet to read from it. Williams does this with enormous gusto.

MARCH/APRIL

Lewis discovers that he owes a large tax bill for money he has given away—he has no grasp of basic economics. Owen Barfield, through his family company of Barfield and Barfield, comes to the rescue and helps Lewis set up a charitable trust. [*Barfield later writes a semi-autobiographical fiction,* This Ever Diverse Pair (1950), *about two London solicitors. At one stage they take on an author, Ramsden, loosely based on Lewis, who unwittingly has fallen foul of the Inland Revenue.*]

APRIL

Lewis gives his first traveling talks at the Royal Air Force base in Abingdon. [*"As far as I can judge," he writes to his friend Sister Penelope some weeks later, "they were a complete failure. . . . One must take comfort in remembering that God used an ass to convert the prophet." His responsibilities to the RAF meant much traveling throughout Britain, with most weekends taken up.*]

APRIL 20 (Mon)

Lewis lectures to the Junior Sisters in the Community of St. Mary the Virgin in Wantage, on "The Gospel in Our Generation." [*Sister Penelope, Lewis's friend at the Anglican community, invites him, and he stays overnight in their Gate House after speaking.*]

APRIL 22 (Wed)

He goes from Wantage to London by train to give the Annual Shakespeare Lecture to the British Academy on "Hamlet: The Prince or the Poem?"

MAY 16 (Sat)

The philosopher C. E. M. Joad reviews *The Screwtape Letters* in the *New Statesman and Nation*, saying, "Mr. Lewis possesses the rare gift of making righteousness readable."

SEPTEMBER 20 (Sun)

Lewis's third series of BBC radio broadcasts begins today.

Lewis's Radio Broadcasts (Series Three)

The third series went out on the Armed Forces network on Sunday afternoons between 2.50 and 3 p.m. Lewis had prepared his usual fifteen-minute talks only to discover that just ten minutes were allocated for each. His cuts were restored for *Christian Behaviour* (1943), with some later changes for *Mere Christianity* (1952).

3. *Christian Behaviour*

BBC Broadcast Talk	*Mere Christianity*, Book 3
First Talk, Sept. 20, 1942	1. "The Three Parts of Morality"
	2. "The Cardinal Virtues"
Second Talk, Sept. 27, 1942	3. "Social Morality"
Third Talk, Oct. 4, 1942	4. "Morality and Psychoanalysis"
Fourth Talk, Oct. 11, 1942	5. "Sexual Morality"
	6. "Christian Marriage"
Fifth Talk, Oct. 18, 1942	7. "Forgiveness"
Sixth Talk, Oct. 25, 1942	8. "The Great Sin"
	9. "Charity"
	10. "Hope"
Seventh Talk, Nov. 1, 1942	11. "Faith"
Eighth Talk, Nov. 8, 1942	12. "Faith"

OCTOBER 8 (Thu)

Oxford University Press publishes Lewis's scholarly *A Preface to "Paradise Lost,"* a book of literary criticism partly inspired by Charles Williams's view on one of Lewis's long-loved authors. Its index contains the entry, *Rabbit, Peter.*

NOVEMBER 29 (Sun)

Lewis's forty-fourth birthday.

1943

The German army surrenders at Stalingrad; the Warsaw Ghetto Uprising takes place; Axis forces surrender in North Africa; the Soviets defeat the Germans at the Battle of Kursk; the Allies invade Sicily, and Italy surrenders.

Pat Barker, Terry Eagleton, Lorna Sage, Rose Tremain, and Joanna Trollope are born.

Laurence Binyon, R. G. Collingwood, E. M. Delafield, R. Austin Freeman, Elinor Glyn, Sarah Grand, Radclyffe Hall, W. W. Jacobs, Beatrix Potter, Sergei Rachmaninov, and Beatrice Webb die.

Warren begins to act as secretary to his brother, using his typewriter (Lewis always writes by hand, including his books). Lewis publishes *Christian Behaviour*, the third series of broadcast talks for the BBC. He also publishes *Perelandra* and *The Abolition of Man*.

FEBRUARY 17 (Wed)

Lewis gives a dinner party at Magdalen for the fantasy writer E. R. Eddison. Afterwards he takes him across to his college rooms for a meeting of the Inklings, attended by Tolkien, Warren, and Charles Williams.

FEBRUARY 18 (Thu)

In the Sheldonian Theatre in Oxford, an honorary M.A. is awarded to Charles Williams, with many of the Inklings in attendance.

FEBRUARY 22 (Mon)–26 (Fri)

Warren accompanies Lewis to Durham by train, where Lewis gives the Riddell Memorial lectures (later to be published as *The Abolition of Man*). [*Edgestow, in Lewis's* That Hideous Strength, *is partly based in Durham, though located in the West Midlands. Like Oxford and Cambridge, the university at Durham is made up of small colleges, including Hatfield, University, and St. Chad's College.*]

APRIL 20 (Tue)

Tolkien writes to Lewis, who has influenza: "My dear Jack, V. sorry to hear you are laid low—and with no U.Q. ["Useless Quack," i.e., Dr. Havard] to suggest that it may be your last illness! I begin to think that for us to meet on Wednesdays is a duty: there seem to be so many obstacles and fiendish devices to prevent it." [*Havard is away serving in the navy. Tolkien is alluding to* The Screwtape Letters *in speaking of fiendish devices. Tolkien and Lewis rarely correspond, presumably because they meet so frequently.*]

MAY 5 (Wed)

Charles Williams, in a letter to his wife Michal, mentions Havard turning up in a naval lieutenant's uniform. Havard, Tolkien, the Lewis brothers, and Charles Williams have dinner at the George Hotel at lunchtime. [*Michal stayed behind in London—Williams has only been evacuated to Oxford because of his work with Oxford University Press.*]

SEPTEMBER 28 (Tue)

Out of the Silent Planet is published in the United States. [*Lewis writes for the dust jacket: "My happiest hours are spent with three or four old friends in old clothes tramping together and putting up in small pubs—or else sitting up till the small hours in someone's college rooms talking nonsense, poetry, theology, metaphysics over beer, tea and pipes."*]

OCTOBER 28 (Thu)

At a meeting of the Inklings in Lewis's rooms in Magdalen College, Charles Williams reads some of his novel in progress, *All Hallows' Eve*. Lewis exclaims that it is much the best thing that Charles Williams has done. [*Some months later Williams records in a letter to Michal that "Magdalen" (i.e., the Inklings) "thinks it 'tender and gay' among all the melodramatic horrors."*]

NOVEMBER 29 (Mon)

Lewis's forty-fifth birthday.

DECEMBER 9 (Thu)

Lewis hears Williams read more of his novel in progress, *All Hallows' Eve*, probably at an Inklings meeting at Magdalen.

DECEMBER 14 (Tue)

Lewis makes a point of inviting Williams over to Magdalen in order to meet Hugo Dyson, who is visiting from Reading, where he teaches at this time.

DECEMBER 24 (Fri)

Lewis has finished *That Hideous Strength*, the third volume of his science-fiction trilogy, and he writes the preface.

—— *Lewis's Science Fiction Planets* ——

In Lewis's science-fiction trilogy, *Out of the Silent Planet* (1938), *Perelandra* (1943), and *That Hideous Strength* (1945), he gives names of the astrological planets of medieval times and the classical world. These names are in the language of Old Solar (spoken, Lewis says, before the fall of humankind; "Handra" in Old Solar means "world," hence the suffixes of some of the names):

The sun = Arbol

Mercury = Viritrilbia

Venus = Perelandra

Earth = Tellus or Thulcandra (the Silent Planet)

Mars = Malacandra

Jupiter = Glundandra

Saturn = Lurga

Lewis returns to the astrological planets in *The Chronicles of Narnia*. In Narnia, the planets are ruled by intelligences, great lords and ladies (rather like the planets in Lewis's science-fiction trilogy). There is not a modern separation, therefore, between astronomy and astrology.

1944

The Allies land at Anzio; the Siege of Leningrad ends; the Allies land in Normandy on D-Day; the first V-bombs land on London; an attempt to assassinate Hitler fails; the Warsaw Uprising takes place; Paris is liberated; the Battle of the Bulge begins in the Ardennes. The Education Act is introduced in Britain by R. A. Butler.

Eavan Boland, David Constantine, Bernard Cornwell, Alison Fell, Craig Raine, and Carol Rumens are born.

Joseph Campbell, Keith Douglas, Jean Giraudoux, Philip Guedalla, Alun Lewis, Thomas Sturge Moore, Robert Nichols, Lucien Pissarro, Sir Arthur Quiller-Couch, Antoine de Saint-Exupéry, and William Temple, the Archbishop of Canterbury, die.

Lewis lectures at Cambridge—the Clark Lectures. He publishes *Beyond Personality*, the final series of radio talks. Charles Williams is reading *All Hallows' Eve* to the Inklings as it is being written. During the spring or summer vacation of this year Williams reads the first two chapters of a work never completed, *The Figure of Arthur*, to Lewis and Tolkien. Lewis describes the scene in his college rooms: "Picture to yourself . . . an upstairs sitting-room with windows looking north into the 'grove' of Magdalen College on a sunshiny Monday Morning in vacation at about ten o'clock. The Professor and I, both on the Chesterfield, lit our pipes and stretched out our legs. Charles Williams in the arm-chair opposite to us threw his cigarette into the grate, took up a pile of the extremely small, loose sheets on which he habitually wrote—they came, I think, from a twopenny pad for memoranda, and began. . . ."

JANUARY 5 (Wed)

Williams tells Michal about a *Time* magazine journalist writing on Lewis. Having interviewed Lewis he wants the view of Williams, as a friend. [*The cover feature eventually appears in September* 1947 *and helps to establish Lewis's popularity in the United States.*]

FEBRUARY 5 (Sat)

Williams writes to Michal, "I have found myself thinking how admirable it would be if I could get a Readership here when I retire. I know it may only be a dream; on the other hand, Lewis and Tolkien are only human, and are likely to take more trouble over a project which would enable them to see a good deal more of me than over anything which didn't." [*Lewis and Tolkien had evidently discussed this aspiration with Williams; a Readership is a senior university appointment.*]

FEBRUARY 22 (Tue)

Lewis's fourth and final series of broadcasts for the BBC, titled "Beyond Personality," starts this evening.

Lewis's Radio Broadcasts
(Series Four)

Transmitted on the BBC Home Service at 10.15 p.m. Talks 2, 6 and 7 were pre-recorded and the remainder broadcast live.

4. *Beyond Personality: The Christian View of God*

BBC Broadcast Talk	*Mere Christianity*, Book 4
1. "Making and Begetting," Feb. 22, 1944	1. "Making and Begetting"
2. "The Three-Personal God," Feb. 29, 1944	2. "The Three-Personal God"
	3. "Time and Beyond Time"
3. "Good Infection," March 7, 1944	4. "Good Infection"
4. "The Obstinate Toy Soldiers," March 14, 1944	5. "The Obstinate Toy Soldiers"
	6. "Two Notes"
5. "Let's Pretend," March 21, 1944	7. "Let's Pretend"
6. "Is Christianity Hard or Easy?" March 28, 1944	8. "Is Christianity Hard or Easy?"
	9. "Counting the Cost"
	10. "Nice People or New Men"
7. "The New Man," April 4, 1944	11. "The New Men"

MARCH 1 (Wed)

In a letter to his son Christopher, Tolkien comments on a description, the "Ascetic Mr. Lewis," in the *Daily Telegraph*. "I ask you! He put away three pints in a very short session we had this morning, and said he was 'going short for Lent.'" Tolkien also notes, "Lewis is as energetic and jolly as ever, but getting too much publicity for his or any of our tastes."

MARCH 29 (Wed)

Tolkien meets up with Lewis and Warren, and then lunches with the former. The "indefatigable" Lewis reads him part of a "new story," and, Tolkien later writes, puts "the screw on me to finish mine." [*The "new story" is probably* The Great Divorce, *which Lewis finishes by the end of the summer.*]

APRIL 12 (Wed)

Lewis spends almost two hours with Tolkien and Williams at The White Horse, a pub they prefer at this time. During this meeting Tolkien reads a recently composed chapter from *The Lord of the Rings*, to the great pleasure of the others.

APRIL 13 (Thu)

In an episodic letter to his son Christopher, on service with the RAF in South Africa, Tolkien writes that he is going to Magdalen College tonight for an Inklings meeting. He anticipates that those attending will be the Lewis brothers, Charles Williams, David Cecil, and probably Dr. Havard (who is "still bearded and uniformed"). He mentions that Warren is writing a book, adding that this activity "was catching." All turn up except David Cecil, and they stay until midnight. The best part of it, according to Tolkien, is Warren's chapter on the subject of the court of Louis XIV. He is not so partial to the concluding chapter of Lewis's *The Great Divorce*.

APRIL 19 (Wed)

Tolkien reads his chapter on the passage of the Dead Marshes from the unfolding *The Lord of the Rings* to an approving Lewis and Charles Williams this morning.

APRIL 24 (Mon)

Lewis and Tolkien are in the habit at this time of meeting on Wednesday mornings. But Tolkien writes to Christopher, "No Lewis this morning, as he has been appointed Clarke Lecturer in Cambridge, and leaves early to lecture there at 5 p.m. on Wednesdays."

MAY 8 (Mon)

Tolkien reads a new chapter of *The Lord of the Rings*, in which Faramir, a new character, comes on the scene. It receives "fullest approbation" from the listeners, Lewis and Williams.

MAY 22 (Mon)

After an exhausting previous day writing a new chapter of *The Lord of the Rings*, Tolkien is rewarded by its enthusiastic reception by Lewis and Williams this morning.

MAY 25 (Thu)

Tolkien records, in a letter to his son Christopher, a long, very enjoyable Inklings meeting. Hugo Dyson attends from Reading. Tolkien thinks him tired looking but still "reasonably noisy." Warren reads another chapter from his book on the times of Louis XIV, and his younger brother reads extracts from *The Great Divorce* (then going by the title of "Who Goes Home?"—which Tolkien quips should rather be called "Hugo's Home").

MAY 29 (Mon)

Tolkien reads the latest two chapters from *The Lord of the Rings* to Lewis in the morning, "Shelob's Lair" and "The Choices of Master Samwise." Lewis approves of them with unusual fervor, and is moved to tears by the second chapter.

JUNE 8 (Thu)

The Inklings assemble in Lewis's rooms at Magdalen College, those present being Tolkien, the Lewis brothers, Williams, and E. R. Eddison, author of a fantasy approved by the Inklings, *The Worm Ouroborous*. There is three and a half hours of reading, including a long chapter from Warren's book on Louis XIV, a new extract from *The Lord of the Rings*, an unnamed piece from Lewis, and a new chapter from Eddison of a work in progress, *The Mezentian Gate*. [*This will remain incomplete at Eddison's death in the following year.*]

JULY 12 (Wed)

Charles Williams with Tolkien visits Lewis in a nursing home. [*Lewis has had a minor operation. For some time he had been troubled by the shrapnel lodged in his body since 1918.*]

AUGUST 14 (Mon)

In a letter to Michal, Williams refers to an ideal life, which includes "a Tuesday drink with the Magdalen set and a sometimes Thursday evening." [*The "Magdalen set" is the Inklings.*]

AUGUST 31 (Thu)

An Inklings evening is attended by Lewis, Charles Williams, and others. Lewis reads a long paper on

Kipling, and Williams reads his essay on Kipling from his book *Poetry at Present*.

SEPTEMBER 21 (Thu)

An Inklings meeting at Magdalen College is attended by the Lewis brothers, Tolkien, and Williams. Warren reads the final chapter of his book in progress on Louis XIV, and they hear from Lewis an unnamed article and a long extract from his translation of Virgil's *The Aeneid* (never published). The Inklings agree that, if they are spared to have one, their victory celebration will consist of hiring a country inn for at least a week, spending the time entirely in beer and talk, totally ignoring any clock. Tolkien walks part of the way home afterwards with Williams, discussing the concept of freedom and its misuses.

OCTOBER 3 (Tue)

At noon Tolkien and Charles Williams look in at the "Bird and Baby" (Eagle and Child) pub. Surprisingly, the Lewis brothers are already there. The conversation becomes lively. Tolkien notices a "strange gaunt man" rather like Strider at the Inn in Bree in *The Lord of the Rings*. He doesn't have the usual "pained astonishment of the British (and American) public" on encountering the Lewises and Tolkien in a pub, but rather has an attentive interest in the conversation. Eventually he interjects a comment on Wordsworth. The stranger turns out to be the right-wing poet and soldier Roy Campbell, recently lampooned by Lewis in the *Oxford Magazine*. There is no ill feeling. He is promptly invited to the next Inklings on Thursday.

NOVEMBER 10 (Fri)

The first installment of *The Great Divorce*, which Lewis has read to the Inklings, is published in a religious weekly.

[From November 10, 1944, to April 14, 1945, The Great Divorce *is published in weekly installments in* The Guardian. (The Guardian *was a religious newspaper which ceased publication in* 1951; *it was not related to the Manchester* Guardian.)]

NOVEMBER 14 (Tue)

After dining out, the Inklings meet at Magdalen College. Colin Hardie gives a paper, which is followed, in Charles Williams's words, by a "learned discussion of dates and texts." The meeting breaks up at 10:30, after which Williams goes back with Lewis to his rooms, where they talk for another hour.

NOVEMBER 23 (Thu)

Tolkien, Williams, and Dr. Havard dine at The Mitre before joining Lewis and Owen Barfield, who have eaten at Magdalen College. Tolkien considers Barfield the only person who can tackle Lewis when in full flood of argument, "interrupting his most dogmatic pronouncements with subtle *distinguo's.*" Writing about the evening later to his son Christopher, Tolkien describes it as "most amusing and highly contentious." Items they hear include a short play by Barfield concerning Jason and Medea, and two sonnets that have been sent to Lewis. They discuss ghosts, the special nature of hymns (following Lewis's involvement with the revision of *Hymns Ancient and Modern* for the Church of England), and other subjects.

NOVEMBER 29 (Wed)

Lewis's forty-sixth birthday.

MID-DECEMBER

Lewis discusses with Tolkien collaborating on a book on language. [*This never materializes.*]

—————— *The BBC Sound Archives* ——————

The BBC Sound Archives has only five extant recordings of Lewis's talks, including one of his wartime broadcast talks.

Program/Date/Duration/Subject

1. "The New Man"/Mar. 21, 1944/14 minutes/The final weekly talk under the title "Beyond Personality." The talk covers the problem of prayer, and how it relates to becoming children of God.

2. "The Great Divorce"/Feb. 27, 1948/2 minutes/Lewis reads his prologue to *The Great Divorce*.

3. "Charles Williams"/Feb. 11, 1949/18 minutes/Lewis's comments on the work of his friend and fellow Inkling, who seems to be acquainted with another world.

4. "The Great Divide"/Apr. 1, 1955/37 minutes/Lewis argues that the "great divide" is not between the Middle Ages and the Renaissance but between old Western culture up to the early nineteenth century and the modern world. Here the radical historical fracture occurs.

5. "Pilgrim's Progress"/Oct.16, 1962/26 minutes/A talk on John Bunyan's *The Pilgrim's Progress*, illustrated with extracts read by Michael Spice and Vivienne Chatterton.

————————— ● ━ ● —————————

1945

In early February Roosevelt, Churchill, and Stalin meet at Yalta; the Allies bomb Dresden; Franklin D. Roosevelt dies without seeing the war's end, and Harry S. Truman succeeds him as U. S. president; the Russians reach Berlin; Mussolini is executed by partisans; Hitler commits suicide; Berlin falls; the concentration camps are liberated; the war ends in Europe; and Stalin, Truman, and Churchill meet at Potsdam. Labour is victorious in the British general election, Clement Attlee replaces Churchill as prime minister. Atomic bombs are dropped on Hiroshima and Nagasaki; Japan surrenders. UNESCO is founded; the United Nations Organization Charter is established. The Nuremberg war trials open.

John Banville, Wendy Cope, Selima Hill, and Shiva Naipaul are born.

Maurice Baring, Béla Bartók, Lord Alfred Douglas, Theodore Dreiser, George Egerton (Mary Chavelita Dunne), Arthur Symons, and Paul Valery die.

Lewis publishes *The Great Divorce* and *That Hideous Strength* ("Williams' influence . . . I think spoiled it," Tolkien writes to his son Michael about the latter).

JANUARY 8 (Mon)

Birth of a son, Richard Francis, to Maureen (née Moore) and Leonard Blake.

JANUARY 27 (Sat)

Auschwitz is liberated by the Russian army.

MAY 8 (Tue)

Germany surrenders.

MAY 9 (Wed)

The war in Europe is ended, and Charles Williams is almost alone in the temporary offices of the Oxford University Press for the last day that he will work. In the evening he walks the streets of Oxford with Anne Spalding (at whose house he is lodged). Victory bonfires are burning everywhere.

MAY 10 (Thu)

Charles Williams is gripped with pain. [*Michal, Williams's wife, arrives from London. He is taken to the Radcliffe Infirmary.*]

MAY 14 (Mon)

Williams is operated on for a condition that had troubled him years before, but he never fully recovers consciousness.

MAY 15 (Tue)

Lewis goes to the infirmary to call on Williams, carrying a book he wants to lend him, before joining the others as usual in the "Bird and Baby" a few minutes' walk away, and is stunned to find that his great friend has passed away. Warren records in his diary the sudden, unexpected death of Williams. "And so vanishes one of the best and nicest men it has ever been my good fortune to meet. May God receive him into His everlasting happiness." [*Charles Williams is buried in St. Cross Churchyard, Holywell, central Oxford, not far from the grave of Kenneth Grahame.*]

MAY 20 (Sun)

Lewis writes to a former student, "I also have become much acquainted with grief now through the death of Charles Williams, my friend of friends, the comforter of all our little set, the most angelic man."

AUGUST 6 (Mon)

The first atomic bomb is dropped on Hiroshima.

AUGUST 9 (Thu)

The second atomic bomb is dropped on Nagasaki.

SEPTEMBER 2 (Sun)

Japan surrenders.

MICHAELMAS (Autumn) TERM

Tolkien becomes Merton Professor of English Language and Literature, and thus a fellow of Merton College. This involves special responsibility for Middle English up to the year 1500. [*Previously he was a fellow of Pembroke College.*]

NOVEMBER 29 (Thu)

Lewis's forty-seventh birthday.

DECEMBER 11 (Tue)–14 (Fri)

There is a "victory" Inklings holiday at The Bull, Fairford. They walk in the countryside round about, which includes the discovery of a pub called The Pig and Whistle and a quiet country church where Tolkien, to Warren's surprise and pleasure, says a prayer. [*The group includes the Lewis brothers and Tolkien, with Dr. Havard in attendance some of the time.*]

DECEMBER 24 (Mon)

Augustus Hamilton dies (Lewis's uncle, brother of Flora Lewis).

Academic Chairs Held by the Inklings

Cambridge University

Professor of Medieval and Renaissance English
1954–1963 C. S. Lewis

Oxford University

Rawlinson and Bosworth Professor of Anglo-Saxon
1925–1945 J. R. R. Tolkien

Merton Professor of English Language and Literature
1945–1959 J. R. R. Tolkien

Merton Professor of English Literature
1957–1966 Nevill Coghill

Professor of Poetry
1938–1943 Adam Fox

1973–1978 John (Barrington) Wain

London University

Goldsmiths' Professor of English Literature
1948–1970 Lord David Cecil

Leeds University

Professor of English Language
1924–1925 J. R. R. Tolkien

CHAPTER SEVEN

The Beginnings of Narnia and the Coming of Joy

(1946–1953)

The years immediately after the war were difficult for C. S. Lewis. Not only was there rationing of food and fuel shortages (he was forced at times to wear a dressing gown over his indoor clothes to keep warm in his college rooms), but Mrs. Moore, his quasi-adopted mother, was physically and mentally in decline. He loyally looked after her, and was unable to take a holiday for a number of years, leading eventually to his own physical exhaustion. Meanwhile he fulfilled his university obligations and continued to write groundbreaking works of literary scholarship, popular theology with philosophical themes, and fiction. It is in this period that he started writing *The Chronicles of Narnia*.

The sudden death of Charles Williams just as the war ended did not fully restore the old intimacy between Lewis and J. R. R. Tolkien; while the latter felt Williams's loss keenly he still considered that Lewis was too taken with him. The continuing influence of Williams on Lewis after his death, reinforced by Tolkien's dislike of Lewis's popular theology, stood between them.

With the friendship remaining somewhat cool Tolkien perhaps found it harder to accept Lewis's well-meant criticisms of *The Lord of the Rings* (particularly the poetry in its pages, and the amount of the narrative devoted to hobbits), despite the enormous encouragement his friend exercised. This, however, did not distract Tolkien from his resolve to place his friend in a university Chair, using his influence as one of the electors for the Chair. Though he considered Lewis's popularizing of theology a flaw in his friend's output he did not sympathize with a general hostility to Lewis in the Oxford hierarchy, reflected in passing over Lewis for the Merton Chair and perhaps in a later failure to give him the Professorship of Poetry in 1951. In fact, he was grateful to his friend as a close ally in the reforms he had accomplished in the syllabus of the Oxford English School.

The Narnian stories, one of Lewis's greatest achievements, complete a developing process of an imaginative communication of what Lewis and Tolkien thought of as "Old Western values" that had began with *The Pilgrim's Regress*. After that first fiction Lewis's skills dramatically improved in writing his science-fiction trilogy, beginning with *Out of the Silent Planet*, then *Perelandra*, and ending with the less successful but nevertheless powerful *That Hideous Strength*. Partly through reading at this time Roger Lancelyn Green's story "The Wood That Time Forgot" (never published), and partly through having the right images in his head, Lewis found a new liberation in writing about Narnia. He felt that the genre of children's stories, like science fiction, gave him a better platform for what he wanted to say than even his immensely popular broadcast talks. These talks, and his accessible spiritual writings like *The Problem of Pain* (1940) and *Miracles* (1947), still limited what the primary "imaginative man" in Lewis wished to communicate. There was a wildness and valid kind of old paganism missing—until Lewis created Aslan, at the center of the Narnian stories, who is famously not a tame lion. Aslan imaginatively embodies the God Lewis portrays so distinctively and momentously in his book *Miracles*.

Ironically, given Tolkien's displeasure at what he saw as didactic elements in *The Lion, the Witch and the Wardrobe*, the writing of the Narnian Chronicles owes a very great deal to Tolkien. He had persistently argued for and demonstrated an allusive approach to the presence of Christian faith in literature. His views, as always, deeply influenced his friend. Lewis knew that Tolkien did not really approve of his popular theology. However, after the plain-language broadcast talks, Lewis's theological message gradually demanded more of its readers; *Miracles*, Lewis's best and most representative theological work, is considerably more intellectual than *Mere Christianity* (the published broadcast talks). Lewis argued the points raised in one chapter with a leading and sympathetic contemporary philosopher, Elizabeth Anscombe. This debate confirmed Lewis's view that modern philosophical writing was for an increasingly specialist audience. After this he took a much more indirect approach to communicating the Christian message. He followed in the spirit of Tolkien, even if not in the letter (Tolkien nevertheless continued to disapprove of Lewis's theologizing).

The first Narnian story, *The Lion, the Witch and the Wardrobe*, began for Lewis with a vivid mental picture of a faun in a snowy wood carrying a parcel—the image had first come to him, he tells us, when he was a young man of about sixteen. A further ingredient was the landscapes of his childhood, including the Mourne mountains of County

Down, the green countryside at their northeastern feet and beyond, with its drumlins and undulating fields and woods, and the wild, bleak moors of County Antrim. These were Narnia and its environs. Significantly, on an occasion when he longed to visit Northern Ireland, but was confined by the illness and decline of Mrs. Moore, he spoke in a letter of Ulster as his "ain countrie," thinking of the hills of County Down and the coastline of County Antrim.

In 1950 Lewis received a letter from an American novelist and poet, Helen Joy Davidman Gresham (1915–1960), which developed into a long correspondence, culminating in their meeting when she visited England. Her marriage was in terminal decline, and she made the decision to move to England permanently with her two young sons. Soon they were visiting The Kilns. Joy had come into Lewis's life with a vengeance.

1946

The first meeting of the United Nations General Assembly takes place. Nationalization of the Bank of England; Churchill's Iron Curtain speech at Fulton, Missouri. Italy becomes a republic. The Fourth Republic is established in France. In Britain the National Health Act is passed.

Howard Barker, Julian Barnes, Alan Bleasdale, Jim Crace, Christopher Hampton, Alan Judd, James Kelman, Brian Patten, Philip Pullman, Peter Reading, and Marina Warner are born.

Harley Granville Barker, John Maynard Keynes, Sir Charles Oman, Ernest Rhys, Damon Runyan, May Sinclair, Logan Pearsall Smith, Gertrude Stein, and H. G. Wells die.

JANUARY 16 (Wed)

William Lewis, uncle of Lewis and Warren, dies.

JANUARY 31 (Thu)

Lewis, writing to his friend Sister Penelope, mentions Mrs. Moore's health: "Jane is up and down: some days miserable and jealous, at other times gentle and even jolly. We have two nice maids at present."

FEBRUARY 1 (Fri)

Derek Brewer, one of Lewis's students at Magdalen College, notes in his diary: "I meet Lewis occasionally in the mornings, he going towards Addison's [Walk], I returning. So we rush past each other, hastily calling out our respective informations about primroses and snowdrops."

MARCH 18 (Mon)–22 (Fri)

Lewis, Warren, and Hugo Dyson take a short holiday in Liverpool; Lewis is there to participate in a *Brains Trust* for the BBC. [*This regular radio program had become very popular during the war.*]

MARCH 28 (Thu)

An Inklings gathering tonight includes Lewis, Warren, Christopher Tolkien, Humphrey Havard, Colin Hardie, and Gervase Mathew. Amongst other things they discuss the possibility of dogs having souls.

JUNE 26 (Wed)–29 (Sat)

Lewis and Warren take the train to Scotland where Lewis is being made a doctor of divinity by the University of St. Andrews on June 28, a rare honor for a layman. As the train crosses into Scotland Warren records in his diary that after "miserable, hungry England," here they have "real porridge, of which I had almost forgotten the taste, plenty of butter, edible sausages, toast, marmalade, coffee!" At the degree ceremony Professor D. M. Baillie, dean of the Faculty of Divinity, says: "With his pen and with his voice on the radio Mr. Lewis has succeeded in capturing the attention of many who will not readily listen to professional theologians, and has taught them many lessons concerning the deep things of God. . . . In recent years Mr. Lewis has arranged a new kind of marriage between theological reflection and poetic imagination, and this fruitful union is now producing works which are difficult to classify in any literary genre: it can only be said in respectful admiration that he pursues 'things unattempted yet in prose or rhyme.'"

JUNE 30 (Sun)

Lewis invites a group of undergraduates to dine and then have a drink together with him and Hugo Dyson. Those present are Philip Stibbe of Merton College, Tom Stock and Derek Brewer of Magdalen, and Peter Bayley of University College. Brewer records in his diary: "We drank some sherry. Lewis came in cursing from a meeting of the tutorial board and its decision to expand the College. A few amusing stories of the shaggy-dog variety were told. . . . The dinner was magnificent, and so were the hock and conversation. . . . Upstairs again after dinner into Tom's room, where we drank excellent port and graduated on to beer. It was an excellent evening, conversation amusing and intelligent and monopolised by no one." [Such invitations from Lewis are a regular occurrence.]

JULY 21 (Sun)

Tolkien writes to Sir Stanley Unwin, his publisher, that Merton College is about to elect a Merton Professor of English Language and Literature. "It ought to be C. S. Lewis, or perhaps Lord David Cecil, but one never knows." [*Tolkien is an elector for the chair. In the event it is taken by F. P. Wilson; Lewis is passed over.*]

————————— *Wit and Wisdom* —————————

Lewis was noted for his humor, love of fun, wit, and pithy repartee.

He mispronounced names, no doubt intentionally: a Mrs. Clare Boothe Luce became "Clara Bootlace," and a Mrs. Caroline Rakestraw transformed into "the very nice Mrs. Cartwheel." It was Mrs. Rakestraw of the Episcopal Radio-TV Foundation of the United States who had to explain to Lewis why they couldn't in the end broadcast his talks on the "Four Loves." Lewis reported later that she said, "Professor Lewis, I'm afraid you brought sex into your talks on Eros." His reply, he said, was, "My dear Mrs. Cartwheel, how can you talk about Eros and *leave it out?*"

On one occasion, Warren wondered aloud why stars twinkled while planets did not. Lewis instantly responded, "Well, obviously, because the stars are lit by gas and the planets by electricity."

His friends shared his inexhaustible appetite for pun. Hugo Dyson once commented on Lewis's domestic situation with Mrs. Moore by quoting Shakespeare's *Othello*: "O cursed spite that gave thee to the Moor."

Lewis had a taste for harmless bawdy stories. One such comes in a taped discussion on science fiction between Lewis, Kingsley Amis, and Brian Aldiss. The reference is to a book called *Flatland*, by "A. Square."

LEWIS: But of course the word *square* hadn't the same sense then.

ALDISS: It's like the poem by Francis Thompson that ends "She gave me tokens three, a book, a word of her winsome mouth, and a sweet wild raspberry"; there again the meaning has changed. It really was a wild raspberry in Thompson's day. [Laughter.]

LEWIS: Or the lovely one about the bishop of Exeter, who was giving prizes at a girl's school. They did a performance of *A Midsummer Night's Dream*, and the poor man stood up afterwards and made a speech and said [piping voice]: "I was very interested in your delightful performance, and among other things I was very interested in seeing for the first time in my life a female Bottom." [Guffaws.]

AUGUST 8 (Thu)

In his diary, Warren notes an Inklings meeting attended by himself, his brother, Hugo Dyson, Dr. Havard, Tolkien, Gervase Mathew, and a visitor, Stanley Bennett of Cambridge University. It is not, he writes, the sort of evening he enjoys: "mere noise and buffoonery." [*Bennett is involved in inviting Lewis to give a lecture series in Cambridge, and a few years later offering him a university Chair there.*]

AUGUST 22 (Thu)

An Inklings meeting takes place in Lewis's college rooms as usual. It is attended by Tolkien, his son Christopher, and the Lewis brothers. Warren records in his diary his brother reading a poem on Paracelsus's view of gnomes, and "Tollers" [Tolkien] reading "a magnificent myth which is to knit up and concludes his Papers of the Notions Club"— on the downfall of Númenor. [The "Notion Club Papers" was never completed. It involves time travel, and was directly inspired by the meetings of the Inklings.]

SEPTEMBER

An American, Chad Walsh, publishes an article, "C. S. Lewis, Apostle to the Skeptics," in the *Atlantic Monthly*. [*He is an associate professor of English at Beloit College in Wisconsin. The article becomes the foundation for a book of the same name, the first serious study of Lewis. It also leads to a close acquaintance with Lewis, and, independently, a friendship and correspondence with Joy Davidman, who will one day marry Lewis. Indeed, he is partly responsible for bringing the two together.*]

SEPTEMBER 10 (Tue)

Dr. Havard picks up the Lewis brothers and Christopher Tolkien from Magdalen College, and drives them out to a favored inn at Godstow, on the edge of north Oxford, called The Trout. The river runs past the pub. It is near here, in Lewis Carroll's story, that Alice goes down the rabbit hole. They sit in the garden and talk about Dr. Johnson, the great eighteen-century writer whose brilliant conversation Lewis rivalled. They discuss the views he probably would have had on contemporary literature. They also talk about the nature of women.

More Wit and Wisdom

On one occasion at the Socratic Club, while Lewis was in the chair, someone very much taken with logical positivism asked during the usual discussion: "How can you prove anything? I mean, how can you prove there isn't a blue cow sitting on that piano?" Lewis responded, "In what sense blue?"

When Lewis invited a group of undergraduates to his college rooms for a drink, and sometimes during meetings of the Inklings, he delighted to get someone to read from a sentimental Victorian novel, *Irene Iddlesleigh*, by Amanda McKittrick Ros. The idea was to see who could read it the longest without laughing. A typical extract might be: "Speak! Irene! Wife! Woman! Do not sit in silence and allow the blood that now boils in my veins to ooze through cavities of unrestrained passion and trickle down to drench me with its crimson hue!"

Often Tolkien and Lewis, when they were together, had a habit of blowing smoke rings with their pipes. E. L. Edmunds, a wartime student of Lewis's, remembers: "Sometimes, each would try for the best sequence of rings, and it is still a source of wonderment to me how they managed to send up one ring and then put two or three more rings through very quickly before the first ring dissipated. Of such smoking habits were those of Gandalf formed?"

Once, Lewis was on his way to the The Eagle and Child with another member of the Inklings. They saw a beggar in the street. Lewis reached into his pocket and gave money to the man. As they walked on, his friend said, "Why did you do that—he'll only spend it on drink?" Lewis said, "Isn't that what we're going to do?"

SEPTEMBER 17 (Tue)

Lewis has lunch with Roger Lancelyn Green, a former student and friend, and deputy librarian of Merton College.
Lewis returns to him the manuscript of a children's story
he had borrowed the year before. Green had called it "The
Wood That Time Forgot." Lewis has much good advice
for Green and assures him that it should be published.
[*Green tries to revise the manuscript into "a fairy tale for adults," but it
is never published. Elements eventually pass into Lewis's conception of*
The Lion, the Witch and the Wardrobe. *Green's story tells of
three children and their undergraduate friend who enter an
Oxfordshire wood. Soon they find themselves in an enchanted forest cut
off by time from their world and in some type of suspended time. The
story features a sort of fallen angel who disguises himself as a kind old
man, and a sweet drink like raspberry-cordial, which tempts one of the
children to go over to the enemy.*]

NOVEMBER 29 (Fri)

Lewis's forty-eighth birthday.

1947

*The partition of India is declared; Pakistan is established under the
premiership of Ali Khan. The Marshall Plan is proposed. The Dead
Sea Scrolls are discovered at Qumran.*

*Jenny Diski, David Hare, Liz Lochhead, Salman Rushdie, and Willy
Russell are born.*

*James Agate, Angela Brazil, G. G. Coulton, Richard Le Gallienne,
Hugh Lofting, Marie Belloc Lowndes, Arthur Machen, Baroness Orczy,
Forrest Reid, Flora Thompson, Sidney Webb, and A. N. Whitehead die.*

This year is one of great strain for Lewis, as life at The
Kilns becomes more and more fraught. It proves exceed-
ingly difficult to retain maids working with Mrs. Moore.

Lewis never knows from one day to the next when he can loose the tether of his duties "as a nurse and a domestic servant (there are psychological as well as material difficulties in my house)." Warren sells his boat, the *Bosphorus*. Lewis publishes *Miracles*.

EARLY MARCH

Mrs. Moore comes down with pneumonia.

MARCH 29 (Sat)

Warren ceases to belong to the Reserve of Officers.

APRIL 4 (Good Friday)

Lewis and Warren leave for a holiday in Maureen's house in Malvern. It is a cold, gray day, and they are glad of their scarves and heavy coats. While they stay in Malvern, Maureen comes to Oxford to take a turn looking after her mother. [*Hugo Dyson joins them in Malvern for some walking.*]

APRIL 17 (Thu)

Upon his return to Oxford Warren writes in his diary about his dread and hatred of The Kilns. "Though I can still force myself to see that it is beautiful objectively, I loathe every stick and stone and sound of it."

JUNE 11 (Wed)

"The incredible has happened," Warren writes in his diary. "I am off on my Irish adventure. . . . I went by taxi at 9.15, feeling very guilty at leaving poor J[ack] alone with that horrid old woman in that abominable house, though if I had stopped there I would not have been allowed to do anything to ease his burden." [*Like his brother, Warren has a deep love and constant longing for his homeland of*

Ireland. He had feared Mrs. Moore's constant illnesses, and her hold over his brother, would thwart his chance to get away from The Kilns.]

JUNE 20 (Fri)

Warren is taken seriously ill ("in very deep waters," as he puts it) while on holiday in Ireland and taken to hospital in Drogheda (north of Dublin)—an illness resulting from alcohol abuse. [Warren has battled for many years with his chronic dependence.]

JUNE 23 (Mon)

Lewis arrives in Drogheda to see his brother. He has rushed over to Ireland upon getting news of his condition. [Lewis stays in the White Horse Hotel for a week, visiting his brother twice daily.]

JUNE 30 (Mon)

Warren is out of the hospital and with his brother in the White Horse. He refuses to return with Lewis to Oxford. [He spends the rest of his holiday at the White Horse, remaining there until July 27. He discovers St. Peter's Anglican Church near the hotel and begins attending.]

JULY 4 (Fri)

Lewis writes to Arthur Greeves, "The daily letter writing without W[arren] to help me is appalling—an hour and a half or two hours every morning before I can get to my own work."

AUGUST 4 (Mon)–18 (Mon)

Lewis, Warren, and Tolkien take a holiday together in Malvern. [Tolkien is present only to August 9. He has been very sympathetic to Warren over his alcoholism.]

SEPTEMBER 8 (Mon)

A *Time* magazine cover feature on Lewis, "Don v. Devil," describes his growing influence, Oxford life, and conversion from atheism, where he "found himself part of a small circle of Christian Oxonians who met informally each week or so to drink and talk." *Time* describes "his handsome, white-panelled college room overlooking the deer park" and "his tiny, book-crammed inner study." The cover picture, painted by Boris Artzybasheff, shows an angel wing on one side and Uncle Screwtape on the other. The article includes Lewis in a growing band of "heretics" like T. S. Eliot, W. H. Auden, Dorothy L. Sayers and Graham Greene—intellectuals who believe in God.

The article begins:

> The lecturer, a short, thickset man with a ruddy face and a big voice, was coming to the end of his talk. Gathering up his notes and books, he tucked his horn-rimmed spectacles into the pocket of his tweed jacket and picked up his mortar board. Still talking—to the accompaniment of occasional appreciative laughs and squeals from his audience—he leaned over to return the watch he had borrowed from a student in the front row. As he ended his final sentence, he stepped off the platform.
>
> The maneuver gained him a head start on the rush of students down the center aisle. Once in the street, he strode rapidly—his black gown billowing behind his gray flannel trousers—to the nearest pub for a pint of ale.

NOVEMBER 13 (Thu)

Warren, in his diary, records an Inklings meeting at Merton (Tolkien's college). Here "Tollers" [Tolkien] reads "a rich melancholy poem on autumn, which J[ack] very aptly described as 'Matthew Arnold strayed into the world of Hobbit.'"

NOVEMBER 27 (Thu)

Warren's diary notes the topics at an Inklings gathering tonight. Tolkien, Lewis, Stevens, Havard, and he attend. "We talked of B[isho]p. Barnes, of the extraordinary difficulty of interesting the uneducated indifferent in religion: savage and primitive man and the common confusion between them: how far pagan mythology was a substitute for theology: bravery and panache."

NOVEMBER 29 (Sat)

Lewis's forty-ninth birthday.

1948

The U. S. Congress adopts the Marshall Plan. The Organisation for European Economic Co-operation (OEEC) is established. Communists take over Czechoslovakia. The British Mandate in Palestine ends; the state of Israel is created. The Berlin airlift starts.

Prince Charles, Clare Boylan, David Edgar, Zoë Fairbairns, Maggie Gee, Ian McEwan, Deborah Moggach, Terry Pratchett, and Nigel Williams are born.

Gordon Bottomley, A. E. W. Mason, and Mary Tourtel (creator of Rupert the Bear) die.

Lewis is elected a fellow of the Royal Society of Literature.

FEBRUARY 2 (Mon)

Elizabeth Anscombe, later Professor of Philosophy at Cambridge, reads her "Reply to Mr. C. S. Lewis's Argument that 'Naturalism is Self-refuting'" to the Socratic

Club. [*Elizabeth Anscombe's argument causes Lewis to revise chapter 3 of* Miracles *when it is reprinted by Fontana in* 1960.]

FEBRUARY 4 (Wed)

Derek Brewer and other undergraduates meet with Lewis and Hugo Dyson, first in Philip Stibbe's rooms at Merton College, then at the Roebuck Hotel, where they eat. Brewer notes in his diary: "None of us at first very cheerful—one has to work hard to keep up with Lewis. He was obviously deeply disturbed by his encounter last Monday with Miss Anscombe who had disproved some of the central theory of his philosophy about Christianity. I felt quite painfully for him. Dyson said—very well—that now he had lost everything and was come to the foot of the Cross—spoken with great sympathy." Lewis describes the Socratic Club meeting to them: His imagery, in Brewer's perception, is all of the fog of war, and of retreat of infantry under heavy attack. (Brewer, like four of the other undergraduates, had been infantry officers at the age of nineteen and had seen action in the recent war, so Lewis's imagery struck home vividly.) Brewer continues: "Much of the evening was spent in cheerful ribaldry, but Lewis was really still miserable and went early. I finally noted, with a young man's cheerful egotism: 'a good evening, and a little less boisterous and exhausting than others.'" [*Elizabeth Anscombe did not agree with this perception of the event. She thought it an example of psychological transference on the part of some of those who attended, or heard of, the debate. In her view, Lewis had put up a robust defense of his position. Indeed, Lewis would later improve and refine his argument.*]

MARCH

Lewis is working on his autobiography, Surprised by Joy. [*It is not published until* 1955.]

Lewis's Library

Lewis gained his spiritual, intellectual and imaginative nurture from old books, or from contemporary writers who shared older values. Some of the books in his library that were important to him spiritually included:

Thomas Aquinas, *Summa Theologiae*

Athanasius, *On the Incarnation of the Word of God*

Augustine, *The City of God* and *The Confessions*

Arthur James Balfour, *The Foundations of Belief*

Richard Baxter, *The Saints' Everlasting Rest*

Bernard of Clairvaux, *On Loving God*

Jakob Boehme, *Dialogues*

Boethius, *The Consolation of Philosophy*

Sir Thomas Browne, *The Religio Medici*

John Bunyan, *The Pilgrim's Progress*

Joseph Butler, *The Analogy of Religion*

G. K. Chesterton, *The Everlasting Man*

Richard Crashaw, *Sacred Poems*

Francis de Sales, *Introduction to the Devout Life*

Johannes Eckhart, *Miscellaneous Writings*

D. E. Harding, *The Hierarchy of Heaven and Earth*

Walter Hilton, *The Ladder of Perfection*

Richard Hooker, *The Certainty and Perpetuity of Faith in the Elect*

Julian of Norwich, *Revelations of Divine Love*

Thomas à Kempis, *The Imitation of Christ*

Willam Law, *A Serious Call to a Devout and Holy Life*

Brother Lawrence, *The Practice of the Presence of God*

George MacDonald, *Unspoken Sermons*

C. F. D. Moule, *The Sacrifice of Christ*

Blaise Pascal, *Pensées*

Francis Quarles, *Emblems*

Thomas Traherne, *Centuries of Meditation*

Baron Friedrich von Hugel, *Letters to a Niece*

William Wordsworth, *The Prelude*

SUMMER

Lewis remarks vaguely to Chad Walsh about "completing a children's book he has begun 'in the tradition of E. Nesbit.'" During the same visit Walsh discovers that Lewis has started writing *Surprised by Joy* as well as working on his volume of the *Oxford History of English Literature*.

Kenneth Tynan, then a student at Magdalen College, remembers Lewis's deep kindness and charity when the young man had been jilted by his fiancée on the eve of what was to have been their marriage: "He reminded me how I had once told him about the parachuted landmine which, dropping from a German bomber during an air-raid in 1940, so narrowly missed our house in Birmingham that next morning we recovered some of the parachute silk from our chimney. (The mine destroyed six houses across the road and blew out all our windows.) But for that hair's-breadth—a matter of inches only—I would already (Lewis gently pointed out) have been dead for eight years. Every moment of life since then had been a bonus, a tremendous free gift, a present that only the blackest ingratitude could refuse. As I listened to him, my problems began to dwindle to their proper proportions; I had entered his room suicidal, and I left it exhilarated."

NOVEMBER 10 (Wed)

Lewis writes to Owen Barfield, whose fiftieth birthday is close to his. "I also will soon be fifty. Just the twenty years more now! A happy birthday to you. If the knowledge that for some twenty-five years you have been always food (and often physic as well) to my mind and heart can contribute to it, well it is so." [*Lewis will come to live only fifteen years more, not twenty. Barfield, however, will continue to live for a little over forty-nine years.*]

NOVEMBER 29 (Mon)

Lewis's fiftieth birthday.

1949

The North Atlantic Treaty is signed and NATO created. The Republic of Eire is formally proclaimed. The Berlin Blockade ends. The Communists take power in Hungary. The Federal Republic of Germany is established; the German Democratic Republic is established. The Communist People's Republic of China is declared. Harry S. Truman starts a second term as U. S. president. George Orwell publishes 1984.

Peter Ackroyd, Martin Amis, James Fenton, Tom Paulin, Michèle Roberts, Minette Walters, and Graham Swift are born.

J. W. Dunne, Douglas Hyde, Hugh Kingsmill, Edith Anna Œnone Somerville, and Richard Strauss die.

Lewis reads aloud to Tolkien from his manuscript of The Lion, the Witch and the Wardrobe.

JANUARY 14 (Fri)

Writing in Latin to his Italian pen friend Father Giovanni Calabria, Lewis confesses that he labors under many difficulties. His "house is unquiet and devastated by women's quarrels." His "aged mother, worn out by long infirmity, is [his] daily care." He asks his friend to pray for peace in his life. [Vera Henry, Mrs. Moore's goddaughter, has come over from Annagasan, Ireland, to stay at The Kilns to help. There is constant friction between the women, exacerbated by the fact that Vera is not a subservient, employed maid.]

JANUARY 24 (Mon)

Lewis has seen the movie King Kong, and comments in a letter to science-fiction writer I. O. Evans, "I thought parts of 'King Kong' (especially where the natives make a stand after he's broken the gate) magnificent, but the New York parts contemptible."

FEBRUARY

Lewis is roughly halfway through writing *The Lion, the Witch and the Wardrobe*, when Warren binges again on alcohol and has to be admitted to the nearby Acland Nursing Home.

MARCH 10 (Thu)

Lewis reads some chapters of *The Lion, the Witch and the Wardrobe* to Roger Lancelyn Green. He tells Green that Tolkien disliked it intensely. He asks, "Is it worth going on with?" Green responds enthusiastically, "Rather." Some feeling of awe comes over him as he listens to Lewis—he distinctly feels that he is listening to one of the great children's books of the world for the first time.

END OF MARCH

Lewis lends the completed *The Lion, the Witch and the Wardrobe* to Green to read in the original handwritten manuscript.

APRIL

When he hears that Green has read Lewis's manuscript Tolkien retorts to him, "It really won't do, you know! I mean to say: *Nymphs and their Ways*, the *Love-Life of a Faun*. Doesn't he know what he's talking about?" [*Tolkien will write in 1964, after Lewis's death, "It is sad that 'Narnia' and all that part of C. S. L.'s work should remain outside the range of my sympathy, as much of my work was outside his."*]

JUNE

Lewis reads to Roger Lancelyn Green the beginning of a second Narnian story. It hauntingly evokes the original fall

———————— *Some Meals in Narnia* ————————

In *The Lion, the Witch and the Wardrobe*:

Mr. Tumnus gives Lucy a wonderful tea that consists of:

a nice brown egg, lightly boiled;
sardines on toast;
buttered toast;
toast with honey;
and sugar-topped cake.

Mrs. Beaver feeds the hungry children:

a jug of creamy milk (Mr. Beaver had his own jug of beer);
jacket potatoes (with a huge dollop of rich butter in the center of the table to put on them);
an immense and perfectly sticky marmalade roll, steaming fresh from the oven;
and a big pot of well-brewed tea to finish up with.

In *The Magician's Nephew*, the hungry children Polly and Digory find breakfast provided in the form of a fruit-bearing tree, which has grown overnight from a candy brought from our world.

The taste of its soft fruit reminds the children of toffee, even though it is soft and juicy, unlike the confectionary.

Fledge, the flying, talking horse, tries a toffee fruit but decides that—at this time in the morning—he prefers the lush grass around them.

———————— ◆—◆ ————————

of humanity. Digory has the gift of understanding the speech of trees and animals but loses it forever when he cuts off a branch of his favorite oak tree to impress Polly. Digory is bereft when he discovers the truth: "The only life he had ever known was a life in which you could talk to animals and trees. If that was to come to an end the world would be so different for him that he would be a complete stranger in it." Green likes how the story starts out but has a problem with Lewis's character, Mrs. LeFay. [*Lewis agrees with Green's assessment and lays the story aside, unfinished, and continues with a sequel to* The Lion, the Witch and the Wardrobe. *This is* Prince Caspian, *then having the working title of "Drawn into Narnia."*]

JUNE 13 (Mon)

Warren returns to The Kilns from a weekend in Malvern to find an ambulance waiting. Lewis is admitted to the Acland Nursing Home. He has streptococcus.

JUNE 14 (Tue)

Warren writes in his diary: "A very anxious day indeed. J[ack] was light-headed during the night, and obviously a very sick man when I went in to see him; he is having injections of penicillin every three hours. I could get little out of Humphrey [Havard, their family doctor] except that it is 'a very serious illness for a man of fifty.' . . . Humphrey explained to me that J's real complaint is exhaustion. . . . To my joy, he added that when he got him on his legs again, he would insist that he accepted no responsibility for J's health unless he took a good holiday away from The Kilns. I got home sick with fright and savage with anger, and let her ladyship have a blunt statement of the facts: stressing the exhaustion motif and its causes. I ultimately frightened her into agreeing to grant J a month's leave." [*According to Warren, this would be the first proper holiday Lewis has had for fifteen years or more.*]

SEPTEMBER 20 (Tue)

Lewis and Barfield lunch with the poet Ruth Pitter at her flat in Chelsea, London. [*Pitter has been in correspondence with*

Lewis *frequently since she has converted to the Christian faith as a result of hearing his wartime broadcasts. She has also visited Oxford several times to see him.*]

AUTUMN

Tolkien finishes writing the final version of *The Lord of the Rings*. He gives the typescript to Lewis to read. [*He recalled many years later, in a BBC interview: "I remember I actually wept at the denouement. . . . I typed the whole of that work out twice and lots of it many times, on a bed in an attic. I couldn't afford of course the typing."*]

OCTOBER 20 (Thu)

"The last Thursday night Inklings" is recorded in Warren's diary. After a ham supper (the ham supplied by an American correspondent of Lewis's) they go over to Lewis's rooms. Hugo Dyson is in fine, effervescent form.

OCTOBER 27 (Thu)

Warren records: "Dined with J[ack] at College. . . . No one turned up after dinner, which was just as well as J has a bad cold and wanted to go to bed early." Lewis writes to Tolkien about the completed typescript of *The Lord of the Rings*: "*Uton herian holbytlas* indeed [Let us praise hobbits]. . . . All the long years you have spent on it are justified." His letter concludes: "I miss you very much." [*Though there is no further record of Thursday Inklings, the Tuesday mornings at The Eagle and Child continue (where there is no reading out of work in progress).*]

AUTUMN

Tolkien gives Milton Waldman of the William Collins publishing house a large manuscript, much of it handwritten, of the unfinished *The Silmarillion*.

NOVEMBER 29 (Tue)

Lewis's fifty-first birthday.

DECEMBER

Lewis finishes the manuscript of what becomes the Narnian story *Prince Caspian* and passes it to Roger Lancelyn Green to read and comment on.

DECEMBER 31 (Sat)

Lewis has a luncheon party in "The Wilde Room" at Magdalen College to meet Pauline Baynes, who is to illus-trate *The Lion, the Witch and the Wardrobe*. The young illus-trator is quite overawed by the occasion. Green attends and returns the handwritten script of *Prince Caspian*, along with his comments. Other guests include the poet Ruth Pitter, Owen Barfield, and Marjorie Milne, at that time a dedicated fan of Lewis's. [*With no Inklings readings anymore, and given Tolkien's antipathy, Lewis has turned to Green—an expert on children's literature—for criticism of the Narnian stories. Pauline Baynes has been chosen as illustrator because Lewis liked her drawings for Tolkien's* Farmer Giles of Ham.]

1950

The Korean War starts. The United States makes plans to build an H-bomb.

Neil Jordan, Sara Maitland, Timothy Mo, Blake Morrison, Grace Nichols, and A. N. Wilson are born.

Warwick Deeping, George Orwell (Eric Arthur Blair), Rafael Sabatini, George Sampson, George Bernard Shaw, and James Stephens die.

Lewis publishes *The Lion, the Witch and the Wardrobe*.

—— *Some More Meals in Narnia* ——

In *The Horse and His Boy*, Shasha enjoys a good meal in the Calormene fashion while he is mistaken for his twin, Prince Corin, in Tashbaan:

lobsters, and salad;

snipe stuffed with almonds;

truffles;

a complex dish of chicken livers, rice, raisins and nuts;

desserts of cool melons, gooseberry fools, mulberry fools, and various delicacies made with ice.

In *Prince Caspian*:

The centaurs provide a typical meal for the prince, on the run from his wicked uncle:

cakes of oaten meal;

apples and herbs;

wine and cheese.

And after the defeat of the Telmarines the Pevensie children share the best of Narnian feasts:

sides of roasted meat with a delicious smell;

wheaten cakes and oaten cakes;

honey and many-coloured sugars and the smoothest of cream, thick like porridge;

and an abundance of fruit—peaches, nectarines, pomegranates, pears, grapes, strawberries, and raspberries.

———————————— •———————————

JANUARY 10 (Tue)

Lewis receives a letter from a thirty-four-year-old New Yorker, Joy Davidman, a published poet and novelist. [*Nearly six years later Warren will comment in his diary: "Until 10 January 1950 neither of us had ever heard of her; then she appeared in the mail as just another American fan, Mrs W. L. Gresham from the neighbourhood of New York. With, however, the difference that she stood out from the ruck by her amusing and well-written letters, and soon J[ack] and she had become 'pen-friends.'"*]

JANUARY 17 (Tue)

The household dog, Bruce, dies in his dotage, to the relief of the Lewis brothers. Warren recalls some of his maddening traits. He would sometimes incessantly bark all night, and then, while he dozed wearily during the day, Mrs. Moore would instruct the "boys" (Lewis and Warren) to make no noise in case they awakened him. He also used to relieve himself in her "overheated" bedroom, stinking out the house. It would be an ordeal to walk past her bedroom door because of the stench.

JANUARY 27 (Fri)

Joy Davidman writes in a letter to her friend Chad Walsh: "Just got a letter from Lewis in the mail. I think I told you I'd raised an argument or two on some points? Lord, he knocked my props out from under me unerringly; one shot to a pigeon. I haven't a scrap of my case left. And, what's more, I've seldom enjoyed anything more. Being disposed of so neatly by a master of debate, all fair and square—it seems to be one of the great pleasures of life, though I'd never have suspected it in my arrogant youth. I suppose it's unfair tricks of argument that leave wounds. But after the sort of thing that Lewis does, what I feel is a craftsman's joy at the sight of a superior performance."

LATE FEBRUARY

Prince Caspian has been typed, and the handwritten script of *The Voyage of the "Dawn Treader"* is ready for Roger Lancelyn Green to read.

APRIL 2 (Sun)

At Lewis's request Green writes a cover blurb for *The Lion, the Witch and the Wardrobe* "with much difficulty." [*Lewis likes the blurb very much, though he confesses he does not understand "Blurbology;" however, the publisher, Geoffrey Bles, does not use it.*]

APRIL 29 (Sat)

Mrs. Moore is admitted to Restholme (a nursing home in Woodstock Road, Oxford). She had fallen out of bed three times during the night. [*Mrs. Moore has been semiparalyzed for some time, and has to be watched almost permanently.*]

JUNE 22 (Thu)

The galley proofs of *The Lion, the Witch and the Wardrobe* are handed around to Lewis's friends gathered at The Eagle and Child.

JULY 26 (Wed)

Green spends most of today, in the words of his diary, "reading Lewis's new story *Narnia and the North* [*The Horse and His Boy*], which is very enthralling—almost the best of the four."

JULY 27 (Thu)

Green writes in his diary of dining "in Magdalen S.[enior] C.[ommon] R.[oom] with Lewis, and then a wonderful evening talking until after 1 a.m. Began by discussing *To Narnia and the North* [*The Horse and His Boy*], made several suggestions etc. . . . Much literary talk, also of life after death, war, killing, the ethics of such things: we got on to life after death by way of Kipling's 'On the Gate' and a [H. G.] Wells story of a similar kind."

SEPTEMBER 12 (Tue)

Warren records an Inklings meeting at The Eagle and Child this morning in his diary. He notes that he went "to the Bird and Baby as usual, where were Tollers [Tolkien], D. G. [Dundas-Grant], MacCallum, & Tom Stevens."

SEPTEMBER 19 (Tue)

The Inklings meet as usual in the morning at The Eagle and Child. Warren writes: "At the Bird, Tollers [Tolkien],

─────────────── *New Inklings* ───────────────

After the war the number of Inklings swelled. The original members were Lewis, Tolkien, Warren Lewis, Hugo Dyson, Dr. Humphrey Havard, Owen Barfield (an occasional member), and Nevill Coghill, with the later addition of Charles Williams, Adam Fox, Charles Wrenn, Colin Hardie, Lord David Cecil, and James Dundas-Grant (1896–1985).

The influx of new members included:

J. A. W. ("Jaw") Bennett (1911–1981)— New Zealander, and colleague of Lewis's at Magdalen College, Oxford, from 1947. In 1964 he took on Lewis's post as Professor of Medieval and Renaissance Literature at Cambridge.

Gervase Mathew (1905–1976)—a contributor to *Essays Presented to Charles Williams*. Educated at Oxford's Balliol College, he joined the Catholic order of Dominicans in 1928 and was ordained a priest in 1934. He lectured in modern history, theology, and English at Oxford, and wrote books on Byzantium and medieval England.

Ronald B. MacCallum (1898–1973)—a historian and fellow of Pembroke College, Oxford, until 1955, when he was elected Master of Pembroke.

Christopher Tolkien (b. 1924)—the third son of Tolkien. He studied at Trinity College, Oxford, and became a fellow at New College. He

Colin [Hardie], D. G., J.[ack] and I. . . . A good and quite unintentional *gaffe* by J; the question was propounded whether Tollers's voice production or Hugo's handwriting gave more trouble to their friends. J. 'Well, there's this to be said for Hugo's writing, there's less of it.' . . . Ham supper in J.'s rooms at 7.30, same party as this morning, plus Tom Stevens. Humphrey I'm sorry to say didn't turn up." [*Dr. Havard's wife was buried the week before—she died of cancer, leaving five children. Hugo Dyson published very little. Tolkien was notorious for his quick, indistinct speech.*]

---

eventually resigned his academic duties to devote himself to editing his father's work.

Courtnay E. "Tom" Stevens (1905–1976)—fellow and tutor in ancient history at Magdalen College from 1934. He acquired the nickname "Tom Brown Stevens" while a schoolboy at Winchester.

John (Barrington) Wain (1925–1994)—a famous student of Lewis's, who in his autobiographical *Sprightly Running* records his experiences of wartime Oxford: "Once a week, I trod the broad, shallow stairs up to Lewis's study in the 'new building' at Magdalen. And there, with the deer-haunted grove on one side of us, and the tower and bridge on the other, we talked about English literature as armies grappled and bombs exploded." In 1947 John Wain became lecturer in English at Reading University, staying there until 1955. His novel *Hurry on Down* (1953) was followed by further novels, as well as books of criticism and poetry. From 1973 to 1978 he was Professor of Poetry at Oxford.

Roger Lancelyn Green (1918–1987)—not considered a member, but worthy of inclusion as visitor to many Tuesday morning Inklings meetings. He was a biographer and important friend of Lewis's. Lewis and his wife, Joy Davidman Lewis, visited Greece with Green and Green's wife June shortly before Joy's death. He wrote an authoritative study of children's literature, *Tellers of Tales* (1946, updated 1953), and composed many significant books for children himself.

SEPTEMBER 20 (Wed)

Warren and Lewis walk from Dorchester Abbey to Oxford (sixteen miles on the old Roman Road).

OCTOBER 16 (Mon)

The Lion, the Witch and the Wardrobe: A Story for Children is published in hardback by Geoffrey Bles. It is dedicated to Lucy Barfield, the adopted daughter of Owen and Maud Barfield.

NOVEMBER 7 (Tue)

The Lion, the Witch and the Wardrobe: A Story for Children is published in hardback in the United States by Macmillan Publishing Company.

NOVEMBER 13 (Mon)

Staying in the guest room at Magdalen College, Roger Lancelyn Green starts "reading Lewis's newest story in MS." This is *The Silver Chair*. [*Green moved from Oxford back to his ancestral home in Cheshire at the end of August.*]

NOVEMBER 14 (Tue)

Green reads more of the new story. After dinner in the college Hall the two go back to Lewis's rooms; Green notes in his diary, "where we sat talking until about 12.30: the usual sort of subjects—children's books, romances of other worlds; I discoursed upon Edgar Rice Burroughs; we planned a story of a trip to Mercury—but couldn't get very far with it." [*It will be Green who later christens the whole series* The Chronicles of Narnia.]

NOVEMBER 29 (Wed)

Lewis's fifty-second birthday.

1951

The Treaty of Paris establishes a "common market" in coal and steel for the Benelux countries. Winston Churchill becomes prime minister for the third time, and the Festival of Britain is celebrated.

Kate Atkinson and Paul Muldoon are born.

Constant Lambert, Algernon Blackwood, André Gide, and Henry de Vere Stacpoole die.

Lewis loses the election for the position of Professor of Poetry at Oxford to C. Day Lewis.

JANUARY 12 (Fri)

Janie King Moore dies at around 5 p.m., in Restholme. [*She is buried in the yard of Holy Trinity Church in Headington Quarry, Oxford.*]

JANUARY 17 (Wed)

Warren writes in his diary: "And so ends the mysterious self-imposed slavery in which J[ack] has lived for at least thirty years."

FEBRUARY 13 (Tue)

Roger Lancelyn Green records in his diary: "To 'Eagle and Child' to meet C. S. L.: a grand gathering—Tolkien, McCallum, Major Lewis, Wrenn, Hardie, Gervase Mathew, John Wain, and others whose names I didn't catch. Discussion on C. Day Lewis (who was elected Professor of Poetry last week, beating C. S. L. by 19 votes): Lewis praised his *Georgics* but considered his critical work negligible."

END OF MAY

Green is again staying as a guest at Magdalen College and Lewis reads to him the first chapter of a new Narnian story (*The Magician's Nephew*). Then he hands him the half of the manuscript which he has so far written. After an evening of fascinating conversation with Lewis, Green reads it with enthusiasm into the small hours of the morning. [*Later in the year, when much more of the book is written, Green points out a structural problem, and Lewis lays aside the book for the time being to work on* The Last Battle.]

AUGUST 14 (Tue)

Lewis and Warren travel to Northern Ireland together. [*Lewis spends the next fortnight with his old friend Arthur Greeves at Crawfordsburn, County Down, which is on the shores of Belfast Lough.*]

MICHAELMAS (Autumn) TERM

Magdalen College grants Lewis a sabbatical year so that he can complete his daunting volume of the *Oxford History of English Literature*, called plainly *English Literature in the Sixteenth Century, excluding Drama*. [*Dame Helen Gardner often saw him working on the book in the Bodleian Library. She observed: "One sometimes feels that the word 'unreadable' had no meaning for him. To sit opposite him . . . when he was moving steadily through some huge double-columned folio in his reading for his Oxford History was to have an object lesson in what concentration meant. He seemed to create a wall of stillness around him."*]

OCTOBER 15 (Mon)

Prince Caspian: The Return to Narnia is published by Geoffrey Bles.

NOVEMBER 29 (Thu)

Lewis's fifty-third birthday.

Dedications

This is a list of individuals to whom Lewis dedicated each of the following works. (Note: the dedications do not appear in all editions.)

Lucy Barfield—adopted daughter of Owen Barfield and Lewis's goddaughter (*The Lion, the Witch and the Wardrobe*)

Owen Barfield—close friend and intermittent Inkling (*The Allegory of Love: A Study in Medieval Tradition*)

Stanley and Joan Bennett—longtime friends (*Studies in Words*)

Geoffrey Corbett—foster son of Owen Barfield (*The Voyage of the "Dawn Treader"*)

Joy Davidman—future wife of Lewis (*Till We Have Faces: A Myth Retold*)

Hugo Dyson—close friend and Inkling (*Rehabilitations and Other Essays*)

Austin and Katherine Farrer—close friends (*Reflections on the Psalms*)

Roger Lancelyn Green—friend and frequent visitor to the Inklings after World War II (*The Discarded Image: An Introduction to Medieval and Renaissance Literature*)

Arthur Greeves—Lewis's childhood friend (*The Pilgrim's Regress: An Allegorical Apology for Christianity, Reason and Romanticism*)

David and Douglas Gresham—Lewis's stepsons (*The Horse and His Boy*)

Dom Bede Griffiths, OSB—friend (*Surprised by Joy: The Shape of My Early Life*)

Nicholas Hardie—eldest son of Colin Hardie (*The Silver Chair*)

Cecil and Daphne Harwood—close friends (*Miracles: A Preliminary Study*)

Mary Clare Havard—daughter of Dr. Humphrey Havard (*Prince Caspian: The Return to Narnia*)

The Inklings—(*The Problem of Pain*)

The Kilmer Family—correspondents with Lewis (*The Magician's Nephew*)

Warren H. Lewis—brother and friend (*Out of the Silent Planet*)

Jane McNeill— friend from Strandtown, Belfast (*That Hideous Strength*)

Cont.

Marjorie Milne—a fan of Lewis's introduced to him by Owen Barfield (*Dymer*, 1950 edition)

Mary Neylan—a student and friend of Lewis (*George MacDonald: An Anthology*)

J. R. R. Tolkien—close friend of nearly forty years and Inkling (*The Screwtape Letters*)

Barbara Wall—sister-in-law of Colin Hardie who typed several manuscripts for Lewis (*The Great Divorce: A Dream*)

Chad Walsh—American scholar who becomes acquainted with Lewis while writing the first study of his work (*The Four Loves*)

Charles Williams—close friend and Inkling (*A Preface to Paradise Lost*)

Florence "Michal" Williams—wife of Charles Williams (*Arthurian Torso: Containing the Posthumous Fragment of the Figure of Arthur by Charles Williams and A Commentary on the Arthurian Poems of Charles Williams*)

DECEMBER

Lewis declines his election to the Order of the British Empire, offered by the ruling Conservative government under Winston Churchill. He does not wish to be identified with the political Right.

1952

King George VI dies on February 6, succeeded by Queen Elizabeth II. The Mau Mau, a secret insurgent organization, are active in Kenya. Britain becomes a nuclear power.

Douglas Adams, William Boyd, Helen Dunmore, Linton Kwesi Johnson, Hilary Mantel, Andrew Motion, Sean O'Brien, Stephen Poliakoff, and Vikram Seth are born.

Marjorie Bowen, Norman Douglas, Jeffrey Farnol, Sir Desmond McCarthy, and Eva Perón die.

MAY 28 (Wed)

Writing to his distinguished friend Dom Bede Griffiths, Lewis corrects a misapprehension about his huge daily mail. It is not primarily men who write to him, he says, but women. He concludes: "The female, happy or unhappy, agreeing or disagreeing, is by nature a much more *epistolary* animal than the male."

JUNE 22 (Sun)

Tolkien finally offers the typescript of *The Lord of the Rings* to his publisher, George Allen & Unwin.

AUGUST

Tolkien records extracts from *The Hobbit* and the unpublished *The Lord of the Rings* on to a tape recorder while a guest of George Sayer in Malvern, Worcestershire. [*George Sayer at that time is a senior English master at Malvern College, and a former student and then friend of Lewis, through whom he met Tolkien and other Inklings.*] Tolkien has never seen such a machine before. He first records the Lord's Prayer in Gothic, to cast out, he says, any demons that may be lurking in it. [*The recordings were brought out as* Poems and Songs of Middle-earth *in* 1967 *and* J.R.R. Tolkien Reads and Sings His Lord of the Rings: The Two Towers/The Return of the King *in* 1975.]

Joy Davidman sails for England, bringing with her a manuscript she has started about the Ten Commandments.

AUGUST 20 (Wed)

Lewis arrives at Crawfordsburn, County Down, for an Irish holiday, in the company of Arthur Greeves.

SEPTEMBER 1 (Mon)

The Voyage of the "Dawn Treader" is published by Geoffrey Bles.

SEPTEMBER 8 (Mon)

Lewis sails from Belfast to Liverpool, on his way home from his Irish holiday.

SEPTEMBER 22 (Mon)

Lewis is awarded an honorary doctorate in literature by Laval University, Quebec.

SEPTEMBER 24 (Wed)

Lewis meets his correspondent, Helen Joy Davidman Gresham, for the first time. She is accompanied by her pen friend, Phyllis Williams, with whom she is staying in London. By invitation, he has lunch with them in the Eastgate Hotel in Oxford, very near Magdalen College. The fourth member of the party is meant to be Warren, but as he cannot attend his place is taken by George Sayer. "The party was a decided success," Sayer recalls. "Joy was of medium height, with a good figure, dark hair, and rather sharp features. She was an amusingly abrasive New Yorker, and Jack was delighted by her bluntness and her anti-American views. Everything she saw in England seemed to her far better than what she had left behind. Thus, of the single glass of sherry we had before the meal, she said: 'I call this civilized. In the States, they give you so much hard stuff that you start the meal drunk and end with a hangover.' She was anti-urban and talked vividly about the inhumanity of the skyscraper and of the new technology and of life in New York City. She attacked modern American literature. . . . 'Mind you, I wrote that sort of bunk myself when I was young.' Small farm life was the only good life, she said. Jack spoke up then, saying that, on his father's side, he came from farming stock. 'I felt that,' she said. 'Where else could you get the vitality?'"

NOVEMBER 29 (Sat)

Lewis's fifty-fourth birthday.

CHRISTMAS

Lewis invites Joy Davidman to The Kilns for the Christmas holiday. He gives her a copy of George MacDonald's *Diary of an Old Soul*. It carries an inscription in the author's handwriting: "Charlotte Kölle with kindest regards from George and Louisa MacDonald, April 27, 1885." Lewis writes in the flyleaf: "Later: C. S. Lewis to Joy Davidman, Christmas 1952." Warren, like his brother, delights in her company. He notes that Joy "liked walking, and she liked beer, and we had many merry days together."

1953

Nikita Khrushchev becomes first secretary of the Communist Party. Dwight D. Eisenhower is elected president of the United States. Edmund Hillary and Tenzing Norgay reach the summit of Mount Everest. In Britain the coronation of Queen Elizabeth II is celebrated.

Sebastian Faulks, Ronald Frame, Frank McGuinness, Tony Parsons, Lisa St. Aubin de Terán, and Jo Shapcott are born.

Hilaire Belloc, Theodore Powys, Dylan Thomas, Queen Mary, and Joseph Stalin die.

Warren publishes *The Splendid Century: Some Aspects of French Life in the Reign of Louis XIV.*

JANUARY 3 (Sat)

Joy leaves The Kilns for London after over a fortnight's stay. She carries the thought that Lewis has advised her to divorce her husband, Bill Gresham, in the light of what she told him about her marriage, and Bill's behavior.

JANUARY 25 (Sun)

Back in America Joy Davidman writes a full account of the visit to The Kilns to Chad Walsh, which, she says, included a visit to a Pantomime: "We all roared enthusiastically at the oldest jokes and joined in the choruses of the songs. I'll never forget Jack coming in loudly on something that went like this:

> Am I going to be a bad boy? No, no, no!
> Am I going to be awful? No, no, no!
> I promise not to put some crumbs in Aunt Fanny's bed,
> I promise not to pour the gravy over Baby's head. . . . etc."

MARCH 11 (Wed)

Lewis writes to his publisher, Geoffrey Bles, that he has completed the seventh and last of *The Chronicles of Narnia*. [*This is eventually called* The Last Battle.]

APRIL 25 (Sat)

Two Cambridge scientists—Francis Crick and James D. Watson— propose the structure of all biological life, a material code of two strands in a double helix, the DNA of a living thing.

JULY

The galleys of the first volume of Tolkien's *The Lord of the Rings*, *The Fellowship of the Ring*, are sent to him, and he works on them during the summer.

AUGUST 20 (Thu)–SEPTEMBER 14 (Mon)

Lewis and Warren set off for Crawfordsburn in Northern Ireland. They have a few days together. They visit Dundalk, and Rostrevor in Carlingford Lough. Lewis tells Warren that this area of County Down is his idea of

Chronology of "Narnia" and "England"

Note: These dates are based on C. S. Lewis's own time-line made after he completed *The Chronicles of Narnia*. "N.T." = Narnian Time; events in Narnian Time are in roman type. "A.D." = *events in the fictional England; they are in italic type.*

A.D. *1888 Digory Kirke born.*

A.D. *1889 Polly Plummer born.*

The Magician's Nephew

1 N.T. Creation of Narnia. Some animals given gift of speech. Digory plants the Tree of Protection. The White Witch Jadis enters Narnia but flees into the far north. Frank I becomes king of Narnia. *Polly Plummer and Digory Kirke carried into other worlds by magic rings and witness Narnia's birth, A.D. 1900.*

180 N.T. Prince Col, younger son of King Frank V of Narnia, leads some followers into Archenland (not then inhabited) and becomes first king of that country.

204 N.T. Outlaws from Archenland cross the southern desert and set up the new kingdom of Calormen. *Peter and Susan Pevensie born, A.D. 1927 and 1928.*

300 N.T. The empire of Calormen spreads dramatically. Calormenes colonize the land of Telmar to the west of Narnia.

Edmund Pevensie born, A.D. 1930.

302 N.T. The Calormenes in Telmar behave wickedly, and Aslan turns them into dumb beasts. King Gale of Narnia delivers the Lone Islands from a dragon and, as a result, is made emperor. *Eustace Scrubb and Jill Pole born, A.D. 1933. Lucy Pevensie born year previously.*

407 N.T. Olvin of Archenland turns the Giant, Pire, to stone.

460 N.T. Pirates stumbling into Narnia's world from ours take possession of Telmar.

898 N.T. The White Witch Jadis enters Narnia again out of the frozen north.

900 N.T. The Long Winter begins.

The Lion, the Witch and the Wardrobe

1000 N.T. The Pevensies arrive in Narnia. Edmund turns traitor, and Aslan sacrifices himself. The White Witch is defeated, ending the Long Winter. Peter becomes high king of Narnia. *The Pevensies, staying with Digory (now Professor) Kirke, reach Narnia through the magic wardrobe, A.D. 1940.*

Cont.

The Horse and His Boy

1014 N.T. King Peter successfully raids the troublesome Northern Giants. Queen Susan and King Edmund visit the Calormene court. King Lune of Archenland is reunited with his long-lost son, Prince Cor, and rebuffs a treacherous attack by Prince Rabadash of Calormen.

1015 N.T. The Pevensies hunt the White Stag and disappear from Narnia.

1050 N.T. Ram the Great follows Cor as king of Archenland.

1502 N.T. Queen Swanwhite of Narnia lives around this time.

1998 N.T. Invading Telmarines overwhelm Narnia. Caspian I becomes king of Narnia.

2290 N.T. Prince Caspian, son of Caspian IX, born. Caspian IX murdered by his brother Miraz, who takes the throne.

Prince Caspian

2303 N.T. Prince Caspian flees from his Uncle Miraz. Civil war falls upon Narnia. Caspian summons the Pevensie children with Queen Susan's magic horn. By their aid and that of Aslan, Miraz's forces are defeated and he is killed by his own side. Caspian becomes King Caspian X of Narnia. *The Pevensies are again drawn into Narnia by the call of the magic horn,* *while returning to school for the summer term A.D.* 1941.

2304 N.T. Caspian X defeats the Northern Giants.

The Voyage of the Dawn Treader

2306–7 N.T. Caspian X's great voyage to the end of the World. *During A.D.* 1942 *Edmund, Lucy, and Eustace are taken into Narnia. They take part in Caspian's voyage.*

2310 N.T. Caspian X marries Ramandu's daughter.

2325 N.T. Prince Rilian born.

2345 N.T. The queen killed by a serpent (the Green Witch). Rilian disappears.

The Silver Chair

2356 N.T. The quest to find Prince Rilian. Death of Caspian X. *Eustace and Jill, from Experiment House school, are caught into Narnia, A.D.* 1942.

2534 N.T. Outlaws become common in Lantern Waste. Towers are built to guard that region.

The Last Battle

2555 N.T. Rebellion of Shift the ape. Eustace and Jill come to King Tirian's aid. Narnia falls into the hands of the Calormenes by confusion. The last battle and end of Narnia. End of the World. *Serious rail accident involving the Bristol train, in which the Friends of Narnia die, A.D.* 1949.

Narnia. After a week, by arrangement, Warren heads back to England on August 28, leaving Lewis to enjoy a couple of weeks with Arthur Greeves. Lewis leaves Belfast for England on Monday, September 14.

SEPTEMBER 7 (Mon)

The Silver Chair is published by Geoffrey Bles.

OCTOBER 30 (Fri)

Warren's *The Splendid Century: Life in the France of Louis XIV* is published. It is dedicated "To My Brother," and portrays the social, moral, and political life of France in the seventeenth century. [*When it is published in the United States in* 1957 *the* New York Times *calls it "social history at its best."*]

NOVEMBER

At the beginning of the month, Joy sails, with her sons David and Douglas, to live in England, arriving in Liverpool on a gray, wet day. After journeying by train to London they take rooms in the Avoca House Hotel, 43 Belsize Park, Hampstead. Joy chooses the location because her pen friend Phyllis Williams and other writers live nearby. She soon installs the boys in Dane Court School near Woking, in Surrey, where they board.

NOVEMBER 29 (Sun)

Lewis's fifty-fifth birthday.

DECEMBER 17 (Thu)

Joy elicits an invitation for herself and her two sons to visit Lewis and Warren at The Kilns for four days. Douglas is disappointed with Lewis at first meeting. He has read the first four Narnia stories. Lewis cuts no heroic figure but looks very "ordinary." Lewis lends the boys the typescript of *The Horse and His Boy*, and promises to dedicate it to them. Writing to Bill Gresham immediately after the visit Joy acknowledges, "I shouldn't dream of visiting Jack often—we're much too exhausting an experience for that quiet bachelor household." [*Writing to Vera Mathews a few weeks later, Lewis confesses: "The energy of the American boy is astonishing: this pair thought nothing of a four-mile hike across broken country as an incident in a day of ceaseless activity, and when we took them up Magdalen tower, they said as soon as we got back to ground, 'Let's do it again.'"*]

CHAPTER EIGHT

Cambridge and Farewell to Shadowlands

(1954–1963)

When English Chairs became vacant at Oxford University C. S. Lewis was passed over several times. In her lengthy obituary of Lewis for the British Academy in 1965, Dame Helen Gardner reflected on Lewis's presence at Oxford at this time, and also the way that he was snubbed:

> In the early 1940s, when I returned to Oxford as a tutor, Lewis was by far the most impressive and exciting person in the Faculty of English. He had behind him a major work of literary history; he filled the largest lecture-room available for his lectures; and the Socratic Club, which he founded and over which he presided, for the free discussion of religious and philosophic questions, was one of the most flourishing and influential of undergraduate societies. In spite of this, when the Merton Professorship of English Literature fell vacant in 1946, the electors passed him over and recalled his own old tutor, F. P. Wilson, from London to fill the Chair.

Helen Gardner put this largely down to the fact that Lewis had become a household name because of writing popular theology such as his *Broadcast Talks* and *The Screwtape Letters*. She observed, "A good many people thought that shoemakers should stick to their lasts and disliked the thought of a professor of English Literature winning fame as an amateur theologian."

Cambridge University came to the rescue in 1954 with the offer of a new Chair of Medieval and Renaissance Literature that seemed tailor-made for Lewis. With a little help from Warren, Tolkien persuaded Lewis to take the post, even though he had declined it not once, but twice, in the face of the Cambridge vice chancellor's persistence. Lewis is most commonly associated in people's minds with Oxford; he was an undergraduate of University College; he was a fellow of Magdalen College for nearly thirty years; together with Tolkien he helped shape the curriculum of the Oxford English School; very many of his academic publications were written there; and, of course, he was the center of the Oxford Inklings. He was, however, to be closely associated with Cambridge University for over eight years, from late 1954 until his early retirement due to ill health in 1963. During those years he resided in his Cambridge college in midweek days during term time, while continuing to live at The Kilns. He would write several important books at Cambridge—*Studies in Words* (1960), *An Experiment in Criticism* (1961), and *The Discarded Image* (1964).

It was in September 1952 that Lewis had first met his future wife Joy Davidman (1915–1960) from New York, after they had corresponded since 1950. She was a poet and novelist who had been converted from Marxism to Christianity partly through reading C. S. Lewis's books. Not quite a year after their first meeting, Joy had come to live in England with her two sons, David (born 1944) and Douglas (born 1945), a dramatic move. She and Lewis now gradually became on closer terms. In retrospect he wrote, "Her mind was lithe and quick and muscular as a leopard. Passion, tenderness and pain were all equally unable to disarm it. It scented the first whiff of cant or slush; then sprang, and knocked you over before you knew what was happening." They eventually married in a civil ceremony in April 1956, with the sole intention at the time, on Lewis's part, of giving her and her sons British nationality.

In the autumn of that year they learned that Joy had terminal cancer. Lewis's affection for Joy was quickly turning into deep love, and a bedside Christian wedding ceremony took place on March 21, 1957. After prayer for healing, Joy had an unexpected reprieve. Her horridly diseased bones rejuvenated against all medical expectations, and by July 1957 she was well enough to get out and about. Throughout this period Lewis continued his work in Cambridge during term time. David and Douglas were away at boarding school. The next year Joy and Lewis had a fortnight's vacation in Ireland, and others followed. The remission was the beginning of the happiest few years of both their lives. Lewis confessed to fellow Inkling Nevill Coghill, "I never expected to have, in my sixties, the happiness that passed me by in my twenties."

The cancer eventually returned, but the Lewises were able to have a trip to Greece in the spring of the year of her death, 1960, a journey much desired by both of them. (The happiness that had come to Lewis so late in life, and subsequent bitter bereavement, has been made into two successful films and a play based around a similar script by William Nicolson, and entitled *Shadowlands*.)

In Warren's view, Lewis's marriage fulfilled "a whole dimension to his nature that had previously been starved and thwarted." It also put paid to a bachelor's doubt that God was an invented substitute for love. "For those few years H.[elen] and I feasted on love," Lewis recalled in A Grief Observed, "every mode of it—solemn and merry, romantic and realistic, sometimes as dramatic as a thunderstorm, sometimes as comfortable and unemphatic as putting on your soft slippers."

After Joy's death Lewis continued to commute between Oxford and Cambridge (by train, on the "Cambridge Crawler"), to write, to enjoy Warren's company, to care for Joy's two sons, and to endure the deep grief he felt at her departure. He recorded the process of that experience—his dark night of the soul—in A Grief Observed. He was increasingly beset by weakening illness, including osteoporosis, and died in November 1963, somewhat over three years after Joy, and a week before what would have been his sixty-fifth birthday. Warren survived him by another ten years.

Lewis's books continued to appear after his death, because of the plenitude of his writing—whether fiction, poetry, letters, essay, or longer literary criticism. Almost all of his work, even juvenilia, is still in print, and the sales of his popular theology writings and fiction have continued to grow throughout the world, with The Chronicles of Narnia becoming perennial bestsellers.

1954

Colonel Nasser takes power in Egypt. French forces are defeated by Vietnamese Communists at Dien Bien Phu; Communist forces occupy Hanoi. Algeria is troubled by terrorism, and France sends in troops. William Golding publishes The Lord of the Flies.

Iain Banks, Louis de Bernières, Alan Hollinghurst, Kazuo Ishiguro, Hanif Kureishi, Adam Mars-Jones, Tim Parks, and Fiona Pitt-Kethley are born.

Sir E. K. Chambers, James Hilton, W. R. Inge, Henri Matisse, and Francis Brett Young die.

JANUARY 23 (Sat)

Writing to his friend Bede Griffiths, Lewis admits a taste for the writings of Charles Dickens. In his view Dickens is the great author when it comes to exploring human affection; only he and Tolstoy—another firm favorite of Lewis's—present it adequately. Lewis goes on to say that Dickens's error is to believe that affection can replace agape, the presence of divine love in the human being. [*Lewis's letters at this time are preoccupied with the "four loves"— friendship, affection, eros (erotic love), and agape (sacrificial love, as in the original meaning of "charity"). In 1960 he will publish a book on the subject entitled* The Four Loves.]

MARCH 31 (Wed)

Cambridge University announces a new Chair of Medieval and Renaissance Literature, and invites applications by April 30, 1954.

MAY 10 (Mon)

As is the custom at both Oxford and Cambridge, the electors for university Chairs are distinguished scholars. Eight of them—including Tolkien and F. P. Wilson, both representing Oxford—assemble at the Old Schools in Cambridge, the university's administrative center. The other electors include Stanley Bennett, Basil Willey and E. M. W. Tillyard, coauthor with Lewis of *The Personal Heresy*. The unanimous verdict of the electors is to invite Lewis to take the post, even though he has not applied, and even though he has voiced his skepticism about the whole idea of the Renaissance in lectures he has given at Cambridge.

MAY 12 (Wed)

Lewis receives the invitation from the Cambridge vice chancellor, Henry Willink. He writes a hasty rejection. One reason he has not applied is because he has encouraged an interested colleague at Magdalen College, the philologist G. V. Smithers, to apply. He gives other reasons for not accepting the invitation—his domestic situation (by which he means the health of his brother, Warren, who is given to severe bouts of alcoholism) and his declining vitality. At fifty-five, Lewis feels that he has lost a lot of the energy of his earlier years, and he knows that the post would make new demands on him.

MAY 14 (Fri)

Willink writes back to Lewis, urging him to reconsider his decision and giving him a fortnight to do this.

MAY 15 (Sat)

Lewis responds, again declining the offer, elaborating on his reasons and specially mentioning Warren's "psychological health." He does, however, raise the issue of residency in Cambridge, almost as a plea or a query, but obviously assuming that he has to be resident during term time at least. [*Receiving Lewis's second refusal, Willink feels that there is no more he can do. After conferring with Basil Willey, he writes a letter of invitation to the "second string," Helen Gardner.*]

MAY 17 (Mon)

Unlike Lewis, Helen Gardner feels that she needs to consider the matter for some time and so does not reply immediately. Tolkien calls on Lewis to discuss the Cambridge business, not knowing of Willink's letter to Helen Gardner. He succeeds in convincing his friend to change his mind. In his persuasive way Tolkien manages to disarm all of Lewis's hesitations. In the first place, he points out, G. V. Smithers is not eligible, as a philologist, for the post, so there is no issue of conscience. Second, the residency arrangements at Cambridge are flexible—Lewis will only need to be in Cambridge part of the week during term time. While he is away, there are Fred Paxford (the groundsman and factotum), and Mrs. Miller (the housekeeper) to keep Warren company. Third, the transfer will do Lewis good. He needs a change of air, and there seems no likelihood of advancement at Oxford, despite the best efforts of Tolkien and Lewis's other friends.

MAY 18 (Tue)

Tolkien writes to the vice chancellor to report the good news and to ask him to reassure Lewis about residency.

MAY 19 (Wed)

Lewis, like Tolkien unaware of the offer to Helen Garner, writes to Willink expressing his willingness to accept Cambridge's welcome invitation and saying how ridiculous and foolish he feels. [*Helen Gardner in the meantime gets wind of the fact that Lewis has become interested in the post. She declines therefore, she later explains, "partly on account of having heard that Lewis was changing his mind, for it was obvious that this ought to be Lewis's chair." She takes up a post instead as reader in Renaissance English literature at Oxford—where she eventually, in 1966, becomes Merton Professor of English Literature.*]

JULY 29 (Thu)

Tolkien's *The Fellowship of the Ring* is published. This first edition Tolkien dedicates to "The Inklings."

AUGUST 5 (Thu)

The divorce proceedings between Bill and Joy (Davidman) Gresham are completed. Bill marries his lover, Renée Pierce, later that same day.

AUGUST 14 (Sat)

Lewis's review of *The Fellowship of the Ring* appears in *Time and Tide*. He writes, "This book is like lightning from a clear sky. To say that in it heroic romance, gorgeous, eloquent, and unashamed, has suddenly returned at a period almost pathological in its anti-romanticism, is inadequate. To us, who live in that odd period, the return—and the sheer relief of it—is doubtless the important thing. But in the history of Romance itself—a history which stretches back to the *Odyssey* and beyond—it makes not a return but an advance or revolution: the conquest of new territory."

SEPTEMBER 9 (Thu)

In a letter to Raynor Unwin, his publisher, Tolkien refers to the remarkable animosity against Lewis in places. "He warned me long ago," writes Tolkien, "that his support might do me as much harm as good. I did not take it seriously, though in any case I should not have wished other than to be associated with him—since only by his support and friendship did I ever struggle to the end of the labour. All the same many commentators seem to have preferred lampooning his remarks or his review to reading the book."

SEPTEMBER 16 (Thu)

English Literature in the Sixteenth Century, excluding Drama, Lewis's masterly contribution to the Oxford History of English Literature, is published.

OCTOBER 1 (Fri)

Lewis's appointment to Cambridge becomes effective, but because of remaining duties at Oxford he is given a dispensation until January 1, 1955.

NOVEMBER 9 (Tue)

Roger Lancelyn Green notes in his diary: "To 'B.[ird] and B.[aby]' to meet Lewis; his brother, McCallum, Tolkien, Gervase M.[athew] there as well. Very good talk, about Tolkien's book, horror comics, who is the most influential and important man in various countries: decided Burke for Ireland, Scott for Scotland, Shakespeare for England—but

————— *Lewis's Cambridge* —————

C. S. Lewis was appointed as Professor of Medieval and Renaissance Literature at Cambridge University in 1954. This beautiful city is dominated by a federation of colleges that make up the university. As at Oxford, students must belong to a college before becoming members of the university.

Magdalene College—Lewis was a fellow here until his retirement due to poor health in 1963. He had rooms in the college where he stayed midweek during term times. The college is famous for its Pepys Library.

Great St. Mary's (the University Church)—he attended services here from time to time.

The Round Church (Holy Sepulchre Church)—he is believed to have attended here from time to time.

Mill Lane Lecture Hall—Lewis gave his memorable inaugural lecture at this hall on November 29, 1954, upon taking up his Chair (afterwards broadcast on BBC radio).

University Library—the location of the high tower (156 feet in height) which dominates the Cambridge skyline and features unflatteringly in Lewis's abandoned science-fiction novel, "The Dark Tower."

there difficulties arose, Pitt and Wellington also being put forward."

NOVEMBER 11 (Thu)

Tolkien's *The Two Towers* is published.

NOVEMBER 29 (Mon)

Lewis's fifty-sixth birthday. He gives his inaugural lecture, *De Description Temporum*, at Cambridge today. Joy Davidman is present as his guest, as are many of his friends from Oxford. Some have to sit on the platform behind him, because of the cramped conditions. Joy finds the occasion "brilliant, intellectually exciting, unexpected, and funny as hell." In the crowded hall, she writes, "there were so many capped and gowned dons in the front rows that they looked like a rookery. Instead of talking in the usual professorial way about the continuity of culture, the value of traditions, etc., he announced that 'Old Western Culture,' as he called it, was practically dead, leaving only a few scattered survivors like himself." [*This lecture gives him a platform in which to set out a defense of "Old Western values" that he and Tolkien have championed in their work.*]

DECEMBER 3 (Fri)

Lewis completes his last tutorial at Magdalen College, Oxford.

1955

West Germany joins NATO. Sir Anthony Eden becomes British prime minister; Hugh Gaitskell becomes leader of the British Labour Party. A state of emergency is declared in Cyprus.

Carol Ann Duffy, Patrick McCabe, and Candia McWilliam are born.

Ruby M. Ayres, Gilbert Cannan, Albert Einstein, Alexander Fleming, Constance Holme, L. P. Jacks, and Thomas Mann die.

Lewis publishes *Surprised by Joy: The Shape of My Early Life* and *The Magician's Nephew*. Joy Gresham publishes *Smoke on the Mountain* (with a foreword by C. S. Lewis, and dedicated to him).

JANUARY 7 (Fri)

Lewis takes up residence in Magdalene College, Cambridge, midweekly during term times, while remaining the rest of the time at The Kilns. He thus switches his academic home from Magdalen College, Oxford. Lewis is delighted to retain an allegiance to Mary Magdalen, describing the change to Nevill Coghill, "I have exchanged the *impenitent* for the *penitent* Magdalen." He is enchanted by Cambridge. Its great charm, he observes, is that it is still a county town, if you rub below the academic sheen.

FEBRUARY

An entire issue of the humanist journal *Twentieth Century* focuses upon what it perceives as disastrous developments at Cambridge, heralded by Lewis's lecture. The editorial proclaims that its twelve contributors, from a variety of disciplines, agree "on the importance of free liberal, humane inquiry, which they conceive to be proper not only to a university community but to any group that claims to be civilized." Novelist E. M. Forster, one of the contributors, sees humanism threatened and religion on the march. Humanism's "stronghold in history, the Renaissance, is alleged not to have existed." [*Many in Cambridge do not like Lewis's inaugural lecture, or the new professor. They interpret Lewis's words as a reactionary attempt to restore a lost Christendom. Ironically, Lewis's deep interest in narrative, fantasy, and in the reader of literature puts him at the forefront of contemporary critical exploration.*]

MARCH 18 (Fri)–20 (Sun)

Joy spends the weekend at The Kilns with Lewis and Warren. While there she has a significant impact on the development of *Till We Have Faces*. Upon her arrival she finds Lewis "lamenting that he couldn't get a good idea for a book." The three of them sink into comfortable chairs and kick "a few ideas around" until one emerges. They have "another whisky each" and bounce the story concept back and forth. The very next day Lewis writes the first chapter, and passes it to Joy to comment on. Lewis then works over it and moves on to a second chapter. He admits to Joy how important he is finding her help on it. She feels that, though she cannot write "one-tenth as well as Jack," she can "tell him how to write more like himself!"

APRIL 29 (Fri)

Joy Davidman writes to Bill Gresham about Lewis's progress in composing *Till We Have Faces*. He is, she says, "now about three-quarters of the way through the book . . . and he says he finds my advice indispensable."

SUMMER

Joy, with her sons David and Douglas, rents No. 10, Old High Street, Headington. This is but a mile from The Kilns. Lewis spends a short holiday in Northern Ireland with Arthur Greeves in early September.

SEPTEMBER 19 (Mon)

Surprised by Joy is published.

SEPTEMBER 25 (Sun)

It is a beautiful autumn day. Lewis reports to Arthur Greeves in a letter that he got back to Oxford sporting a

"100 horse-power cold" to find The Kilns deserted. [*Warren had been drunk for a fortnight and is ensconced in a nursing home.*]

———————— *"Till We Have Faces"* ————————

Till We Have Faces, published in 1956 and dedicated "To Joy Davidman," is considered by many one of Lewis's best books. In it he retells the ancient story of Cupid and Psyche from Apuleius's *The Golden Ass*. In Apuleius's story, Psyche is so beautiful that Venus becomes jealous of her. Cupid, sent by Venus to make Psyche fall in love with an ugly creature, himself falls in love with her. After bringing her to a palace, he only visits her in the dark and forbids her to see his face. Out of jealousy, Psyche's sisters tell her that her lover is a monster who will devour her. She takes a lamp one night and looks at Cupid's face, but a drop of oil awakes him. In anger, the god leaves her. Psyche seeks her lover throughout the world. Venus sets her various impossible tasks, all of which she accomplishes except the last, when curiosity makes her open a deadly casket from the underworld. At last, however, she is allowed to marry Cupid.

In *Till We Have Faces*, Lewis essentially follows the classical myth, but retells it through the eyes of Orual, Psyche's half-sister, who seeks to defend her actions to the gods as being the result of deep love for Psyche, not jealousy. Psyche's outstanding beauty contrasts with Orual's ugliness (in later life she wears a veil). Orual's account records the bitter years of her suffering and grief at the loss of Psyche, haunted by the fantasy that she can hear her sister weeping. Orual records a devastating "undeception" she undergoes at the end of her life whereby, in painful self-knowledge, she discovers how her affection for Psyche has become poisoned by possessiveness.

In a letter, Lewis explains that Psyche represents a Christ-likeness, though she is not intended as a figure of Christ. Psyche in Lewis's novel is able to see a glimpse of the true God himself, in all his beauty, and in his legitimate demand for a perfect sacrifice. A further key to this story lies in the theme of the conflict of imagination and reason, so important to Lewis himself throughout his life. The final identification of the half-sisters Orual and Psyche in the story represents the harmony and satisfaction of reason and imagination, mind and soul, made fully possible, Lewis believes, only within the Christian worldview. The

Cont.

novel explores the depths of insight possible within the limitations of the pagan imagination, which foreshadows the marriage of myth and fact in the Gospel narratives of the New Testament.

Just as much of Lewis's *That Hideous Strength* was influenced particularly by Charles Williams, it could be said that *Till We Have Faces* bears the impression of Joy Davidman. Lewis likely enough owes to Joy his confidence to write the story from a female's perspective.

OCTOBER 20 (Thu)

The third and final volume of *The Lord of the Rings*, *The Return of the King*, is published.

Billy Graham meets privately with Lewis, along with John Stott, an Anglican church leader, on the eve of Graham's Cambridge University mission. In his autobiography Graham recalls: "We met in the dining room of his college, St. Mary Magdalene's, and we talked for an hour or more. I was afraid I would be intimidated by him because of his brilliance, but he immediately put me at my ease. I found him to be not only intelligent and witty but also gentle and gracious; he seemed genuinely interested in our [mission] meetings. 'You know,' he said as we parted, 'you have many critics, but I have never met one of your critics who knows you personally.'"

NOVEMBER 29 (Tue)

Lewis's fifty-seventh birthday.

1956

Egypt faces the Suez crisis. In Hungary a revolution is crushed by the Soviets.

Janice Galloway is born.

Michael Arlen, Sir Max Beerbohm, E. C. Bentley, Bertolt Brecht, Walter de la Mare, and A. A. Milne die.

FEBRUARY 8 (Wed)

Lewis sends Bede Griffiths, to whom the book is dedicated, a copy of his autobiography, *Surprised by Joy*. [*It had been published several months before, but Lewis had lost Bede Griffith's address in India.*] Lewis refers to his friend's explorations of Hinduism in relation to Christianity, and expresses anticipation for Griffith's forthcoming book on mysticism, which he has learned is soon to be published.

MARCH 19 (Mon)

Lewis publishes *The Last Battle*, the last of the Narnian Chronicles. [*It is awarded the Carnegie Medal, a prestigious award for children's books.*]

APRIL 23 (Mon)

It is St. George's Day. Lewis and Joy Davidman are married in a civil ceremony at the Oxford Registry Office, with the purpose of giving her and thus also her two sons British nationality. This is in order to prevent her threatened deportation by British immigration authorities. [*Lewis tells Roger Lancelyn Green (whom he treats as his future biographer) that the marriage is purely a matter of expediency and friendship. Lewis and Joy do not live together until after their Christian wedding at her bedside in Wingfield Hospital, Oxford, in March* 1957.]

MAY 13 (Sun)

Writing to Arthur Greeves, Lewis mentions his autobiography, *Surprised by Joy*. He tells Arthur that "Humphrey" Havard has expressed the view that the book leaves out too much. Havard has threatened to supplement it with a book entitled *Suppressed by Jack*.

SEPTEMBER 30 (Sun)

The *New York Times Book Review* carries a piece by Chad Walsh on the final volume of *The Chronicles of Narnia*. In it he says that *The Last Battle* "is one of the best . . . The Christian symbolism is clear enough, but the book can stand on its own feet as a deeply moving and hauntingly lovely story apart from the doctrinal content."

AUTUMN

Joy learns that she has cancer, and that it is inoperable. It is sudden, unexpected news, and Lewis is deeply shocked. Cancer is an old acquaintance. Joy's two boys are then

---
Top Ten Books

Near the end of his life, Lewis responded to a question from the *Christian Century*: "What books did most to shape your vocational attitude and your philosophy of life?" This was his list:

Phantastes, by George MacDonald

The Everlasting Man, by G. K. Chesterton

The Aeneid, by Virgil

The Temple, by George Herbert

The Prelude, by William Wordsworth

The Idea of the Holy, by Rudolf Otto

The Consolation of Philosophy, by Boethius

Life of Samuel Johnson, by James Boswell

Descent into Hell, by Charles Williams

Theism and Humanism, by Arthur James Balfour

about the same age as the Lewis brothers had been when their mother died; the parallels are haunting.

NOVEMBER 14 (Wed)

Joy is seriously ill, and Lewis determines to renew their vows in a Christian wedding ceremony.

NOVEMBER 29 (Thu)

Lewis's fifty-eighth birthday.

CHRISTMAS EVE (Mon)

Because it has become necessary to make known their private marriage back in April, an announcement put by Lewis appears in the *Times*: "A marriage has taken place between Professor C. S. Lewis of Magdalene College Cambridge, and Mrs. Joy Gresham, now a patient in the Churchill Hospital, Oxford. It is requested that no letters be sent." [*Joy is later transferred to the Wingfield Hospital, Oxford.*]

1957

Anthony Eden resigns; Harold Macmillan becomes British prime minister. The European Economic Community (EEC) is established with the Treaty of Rome. The USSR launches Sputnik I.

Nick Hornby and Irvine Welsh are born.

Roy Campbell, Joyce Cary, A. E. Coppard, Lord Dunsany, Oliver St. John Gogarty, Ronald Knox, Wyndham Lewis, Malcolm Lowry, John Middleton Murry, Michael Sadleir, and Dorothy L. Sayers die.

Lewis continues his work in Cambridge on midweek days during term time. David and Douglas are away at boarding school. During this year Joy experiences an extraordinary remission from her near-terminal struggle with cancer.

FEBRUARY 18 (Mon)

In London, BBC television broadcasts the first in a series of a new magazine program, called Tonight.

MARCH 21 (Thu)

A bedside Christian wedding ceremony takes place in the Wingfield Hospital, Oxford, where Joy is being treated. Lewis and Joy are married by the Reverend Peter Bide, in accordance with the procedures of the Church of England. The vicar, at Lewis's request, prays for Joy's healing, and lays hands on her. He has a ministry of healing. [*Joy comes home to The Kilns to die, joined by David and Douglas. But she has an unexpected reprieve. Her horridly diseased bones soon rejuvenate against all medical expectations.*]

APRIL 5 (Fri)

Lewis writes to Arthur Greeves to tell him that there is no prospect of an Irish vacation for him this year. Joy is now back at The Kilns. The hospital, he says, has sent her home, not because she is recovering, but because there is nothing more they can do for her. She is totally bed-ridden, even having to be lifted on to the bedpan.

JUNE 21 (Fri)

When Roger Lancelyn Green meets Joy for the first time at The Kilns she is still confined to bed. The bed is in the sitting room. She is attended by a day nurse and a night nurse.

AUGUST 21 (Wed)

It is sunny this morning for the first time after many days. Writing to Arthur Greeves Lewis reports on his present troubles. Warren is in Our Lady of Lourdes Hospital in

Drogheda, Ireland, recovering from an alcoholic bout, and talking of a serious heart complaint. Lewis himself is suffering from painful osteoporosis. He reveals that the combined woes of Joy's suffering, Warren's plight, and his own pain have made him very tired.

SEPTEMBER 24 (Tue)

Roger and June Lancelyn Green, with their elder son, call at The Kilns to pick up Douglas. They are en route to Dane Court School in Surrey, where their son is to start his first term and where Douglas is already a student. They find Joy up from her bed, but still in an invalid chair.

NOVEMBER 29 (Fri)

Lewis's fifty-ninth birthday.

DECEMBER 10 (Tue)

Lewis writes, "Joy is now walking: with a stick and a limp, but we never dreamed of getting so far."

1958

There is the Algerian crisis, and General de Gaulle is elected president of the Fifth French Republic.

Roddy Doyle, Helen Fielding, Caryl Phillips, and Benjamin Zephaniah are born.

F. Tennyson Jesse, Rose Macaulay, G. E. Moore, Charles Morgan, Alfred Noyes, Lennox Robinson, Sir John Collings Squire, Marie Stopes, H. M. Tomlinson, and Ralph Vaughan Williams die.

Lewis is elected an honorary fellow of University College, Oxford. Warren publishes *Assault on Olympus: The Rise of the House of Gramont between 1604 and 1678*.

MARCH 26 (Wed)

Writing to Arthur Greeves, Lewis speaks of things being wonderful at the moment. This is because Joy is able to be up all day, and can use the stairs and get into and out of cars. She is, inevitably, even redecorating The Kilns.

MAY

Joy writes to Roger Lancelyn Green: "The Kilns is now a real home with paint on the walls, ceilings properly repaired, clean sheets on the beds—we can receive and put

─────── *The Four Loves* ───────

The four loves distinguished by Lewis are affection, friendship, eros, and charity (divine love).

Affection is the humblest and most widespread of the four loves. It is not a particularly appreciative love. In human life, the other loves operate through it.

Friendship is the least instinctive, biological, and necessary of our loves. Lewis points out that the ancients put the highest value upon this love, as in the friendship between David and Jonathan. Friendship, as the least biological of the loves, refutes sexual or homosexual explanations for its existence. Friendship, reckoned Lewis, made good people better and bad people worse.

Eros is the kind of love that lovers are within or "in"—the state of being in love. Eros is an important theme in his science-fiction story *That Hideous Strength* (in the marriage of Jane and Mark Studdock), and in *Till We Have Faces* (in Psyche's love for the god of the mountain, the Westwind).

Charity, or divine love, the fourth love, transcends all earthly loves in being a gift-love. All human loves are by nature need-loves. Our human loves are potential rivals to the love of God, and can only take their proper place if our first allegiance is to God. It is the divine likeness in all our human loves (affection, friendship, and eros) that is their heavenly, and thus permanent, element. Our own loves, like our moral choices, judge us.

up several guests. . . . I've got a fence round the woods and all the trespassers chased away; I shoot a starting pistol at them and they run like anything! We'd love a visit."

EARLY JULY

Joy and Lewis have what they consider a belated fort-night's honeymoon in Ireland, in perfect weather. They visit counties Louth, Down, and Donegal. For both, it is their first airflight, and they are enchanted by the cloud formations, viewed from above.

JULY 26 (Sat)

Lewis and Joy visit Dane Court School to see Douglas for the end-of-term display and prize-giving.

AUGUST 19/20 (Tue/Wed)

Lewis records ten talks on *The Four Loves* in London for air-ing in the United States.

SEPTEMBER 8 (Mon)

Reflections on the Psalms is published in London by Geoffrey Bles, Lewis's first book in two years.

NOVEMBER 11 (Tue)

Death of Warren's friend, Lt. Col. Herbert Denis Parkin.

NOVEMBER 29 (Sat)

Lewis's sixtieth birthday.

1959

Fidel Castro seizes power in Cuba. The European Free Trade Association (EFTA) is established.

Dermot Bolger, Ben Okri, and Jeanette Winterson are born.

G. D. H. Cole, Jacob Epstein, Sir Walter Wilson Greg, Laurence Housman, Edwin Muir, Stanley Spencer, and G. M. Young die.

Lewis is awarded the honorary degree of doctor of litera-ture by the University of Manchester. Warren Lewis pub-lishes *Louis XIV: An Informal Portrait.*

JANUARY

"I have stood by the bedside of a woman whose thighbone was eaten through with cancer," writes Lewis in *Atlantic Monthly.* She "had thriving colonies of the disease in many other bones as well. It took three people to move her in bed. The doctors predicted a few months of life; the nurs-es (who often know better), a few weeks. A good man laid his hands on her and prayed. A year later the patient was walking (uphill, too, through rough woodland) and the man who took the last X-ray photos was saying, 'These bones are as solid as rock. It's miraculous.'"

MARCH 23/24 (Mon/Tue)

Sometime during the night Jane McNeill, a lifelong Belfast friend of the Lewis brothers, dies unexpectedly. [*Lewis had dedicated* That Hideous Strength *to her, where the main character is called Jane.*]

MARCH 25 (Wed)

The death of Jane McNeill highlights to Warren the loss of his brother's company because of Lewis's life with Joy. He notes in his diary: "There was no illness, & she [Jane McNeill] had been at a lunch party on Monday 23rd. Lord teach us to number our days. . . . I shall miss her dreadful-ly, for though we didn't often meet, we exchanged long letters four or five times a year, and she, Grundy

[Gundreda] & K. [Kelsie] were the only three people left with whom I could share a part of my life. . . . Now that Janie is gone, & I have also lost the SPB [i.e., his brother], there is no one whom I can ever remind again of the horrible winter activities of Strandtown, the Henrys, Leslie, Stokeses and so on, & little reminiscent jokes wh. no one can share with me. And now I shall never know what my dear Janie thought of Joy!"

APRIL 29 (Wed)

Lewis writes in consolation to Rev. Peter Bide, who prayed for Joy's healing at her bedside, and whose own wife, Lewis has learned, is dying from cancer. He refers to the horror of the monotony of anxiety. He suggests that his friend, so far as is possible, treats his anxiety as being also an illness. The mental anguish of fear is something that has to be suffered before he and his wife are "out of the wood." Any amount of faith cannot reduce the dismay of their situation. [*Margaret Bide will die in September 1960, leaving four children.*]

JUNE 5 (Fri)

Tolkien delivers his "valedictory address" in Oxford as Merton Professor of English Language and Literature. He says, "Philology is the foundation of humane letters." He also refers to his African birth, and adds: "I have the hatred of *apartheid* in my bones; and most of all I detest the segregation or separation of Language and Literature. I do not care which of them you think White."

OCTOBER 21 (Wed)

Lewis reveals in a letter to Chad Walsh a dreadful blow: a routine X-ray on Joy shows that the cancer has returned to bones in several parts of her body. [*The healing has been a remission rather than a lasting cure.*]

NOVEMBER 29 (Sun)

Lewis's sixty-first birthday.

1960

The Sharpeville massacre occurs in South Africa. An American U-2 aircraft is shot down by the USSR. Princess Margaret marries Anthony Armstrong-Jones. Leonid Brezhnev becomes president of the USSR. Adolf Eichmann is arrested. France becomes a nuclear power.

Prince Andrew and Ian Rankin are born.

Aneurin Bevan, Sir Herbert Grierson, Sir Lewis Namier, Sylvia Pankhurst, Boris Pasternak, Eden Phillpotts, Sir Leonard Woolley, and Dornford Yates die.

Despite the remorseless return of Joy's cancer, the Lewises are able to take a trip to Greece this spring, a journey much desired by both of them. Three months later, in July, Joy dies.

JANUARY 17 (Sun)

It is 9.50 in the morning. Lewis has been answering his voluminous correspondent as fast as he can, pushing his dip pen across the paper for an hour and a half solid. He tells one correspondent, Mrs. Vera Gebbert, as he writes to her in his small handwriting, that he is keeping pretty well, even though he always feels very tired.

MARCH 28 (Mon)

Lewis publishes *The Four Loves*, including reflections on friendship inspired by his friendship with Tolkien, Charles Williams, and the Inklings.

APRIL 3 (Sun)–14 (Thu)

Lewis and Joy, accompanied by Roger Lancelyn Green and his wife, June, travel to Greece, visiting Athens, Mycenae,

Rhodes, Herakleon, and Knossos. There is a one-day stop in Pisa on the return. Lewis, jokingly, finds it hard not to relapse into paganism in Attica; it proves difficult, at Daphni, not to pray to Apollo the Healer for Joy.

APRIL 4 (Mon)

From Green's diary: "Joy was able to get right up to the Acropolis, where she and Lewis found a seat on the steps

Ten Things Lewis Believed about Heaven

1. Heaven is a literal place, though, in our present, fallen situation, it will not be discovered by searching through the universe in space rockets.

2. It is a new nature that God has planned, the ultimate context of a fully human life, bodies and all.

3. Heaven is closely linked with "joy" as Lewis understood it, as an inconsolable longing that signals our ultimate happiness.

4. As heaven is part of creation, it is not worthy of our ultimate aim.

5. It is no more mercenary, however, to desire heaven than to wish to marry the person one loves.

6. In this present life, the situation is like being on the wrong side of a shut door, with heaven on the other side.

7. Heaven is like the morning—we respond to the freshness and purity of morning, but that does not make us fresh and pure.

8. Heaven is founded upon the paradox that, the more we abandon ourselves to God, the more fully ourselves we become.

9. Heaven is varied; hell monotonous. Heaven is brimful of meaning; hell is the absence of meaning. Heaven is reality itself, hell a ghost or shadow.

10. Heaven is not without work: humans there shall be office bearers of responsibility in the universe.

of the Propylaea and sat drinking in the beauty of the Parthenon and Erechtheum—columns of honey gold and old ivory against the perfect blue sky, with an occasional white cloud."

APRIL 5 (Tue)

From Green's diary: "When we got to Mycenae we had ideal weather: a great lowering dark cloud over the citadel, but blue sky beyond. Jack was immensely impressed by the entrance between the towering walls of Cyclopean masonry and through the Lion Gate: I shall never forget the way he paused suddenly and exclaimed: 'My God! The Curse is still here,' in a voice hushed between awe and amazement."

APRIL 12 (Tue)

On an all-day excursion across Crete the tourist group stops for lunch. Green records, "On a balcony overlooking the Phaistos ruins we all sat at a big table: Minos wine 'off the wood' flowed in abundance, and Jack was the life and soul of the party, keeping 'the table in a roar.' . . . We'd realized for some time that Joy was often in pain, and alcohol was the best alleviation: so I had become adept at diving into the nearest taverna, ordering 'tessera ouzo.'"

APRIL 18 (Mon)

It is Joy's forty-fifth birthday.

MAY

Joy and Edith Tolkien are in hospital together at the Acland Nursing Home—Joy for her cancer and Edith because of her severe arthritis. While Tolkien is visiting Edith Lewis introduces Joy to him.

MAY 3 (Tue)

Roger Lancelyn Green stays with Lewis at Magdalene College, Cambridge, and finds him working on a new novel, *After Ten Years*. [*With Joy's death, the inspiration ends, and only a fragment of the novel remains.*]

MAY 20 (Fri)

Joy undergoes further cancer treatment, and, in her words, is "made an amazon" in surgery on her right breast.

JUNE 16 (Thu)

Today is Warren's birthday. Though gravely ill, Joy gives him a present of a dozen handkerchiefs.

LATE JUNE

Joy is able to return home to The Kilns to die.

JULY 12 (Tue)

Though remaining in bed, Joy feels much better. She feels in good spirits, does a crossword puzzle with Lewis, and in the evening they play a game of Scrabble.

JULY 13 (Wed)

Warren, who sleeps in the bedroom above the room in which Joy is sleeping, hears her suddenly begin screaming, at 6.15 in the morning, something she has never done before, in all her pain. He runs down to her, and Lewis, following, telephones the doctor. He arrives in a little over half an hour and injects her with painkiller. At 1.30 p.m. Lewis accompanies her to the hospital in an ambulance. She is conscious much of the time and able to talk to Lewis for the last hours of her life, and in little pain because of drugs she is given. At one point, after the surgeon private-ly informs Lewis that Joy is dying rapidly, he returns to her bedside to tell her. At 11.20 p.m. Joy says, "I am at peace with God," smiles, and dies. Twenty minutes later Lewis is back at The Kilns, reporting the news to his anx-ious brother. [Joy's body will be cremated on July 18, at the nearby Oxford crematorium. Later, a poem in her memory by Lewis is engraved on a plaque near where her ashes have been scattered.]

AUGUST 5 (Fri)

In a letter to a correspondent Lewis affirms his faith in the resurrection of the body, but finds the state of those who have died until the resurrection unimaginable. He wonders if Joy is in the same time as those left alive; if not, it makes no sense to wonder where she is now.

SEPTEMBER 9 (Fri)

Lewis's *Studies in Words* is published by Cambridge University Press (exploring words like "Nature," "Sad," "Free," and "Conscience and Conscious").

NOVEMBER 29 (Tue)

Lewis's sixty-second birthday.

1961

John F. Kennedy is inaugurated as president of the United States. Yuri Gagarin becomes the first man in space. The Berlin Wall is built. U.N. Secretary-General Dag Hammarskjöld is killed in an air crash.

Jonathan Coe, Arundhati Roy, and Will Self are born.

H. C. Bailey, Oliver Onions, Frank Richards, Angela Thirkell, Ernest Hemingway, and Carl Jung die.

Lewis publishes *A Grief Observed*. Warren Lewis publishes *The Scandalous Regent: A Life of Philippe, Duc d'Orleans, 1674–1723*, and of his family.

JANUARY 25 (Wed)

Arthur Greeves is planning to visit England. Lewis warmly invites Arthur to stay at The Kilns during his visit.

FEBRUARY 28 (Tue)–MARCH 1 (Wed)

Lewis meets with the other members of the Anglican Commission to Revise the Psalter, at Lambeth Palace in London. The Commission includes the poet T. S. Eliot. This is one of several occasions when they work on modernizing the sixteenth-century translation of the psalms then in use. [*The Commission is charged with producing "for the consideration of the Convocations a revision of the text of the Psalter designed to remove obscurities and serious errors of translation yet such as to retain, as far as possible, the general character in style and rhythm of [Miles] Coverdale's version and its suitability for congregational use."*]

MAY 9 (Tue)

From Magdalene College, Cambridge, Lewis writes to Mrs. Margaret Gray, who has asked him to recommend some reading. Like Lewis she is an adult convert to Christianity. As well as suggesting from his own books, *Transposition*, *The Great Divorce*, or *The Four Loves*, he includes a long list of titles from a range of writers past and present, including G. K. Chesterton, Charles Williams, Dorothy L. Sayers, St. Augustine, and George Herbert.

JUNE 22 (Thu)

Lewis and his driver collect Arthur Greeves from London. [*The two days vacation they have together in Oxford Lewis later describes to Arthur as the happiest he has had for a considerable time.*]

JULY 2 (Sun)

Lewis is supposed to have an operation for his enlarged prostate gland, but it is deemed too dangerous, as his kidneys are also infected. He is fitted with a catheter and put on a low-protein diet instead. [*Later in the year Lewis will receive blood transfusions every few weeks.*]

SEPTEMBER 5 (Tue)

In his diary, Warren complains of the "discomforts of Kiln life." This is partly to do with the presence of David and Douglas over the holidays, whose teenage behavior he finds difficult to cope with. However, he also has "constant anxiety about J.[ack], overworked." The discomfort is affecting his sleep. "There have been nights this summer when I woke suddenly in sheer terror, telling myself that I was trapped without hope in this hell hole wh. I wd. never leave again until I do so in a hearse."

OCTOBER 20 (Fri)

In the privacy of his diary Warren notes gladly that, during the year to this date, he has been a teetotaller for 355 days. [*The next year he will abstain for 298 days.*]

NOVEMBER 29 (Wed)

Lewis's sixty-third birthday.

NOVEMBER 30 (Thu)

Warren Lewis publishes *Levantine Adventurer: The Travels and Missions of the Chevalier d'Arvieux, 1653–1697.*

1962

Adolf Eichmann is executed. Algerian independence is established. The Telstar satellite is launched. The Cuban Missile Crisis takes place.

Richard Aldington, Clifford Bax, Wilfrid Gibson, Patrick Hamilton, Vita Sackville-West, R. H. Tawney, and G. M. Trevelyan die.

During this year Lewis is forced to spend much of his time at home because of his afflictions. On Wednesday evenings his local parish priest, Ronald Head, serves him Communion at The Kilns. Friends will take him out to The Lamb and Flag for beer, and to The Trout at Godstow for a meal afterwards. He has many visits from friends, such as Owen Barfield, Cecil Harwood, Roger Lancelyn Green, George Sayer, John Wain, Kenneth Tynan, and Christopher Derrick.

MAY 22 (Tue)

Lewis writes to T. S. Eliot from The Kilns: "You need not sympathize too much: if my condition keeps me from doing some things I like, it also excuses me from doing a good many things I don't!" He expresses a wish to discuss with Eliot the topical issue of punishment—he feels the modern view has dangerously excluded the element of retribution. Superficially this seems humane, but in fact is introducing a "vile tyranny."

AUGUST 10 (Fri)

In a letter to Christopher Derrick, Lewis discusses art history, in which they have a mutual interest. Lewis praises the work of E. H. Gombrich, giving him an alpha, with as many plusses, he says, as Derrick pleases. He believes that writers on art have far outstripped contemporary writers on literature.

SEPTEMBER 13 (Thu)

Joy's ex-husband, Bill Gresham, takes a fatal overdose of sleeping pills after discovering that he has cancer of the throat and tongue, and would also likely become blind.

OCTOBER 28 (Sun)

Nikita Khrushchev promises that Russian missiles based in Cuba will be dismantled and sent back to the Soviet Union. In return John F. Kennedy assures Russia that he will not invade Cuba and will lift the blockade. Thus the world steps back from the brink of nuclear war.

NOVEMBER 20 (Tue)

Lewis replies to Tolkien's invitation to attend a dinner to celebrate publication of *English and Medieval Studies Presented to J. R. R. Tolkien on the Occasion of his Seventieth Birthday* (1962). "Dear Tollers—What a nice letter. I also like beer less than I did, tho' I have retained the taste for general talk. But I shan't be at the Festschrift dinner. I wear a catheter, live on a low protein diet, and go early to bed. I am, if not a lean, at least a slippered, pantaloon."

NOVEMBER 29 (Thu)

Lewis's sixty-fourth birthday.

CHRISTMAS EVE (Mon)

Lewis replies to a letter from Tolkien: "All my philosophy of history hangs upon a sentence of your own, 'Deeds were done which were not wholly in vain.' " [*He refers to a line in* The Fellowship of the Ring (Book 1, Chapter 2): "*There was sorrow then too, and gathering dark, but great valour, and great deeds that were not wholly in vain.*"]

1963

Charles de Gaulle vetoes British membership in the EEC. Sir Alec Douglas-Home is elected British prime minister. John F. Kennedy is assassinated; Lyndon B. Johnson becomes president of the United States.

Simon Armitage, Don Paterson, and Meera Syal are born.

Remarkable Memory

The critic Kenneth Tynan describes a remarkable instance in an interview with Stephen Schofield:

> [C. S. Lewis] had the most astonishing memory of any man I have ever known. . . . Once when I was invited to his rooms after dinner for a glass of beer, he played a game. He directed, "Give me a number from one to forty."
>
> I said, "Thirty."
>
> He acknowledged, "Right. Go to the thirtieth shelf in my library." Then he said, "Give me another number from one to twenty."
>
> I answered, "Fourteen."
>
> He continued, "Right. Get the fourteenth book off the shelf. Now let's have a number from one to a hundred."
>
> I said, "Forty-six."
>
> "Now turn to page forty-six! Pick a number from one to twenty-five for the line of the page."
>
> I said, "Six."
>
> "So," he would say, "read me that line." He would always identify it—not only by identifying the book, but he was also usually able to quote the rest of the page. This is a gift. This is something you can't learn. It was remarkable.

Phyllis Bottome, Jean Cocteau, Robert Frost, Christopher Hassall, Aldous Huxley, Louis MacNeice, Sylvia Plath, and John Cowper Powys die.

JANUARY 25 (Fri)

Bad weather conditions in Oxfordshire and elsewhere resemble the bitter winter of 1947. Warren records in his diary the "34th consecutive day of the worst winter this country has endured since 1882." He and his brother, he notes, have not been able to attend church, at Holy Trinity, Headington Quarry, since Christmas Day.

MARCH 3 (Sun)

Writing to Arthur Greeves to arrange a vacation in Ireland with him, Lewis observes: "I saw snowdrops for the first time last week." [*The vacation is eventually cancelled because of Lewis's serious heart trouble.*]

MAY 7 (Tue)

Sherwood E. Wirt interviews Lewis in his rooms at Magdalene College, Cambridge. In it Lewis reaffirms his full commitment to "mere Christianity."

JUNE 17 (Mon)

In his diary Roger Lancelyn Green notes perhaps the last record of The Inklings: "To 'Lamb and Flag' about 12, there joined CSL. Several others—Gervase Mathew, Humphrey Havard, Colin Hardie, and a young American, Walter Hooper, who is writing some sort of book or thesis about Jack." [*After Lewis's death Ronald McCallum will try to restart the Monday morning Inklings meetings, but Lewis's presence proves to be indispensable and the experiment is dropped.*]

JULY 15 (Mon)

Lewis is admitted to Acland Nursing Home for a blood transfusion (due to his kidney complaint) and has a heart attack at 5 p.m.

JULY 16 (Tue)

Lewis is in a coma and given Extreme Unction (in which a dying person, unable to take Christian Communion, is anointed). To everyone's surprise, Lewis comes out of unconsciousness and asks for a cup of tea. [*During this week he is visited by Maureen Blake and Tolkien. Lewis tells George Sayer that he has engaged Walter Hooper, a "young American," as his "secretary." Warren, who has served as his brother's secretary for many years, is in Ireland at the time and recovering from an alcoholic binge, thus oblivious to his brother's brush with death.*]

SUMMER

Lewis resigns his position at Cambridge during the summer and is then elected an honorary fellow of Magdalene College, Cambridge.

AUGUST

Lewis returns to The Kilns. He has much-needed secretarial help from Walter Hooper, who comes in daily. A nurse is in residence to care for him.

SEPTEMBER

Warren returns home to The Kilns after having been in Ireland for several months.

AUTUMN

Tolkien and his eldest son John visit Lewis at The Kilns. John Tolkien remembers: "We drove over to The Kilns for what turned out to be a very excellent time together for about an hour. I remember the conversation was very much about the *Morte d'Arthur* and whether trees died."

EARLY OCTOBER

Warren writes, in his *Memoir of C. S. Lewis*: "In their way, these last weeks were not unhappy. Joy had left us, and once again—as in the earliest days—we could turn for comfort only to each other. The wheel had come full circle: once again we were together in the little end room at home, shutting out from our talk the ever-present knowledge that the holidays were ending, that a new term fraught with unknown possibilities awaited us both."

NOVEMBER 22 (Fri)

Today begins much as any day. Lewis and Warren breakfast together, they tackle the correspondence, and afterwards settle to the crossword from the newspaper. After lunch Lewis nods off in his chair; Warren suggests that he will be better in bed, and Lewis goes off to his room. At four, as usual, Warren prepares a pot of tea. He finds his brother comfortable and drowsy. The few words that they exchange are their last words together. An hour and a half later, when all is quiet except for the ticking of the clock, Warren hears a crash. He is instantly at his feet and running into Lewis's room. His brother is lying slumped by the foot of his bed. His breathing stops within three or four minutes. He is dead. In the horror of that realization, the thought flashes across Warren's mind that, whatever happens to him in the future, it can be nothing worse than this.

It is one week before C. S. Lewis's sixty-fifth birthday.

The same day President John F. Kennedy is assassinated, and Aldous Huxley dies.

[*Lewis dies from a combination of "old man's troubles"—afflictions of bladder, prostate, and weakened heart—and indifferent medical care. His grave is in the yard of Holy Trinity Church in Headington Quarry, Oxford.*]

NOVEMBER 26 (Tue)

In a letter to his daughter Priscilla, written immediately after Lewis's funeral that day, Tolkien says: "So far I have felt the normal feelings of a man of my age—like an old

Churches Associated with C. S. Lewis

St. Mark's Church, Dundela, Belfast. Church of Ireland (i.e., Anglican). The first rector of St. Mark's was Lewis's grandfather, Rev. Thomas Hamilton, who lived in the Old Rectory within the church grounds. The infant C. S. Lewis was baptized by his grandfather on January 29, 1899, at the font to the west end of the church. Lewis's father, Albert, served as a church warden, trustee, and the first Sunday School super-intendent. Albert gave the church silver vessels used for the sacrament of Communion to this day. Some stained-glass windows were present-ed in memory of their parents by the Lewis brothers in 1932. The win-dows, which are in the south aisle and portray Mark, Luke, and James, were made by Michael Healy, a Dublin artist. The church magazine is called *The Lion*, after the traditional symbol of St. Mark.

Magdalen College Chapel, Oxford. Lewis began attending daily services here regularly during term time while on his journey from theism (when he accepted God, after having been an atheist) to belief in Christ. Work on the original chapel was completed in 1480, and its interior was sub-stantially restored and renovated between 1828 and 1835. In the antechapel there is a brass memorial to Lewis.

Holy Trinity Church, Headington Quarry, Oxford. About a mile from The Kilns, this was Lewis's parish church, which he attended regularly. He is buried here in a simple grave together with his brother, Warren. Mrs. Janie Moore is buried in the same churchyard. Lewis was invited to preach several times, and got the idea for *The Screwtape Letters* during a Sunday morning service here. On the left side of the church a brass pew marker commemorates where Lewis and Warren habitually sat. Lewis would arrive late and leave early to avoid the embarrassment of celebrity. Near the marked pew is a window on which characters and scenes from Narnia are delicately etched. It was dedicated in 1991 in memory of two people who died in childhood.

The University Church of St. Mary the Virgin, High Street, Oxford. This venera-ble church stands right in the center of the original walled town of Oxford, and the university grew around it as various colleges were founded. St. Mary's has been a parish church since Anglo-Saxon times, but by the thirteenth century it had become part of the university

Cont.

institution, housing the university government and its first library, the place where degrees were conferred and learned debate took place. It was not until the middle of the seventeenth century that all university business was transferred from the church. Lewis preached two of his most notable sermons here—"Learning in Wartime" (October 22, 1939) and "The Weight of Glory" (June 8, 1941). On both occasions the church was heaving with undergraduates and scholars. The church has many other historical associations, with, for example, John Wesley and with the martyrs Latimer, Ridley, and Cranmer.

The Church of St. Cross, Holywell, Oxford. A number of the Inklings and others of Lewis's friends or associates are buried here: Charles Williams, H. V. D. "Hugo" Dyson, Austin and Katharine Farrer, Stella Aldwinckle, George S. Gordon (who taught Lewis), and Kenneth Tynan (ex-student of Lewis's and renowned playwright and literary critic). Also resting here are Kenneth Grahame (author of *The Wind in the Willows*) and James Blish (science-fiction author, who once dedicated a book to Lewis). Charles Williams often attended this church.

---

tree that is losing all its leaves one by one: this feels like an axe-blow near the roots. Very sad that we should have been so separated in the last years; but our time of close communion endured in memory for both of us. I had a mass said this morning, and was there, and served; and Havard and Dundas Grant were present."

1964

Letters to Malcolm: Chiefly on Prayer is published, prepared by Lewis for publication before his death. Warren brings out *Memoirs of the Duc de Saint-Simon.*

1965

Warren suffers a minor stroke that leaves his right hand slightly paralyzed. He also experiences a temporary speech impairment.

Endnotes

CHAPTER 1

Page 3: "chivalrous mice and rabbits who rode out in complete mail": from
C. S. Lewis, *Surprised by Joy* (London: Bles), 1955, ch. 1.

Page 4: "All settled happiness, all that was tranquil and reliable": *Surprised
by Joy*, ch. 1.

Page 10: "He never actually obeyed you": *Surprised by Joy*, ch. 10.

Page 15: "She was the most beautiful woman": *Surprised by Joy*, ch. 3.

Page 24: "I . . . certainly wish I could have been with you": C. S. Lewis,
Collected Letters, Vol. I (London: HarperCollins), 2000, p. 188.

Page 27: "to combine my two chief literary pleasures": *Surprised by Joy*, ch. 1.

Page 27: Quotations from "My Life. By Jacks Lewis, 1907" quoted in Walter
Hooper, *C. S. Lewis: A Companion and Guide* (London: HarperCollins), 1996,
pp. 5-6, and A. N. Wilson, *C. S. Lewis: A Biography* (London: Collins),
1990, p.18.

Page 31: "You have never refused me anything": *Lewis Papers: Memoirs of the Lewis
Family 1850-1930*, II: 146.

CHAPTER 2

Page 34: "The only stimulating element in the teaching": *Surprised by Joy*, ch. 2.

Pages 34-5: "In spite of Capron's policy of terror the school": from the diaries
of Warren Lewis.

Page 41: "Here indeed my education really began": *Surprised by Joy*, ch. 4.

Page 47: "I can't say I'm surprised": from the *Lewis Papers*.

Page 48: "a noisy, cheerful function, of which all I remember": from W. H.
Lewis, "Memoir of C. S. Lewis," in *Letters of C. S. Lewis* (London: Bles),
1966, p. 4.

Page 48: "I can remember going with him": from letter to Roger Lancelyn
Green, quoted in Walter Hooper and Roger L. Green, *C. S. Lewis: A Biography*
(London: HarperCollins), third edition, 2002, p. 20.

Page 50: "The fact is that he should never have been sent": from W. H. Lewis,
"Memoir of C. S. Lewis," p. 5.

Page 51: "His friendship with Arthur Greeves": from G. B. Tennyson (Ed.),
Owen Barfield on C. S. Lewis (Middletown, CT: Wesleyan University Press),
1989, p. 126.

Page 51: "Many thousands of people have had the experience": *Surprised by Joy*,
ch. 8.

Page 55: "*The Lion* all began with a picture of a Faun": from *Of This and Other
Worlds* (London: Collins Fount), 1982, p. 79.

Page 56: "My relations to my father": *Surprised by Joy*, ch. 10.

Page 65: "I have never concealed the fact": from preface to C. S. Lewis (Ed.),
George MacDonald: An Anthology (New York: Macmillan), 1947, p. xxxii.

Page 68: "Climbing to the top of the cliff": quoted in *Collected Letters, Vol. I*,
p. 195.

Page 69: "What was your very first impression of death?": quoted in David
Bratman, "Hugo Dyson: Inkling, Teacher, Bon Vivant," in *Mythlore* vol. 21,
no. 4 (Winter 1997), pp. 19-34.

CHAPTER 3

(WCOH = The Wade Center Oral History collection)

Page 73: "Before my brother went out to the trenches": WCOH.

Page 80: "Rather slim, but nice looking, talkative": WCOH.

Page 80: "Perhaps the first thing you noticed about him": Professor A. G.
Dickens, WCOH.

Page 80: "Lewis was a big, full-blown man": Dr. R. E. Havard, WCOH.

Page 80: "He was not naturally impressive": Stuart Barton Babbage, "To the
Royal Air Force," in Carolyn Keefe (Ed.), *C. S. Lewis: Speaker and Teacher*
(London: Hodder and Stoughton), 1974, pp. 96-7.

Page 80: "I am tall, fat, clean shaven, don't wear glasses": C. S. Lewis,
Collected Letters, Vol. II (London: HarperCollins), 2004, p. 610.

Page 80: "A slightly stooped, round-shouldered, balding gentleman": Douglas
Gresham, *Lenten Lands: My Childhood with Joy Davidman and C. S. Lewis* (London:
Collins), 1989, p. 55.

Page 88: Poem "French Nocturne": from the collection by C. S. Lewis (writing
as Clive Hamilton), *Spirits in Bondage* (1919), now in the public domain.

Page 91: "Through the winter, weariness and water": *Surprised by Joy*, ch. 12.

Page 92: "*The magpies in Picardy*": quoted in Martin Gilbert, *First World War*
(London: Weidenfeld and Nicolson), 1994, p. 408.

Page 93: "Even then they attacked not us but the Canadians": *Surprised by Joy*,
ch. 12.

Page 95: "The Board find he was struck by shell fragments": quoted in Hooper
and Green, *C. S. Lewis: A Biography*, p. 44.

Page 96: Poem "Satan Speaks": from the collection by C. S. Lewis (writing as
Clive Hamilton), *Spirits in Bondage* (1919), now in the public domain.

Page 96: "Come and see me. I am homesick, that is the long and short of it":
from *Collected Letters, Vol. I*, p. 386.

Page 97: "One would have thought that it would have been impossible":
from W. H. Lewis, "Memoir of C. S. Lewis", pp. 9-10.

Pages 99-100: "I was in the office at about 9 p.m.": W. H. Lewis, *Brothers and
Friends: The Diaries of Major Warren Hamilton Lewis* (San Francisco: Harper &
Row), 1982, pp. 3-4.

Pages 100-1: "A red letter day. We were sitting in the study": from the diaries
of W. H. Lewis, quoted in the *Lewis Papers*, VI: 79.

CHAPTER 4

Pages 107-8: "After the interval the usual informal discussion followed": from
the minutes of the Martlets, quoted by Walter Hooper, "To the Martlets,"
in Carolyn Keefe (Ed.), *C. S. Lewis: Speaker and Teacher*, pp. 49-83.

Page 112: "with a man who has been asking me for some time to go and 'walk'
with him": quoted in Hooper and Green, *C. S. Lewis: A Biography*, p. 55.

Pages 112/114: Paper to the Martlets on narrative poetry: from the minutes
of the Martlets, quoted by Walter Hooper, "To the Martlets," in Carolyn
Keefe (Ed.), *C. S. Lewis: Speaker and Teacher*, pp. 49-83.

Pages 115-6: "I walk and ride out into the country": from *Collected Letters, Vol. I,*
p. 566.

Page 116: "During those early years I was given no hint": from Owen Barfield,
foreword to Walter Hooper (Ed.), C. S. Lewis, *All My Road Before Me:
The Diary of C. S. Lewis 1922-1927* (London: HarperCollins), 1991.

Page 116: "The thing most puzzling to myself and to Jack's friends": from
W. H. Lewis, "Memoir of C. S. Lewis," p. 12.

Page 125: "We used to foregather in our rooms": from Nevill Coghill, "The
Approach to English," in Jocelyn Gibb (Ed.), *Light on C. S. Lewis* (London:
Bles), 1965, pp. 54-5.

Page 126: "Isn't it a damned world—and we once thought": from *Collected
Letters, Vol. I,* p. 606.

Page 128: "though improved by Warnie's presence, were as usual three weeks
too long": from C. S. Lewis, *All My Road Before Me,* p. 279.

CHAPTER 5

Page 138: The Inklings as an "undetermined and unelected circle of friends
who gathered around C. S. L": from Humphrey Carpenter (Ed.), J. R. R.
Tolkien, *The Letters of J. R. R . Tolkien* (London: George Allen and Unwin),
1981, p. 388.

Page 139: "Rum thing. All that stuff of Frazer's": *Surprised by Joy*, ch. 14.

Page 140: "We somehow got on the historical truth of the Gospels":
C. S. Lewis, *All My Road Before Me,* p. 379.

Page 140: "a smooth, pale, fluent little chap": from C. S. Lewis, *All My Road
Before Me,* p. 393.

Page 141: "It is as if, not content with seeing with your eyes": from
C. S. Lewis, *All My Road Before Me,* p. 394.

Page 144: "unholy muddle . . . undigested scraps of anthroposophy": from
C. S. Lewis, *All My Road Before Me,* pp. 431-2.

Page 144: "what we get in imagination at its highest is real in some way":
from C. S. Lewis, *All My Road Before Me,* p. 432.

Page 146: "I think in general that I am going to agree": from *Collected Letters,
Vol. I,* p. 762.

Page 148: "I gave in, and admitted that God": from *Surprised by Joy*, ch. 14.

Page 148: "I never had the experience of looking for God": from C. S. Lewis,
Christian Reflections (London: Bles), 1967, ch. 14.

Page 149: "Where Allie is such good fun": from *Lewis Papers,* II: 64.

Page 149: "discoursing of the gods & giants": from *Collected Letters, Vol. I,*
p. 838.

Page 150: "I can quite honestly say": from J. R. R. Tolkien, *The Lays of Beleriand*
(London: George Allen and Unwin), 1985, p. 151.

Page 151: "A broad tree lined avenue led up to the Buddha": W. H. Lewis,
Brothers and Friends, p. 20.

Page 152: "You'd better come on Monday at the latest or I may have entered a
monastery": from *Collected Letters, Vol. I,* p. 883.

Page 153: "The eight-acre garden is such stuff": W. H. Lewis, *Brothers and Friends*, p. 58.

Page 155: "I started to say my prayers again": W. H. Lewis, *Brothers and Friends*, pp. 79-80.

Page 155: "When we set out I did not believe": C. S. Lewis, *Surprised by Joy*, ch. 15.

Page 157: "Sometimes we talk English school politics": from *Collected Letters*, Vol. II, p. 16.

Page 160: "A religious work, based on the opinion of some": W. H. Lewis, *Brothers and Friends*, pp. 102-3.

Page 161: "Of course there was no reading on Tuesday": W. H. Lewis's unpublished biography of C. S. Lewis, The Wade Center, p. 270.

Page 162: "In the afternoon J.[ack] and I and the dogs did the Railway walk": W. H. Lewis's diary, The Wade Center, November 5, 1933.

Page 164: "Mr C. S. Lewis read a paper on 'Is Literature an Art?'": quoted by Walter Hooper, "To the Martlets," in Carolyn Keefe (Ed.), *C. S. Lewis: Speaker and Teacher*, pp. 75-76.

Page 165: "[Mrs Moore] nags J[ack] about having become a believer": W. H. Lewis, *Brothers and Friends*, p. 128.

Page 169: "My father is dead and my brother has retired": from *Collected Letters*, Vol. II, p. 161.

Page 171: "If you had delayed writing another 24 hours": quoted in Hooper and Green, *C. S. Lewis: A Biography*, p. 137.

Page 171: "there is too little of what we really like in stories": see J. R. R. Tolkien, *The Lost Road* (London: Unwin Paperbacks), 1989, pp. 7-9.

Page 173: "I lent *The Silver Trumpet* to Tolkien": from *Collected Letters*, Vol. II, pp. 198-9.

Page 176: "I am personally immensely amused by hobbits as such": J. R. R. Tolkien, *The Return of the Shadow* (London: Unwin Paperbacks), 1990, p. 108.

Pages 176-7: "In describing the various types of men": Hooper and Green, *C. S. Lewis: A Biography*, p. 146.

CHAPTER 6

Page 180: "While C. S. Lewis attacked on a wide front": from John Wain, *Sprightly Running* (London: Macmillan), 1962, p. 182.

Page 182: "I go to Cambridge to lecture once a week this term": from *Collected Letters*, Vol. II, pp. 246-7.

Page 184: "until his death we met one another about twice a week": from C. S. Lewis (Ed.), *Essays Presented to Charles Williams* (London: Oxford University Press), 1947, pp. viii-ix.

Page 188: "the usual party assembled on Thursday night": from *Collected Letters*, Vol. II, p. 336.

Page 191: "The stupid creature had either forgotten her": from *Collected Letters*, Vol. II, p. 404.

Page 192: "had passed from the status of a sense-object to that of a mental picture": from *Collected Letters*, Vol. II, p. 416.

Page 195: "One reader, a country clergyman, cancels his subscription": from C. S. Lewis, preface to *The Screwtape Letters and Screwtape Proposes a Toast* (London: Bles), 1961, p. 5.

Pages 195-6: "It is a serious thing to live in a society of possible gods": from "The Weight of Glory," in C. S. Lewis, *Essay Collection and Other Short Pieces* (London: HarperCollins), 2000, p. 105.

Page 198: "He is an ugly man with rather a cockney": from *Collected Letters*, *Vol. II*, p. 501.

Page 198: "The moons I think finally were the moons": from the BBC Radio 4 interview with Denis Gueroult, *Now Read On*, December 16, 1970.

Pages 198/200: "I have a strong visual memory of these evenings": from Helen Tyrrell Wheeler, "Wartime Tutor," in David Graham (Ed.), *We Remember C. S. Lewis* (Nashville: Broadman and Holman), 2001, p.51.

Page 201: "As far as I can judge": from *Collected Letters*, Vol. II, p. 485.

Page 204: "My dear Jack, V. sorry to hear you are laid low": from Humphrey Carpenter (Ed.), *The Letters of J. R. R. Tolkien*, p. 59.

Page 207: "Picture to yourself . . . an upstairs sitting-room": from C. S. Lewis, introduction to *Arthurian Torso* (London: Oxford University Press), 1948.

Pages 208-9: "I ask you! He put away three pints": from Humphrey Carpenter (Ed.), *The Letters of J. R. R. Tolkien*, p. 68.

Page 210: "No Lewis this morning, as he has been appointed": from Humphrey Carpenter (Ed.), *The Letters of J. R. R. Tolkien*, p.74.

Page 212: Tolkien notices a "strange gaunt man": from Humphrey Carpenter (Ed.), *The Letters of J. R. R. Tolkien*, p. 95.

Page 213: "interrupting his most dogmatic pronouncements": from Humphrey Carpenter (Ed.), *The Letters of J. R. R. Tolkien*, p. 103.

Page 216: "I also have become much acquainted with grief": from W. H. Lewis (Ed.) *Letters of C. S. Lewis*, p. 206.

CHAPTER 7

Page 222: "Jane is up and down: some days miserable": from *Collected Letters*, *Vol. II*, p. 702.

Page 222: "I meet Lewis occasionally in the mornings": from Derek Brewer, "The Tutor: A Portrait," in James T. Como (Ed.), *C. S. Lewis at the Breakfast Table* (London: Collins), 1980, p. 55.

Page 223: "With his pen and with his voice on the radio": from *St Andrews Citizen*, 29 June 1946.

Page 223: "We drank some sherry. Lewis came in cursing": from Derek Brewer, "The Tutor: A Portrait," in James T. Como (Ed.), *C. S. Lewis at the Breakfast Table*, p. 58.

Page 224: "LEWIS: But of course the word *square* hadn't the same sense then.": from "Unreal Estates," in C. S. Lewis, *Essay Collection and Other Short Pieces*, p. 538.

Page 228: His duties "as a nurse and a domestic servant": from *Collected Letters*, *Vol. II*, p. 766.

Page 228: "Though I can still force myself to see": from W. H. Lewis, *Brothers and Friends*, p. 200.

Page 228: "The incredible has happened. I am off": from W. H. Lewis, *Brothers and Friends*, p. 201.

Page 229: "The daily letter writing without W to help": from *Collected Letters*, *Vol. II*, p. 789.

Page 230: "The lecturer, a short, thickset man with a ruddy face": from "Don v. Devil," *Time* magazine, 8 September 1947.

Page 231: "We talked of Bp. Barnes, of the extraordinary difficulty": from W. H. Lewis, *Brothers and Friends*, p. 216.

Page 232: "None of us at first very cheerful": from Derek Brewer, "The Tutor: A Portrait," in James T. Como (Ed.), *C. S. Lewis at the Breakfast Table*, p. 59.

Page 234: "Lewis remarks vaguely to Chad Walsh": from Chad Walsh, *C. S. Lewis: Apostle to the Skeptics* (New York: Macmillan), 1949, p. 10.

Page 234: "He reminded me how I had once told him": from John Lahr (Ed.), *The Diaries of Kenneth Tynan* (London: Bloomsbury), 2001.

Page 234: "I also will soon be fifty": from *Collected Letters*, Vol. II, pp. 889-90.

Page 235: "I thought parts of 'King Kong'": from *Collected Letters*, Vol. II, p. 910.

Page 236: "It is sad that 'Narnia' and all that part": from Humphrey Carpenter (Ed.), *The Letters of J. R. R. Tolkien*, p. 252.

Pages 237-8: "The only life he had ever known was a life": quoted in Walter Hooper, *Past Watchful Dragons* (London: Collins Fount), 1980, p. 69.

Page 239: "I remember I actually wept": from the BBC Radio 4 interview with Denis Gueroult, *Now Read On*, December 16, 1970.

Page 239: "Dined with J[ack] at College. . . . No one turned up": from W. H. Lewis, *Brothers and Friends*, p. 230.

Page 239: "*Uton herian holbytlas* indeed. . . . All the long years": from *Collected Letters*, Vol. II, p. 990.

Pages 241-2: "Until 10 January 1950 neither of us": from W. H. Lewis, *Brothers and Friends*, p. 244.

Page 242: "Just got a letter from Lewis in the mail": from Lyle Dorsett, *And God Came In* (New York: Macmillan), 1983, p. 70.

Page 243: "reading Lewis's new story *Narnia and the North*": from Hooper and Green, *C. S. Lewis: A Biography*, p. 310.

Page 243: "in Magdalen S. C. R. with Lewis, and then a wonderful": from Hooper and Green, *C. S. Lewis: A Biography*, p. 310.

Page 245: "Once a week, I trod the broad, shallow stairs": from John Wain, *Sprightly Running*, p. 137.

Page 246: "where we sat talking until about 12.30": from Hooper and Green, *C. S. Lewis: A Biography*, p. 310.

Page 247: "To 'Eagle and Child' to meet C. S. L.": from Hooper and Green, *C. S. Lewis: A Biography*, p. 178.

Page 248: "One sometimes feels that the word 'unreadable'": from Helen Gardner, "C. S. Lewis: 1898-1963," in *Proc. British Academy* 51 (1965), p. 419.

Page 252: "The party was a decided success. Joy was of medium height": from George Sayer, *Jack* (London: Macmillan), 1988, pp. 214-5.

Page 254: "We all roared enthusiastically at the oldest jokes": from Lyle Dorsett, *And God Came In*, p. 88.

Page 258: "I shouldn't dream of visiting Jack often": from Lyle Dorsett, *And God Came In*, p. 105.

CHAPTER 8

Page 259: "In the early 1940s, when I returned to Oxford as a tutor": from Helen Gardner, "C. S. Lewis: 1898-1963," in *Proc. British Academy* 51 (1965), p. 424.

Page 261: "Her mind was lithe and quick and muscular": from C. S. Lewis, *A Grief Observed* (London: Faber and Faber), 1966, p. 8.

Page 262: "For those few years H.[elen] and I feasted on love": from C. S. Lewis, *A Grief Observed*, p. 10.

Page 266: "This book is like lightning from a clear sky": quoted in Humphrey Carpenter, *J. R. R. Tolkien: A Biography*, p. 219.

Page 266: "He warned me long ago": from Humphrey Carpenter (Ed.), *The Letters of J. R. R. Tolkien*, p. 184.

Pages 267-8:"To 'B. and B.' to meet Lewis; his brother, McCallum, Tolkien": from Hooper and Green, *C. S. Lewis: A Biography*, p. 178.

Page 268: "brilliant, intellectually exciting, unexpected, and funny as hell": quoted in Hooper and Green, *C. S. Lewis: A Biography*, p. 351.

Page 269: "An entire issue of . . . *Twentieth Century*": see Brian Barbour, "Lewis and Cambridge," in *Modern Philology*, 96, no. 4 (May 1999).

Page 270: "lamenting that he couldn't get a good idea for a book": from Hooper and Green, *C. S. Lewis: A Biography*, pp. 353-4.

Page 272: "We met in the dining room of his college": from Billy Graham, *Just as I Am* (London: HarperCollins), 1997, p. 258.

Pages 278-9: "'The Kilns' is now a real home with paint on the walls": from Hooper and Green, *C. S. Lewis: A Biography*, p. 386.

Page 280: "I have stood by the bedside of a woman": from *Atlantic Monthly*, CCIII, January 1959.

Page 281: "Philology is the foundation of humane letters": from "Valedictory Address," in J. R. R. Tolkien, *The Monsters and the Critics and Other Essays* (London: George Allen and Unwin), 1983, pp. 224-240.

Pages 283-4: "Joy was able to get right up to the Acropolis": from Hooper and Green, *C. S. Lewis: A Biography*, p. 393.

Page 284: "When we got to Mycenae": from Hooper and Green, *C. S. Lewis: A Biography*, p. 393.

Page 284: "On a balcony overlooking the Phaistos ruins": from Hooper and Green, *C. S. Lewis: A Biography*, p. 396.

Page 289: "You need not sympathize too much": from *Letters of C. S. Lewis*, p. 304.

Page 291: "[C. S. Lewis] had the most astonishing memory of any man": from Kenneth Tynan, "Exhilaration," in Stephen Schofield (Ed.), *In Search of C. S. Lewis* (South Plainfield, NJ: Bridge Publishing), 1983, pp. 6-7.

Page 292: "To 'Lamb and Flag' about 12, there joined CSL": from Hooper and Green, *C. S. Lewis: A Biography*, p. 178.

Page 293: "We drove over to The Kilns": from Hooper and Green, *C. S. Lewis: A Biography*, p. 430.

Pages 293-4: "In their way, these last weeks were not unhappy": from W. H. Lewis, "Memoir of C. S. Lewis" in *Letters of C. S. Lewis*, p. 24.

Pages 294/296: "So far I have felt the normal feelings of a man of my age": from Humphrey Carpenter (Ed.), *The Letters of J. R. R. Tolkien*, p. 341.

Acknowledgements

The quotation on page 80 from the Oral History Interview with Professor A. G. Dickens is used with the permission of the copyright owner, The Marion E. Wade Center, Wheaton College, Wheaton, Illinois, USA© 1989 (and may not be further reproduced without written permission from the copyright owner).

Quotations from the diaries of Warren Lewis (published as *Brothers and Friends: The Diaries of Major Warren Hamilton Lewis*, San Francisco: Harper & Row, 1982) are used with the permission of the copyright owner, The Marion E. Wade Center, Wheaton College, Wheaton, Illinois, USA (and may not be further reproduced without written permission from the copyright owner).

Quotations from the letters of Flora Lewis, the letters and diaries of Albert Lewis, the letters of W. T. Kirkpatrick, and Robert Capron are taken from the *Lewis Papers: Memoirs of the Lewis Family 1850-1930*, 11 volumes, held at The Marion E. Wade Center, Wheaton College, Wheaton, Illinois, USA, and the Bodleian Library, Oxford, UK.